ASTRONOMY & SPACE

ASTRONOMY & SPACE

From the Big Bang to the Big Crunch

PHILLIS ENGELBERT

volume 3
Q-Z

DETROIT · NEW YORK · TORONTO · LONDON

AN IMPRINT OF GALE

Astronomy & Space:
From the Big Bang to the Big Crunch

by Phillis Engelbert

Staff

Jane Hoehner, *U·X·L Developmental Editor*
Carol DeKane Nagel, *U·X·L Managing Editor*
Thomas L. Romig, *U·X·L Publisher*

Mary Beth Trimper, *Production Director*
Evi Seoud, *Assistant Production Manager*
Shanna Heilveil, *Production Associate*

Cynthia Baldwin, *Product Design Manager*
Barbara J. Yarrow, *Graphic Services Supervisor*
Tracey Rowens, *Cover Designer*
Pamela A.E. Galbreath, *Page Designer*

Susan Salas, *Permissions Associate (Pictures)*

Marco Di Vita, Graphix Group, *Typesetting*

Library of Congress Cataloging-in-Publication Data
Engelbert, Phillis
  Astronomy and space: from the big bang to the big crunch/
  by Phillis Engelbert.
       p. cm.
  Includes bibliographical references and index. Contents: v. 1. A-Her v. 2. Hes-P v. 3 Q-Z
   ISBN 0-7876-0942-0 (set); 0-7876-0943-9 (v.1); 0-7876-0944-7 (v.2); 0-7876-
0945-5 (v.3); (acid-free paper)
    1. Astronomy—Encyclopedias, Juvenile. 2. Outer space—Encyclopedias, Juvenile.
  3. Astronautics—Encyclopedias, Juvenile. [1. Astronomy—Encyclopedias. 2. Outer space—
  Encyclopedias. 3. Astronautics—Encyclopedias.] I. Engelbert, Phillis.
  qb14.a874   1996
  500.5'03—dc20
                                                                    96-12522
                                                                    CIP
                                                                    AC

Printed in the United States of America

10 9 8 7 6 5 4 3

Table of Contents

Table of Contents

Table of
Contents

Table of Contents

Table of Contents

Reader's Guide

Astronomy & Space: From the Big Bang to the Big Crunch provides a comprehensive overview of astronomy and space exploration in three hundred alphabetically arranged entries. The topics included in *Astronomy & Space* can be grouped loosely into the following categories: space objects and phenomena (such as planets, black holes, comets, and solar wind); piloted space missions and scientific satellites; famous astronomers and astronauts; the history of astronomy; observatories; and technological advances in the field. Chronologically, *Astronomy & Space* begins fifteen to twenty billion years ago with the Big Bang, and continues on to recent discoveries such as planets beyond our solar system and the possibility of life on Mars. It extends to the future by describing projects—such as the International Space Station and *Pluto Express*—coming early in the twenty-first century and one possible fate of our universe, the Big Crunch.

The approach taken in *Astronomy & Space* is interdisciplinary and multicultural. The writing is interdisciplinary in that it does not merely address the exploration of the cosmos in a scientific sense, but it also places it in a social and historical context. For example, the entry on rockets includes a discussion of World War II and the entry on the space race addresses the cold war. The set is multicultural in that it features astronomers, observatories, astronomical advances, and space programs from around the world.

Scope and Format

The three hundred entries in *Astronomy & Space* are arranged alphabetically over three volumes. Articles range from one to four pages in length. The writing is nontechnical and is geared to challenge, but not overwhelm, students. More than two hundred photographs and illustrations and numerous sidebars keep the volumes lively and entertaining. Each volume begins with a historical timeline depicting major events in astronomy and space. Boldfaced terms throughout the text can be found in the glossary, while cross-references concluding each entry alert the reader to related entries. A cumulative index in all three volumes provides easy access to the topics discussed throughout *Astronomy & Space*.

Advisors

Thanks are due for the invaluable comments and suggestions provided by:

Teresa F. Bettac
Advanced Science for Kids Teacher, Willis Middle School
Delaware, Ohio

Patricia A. Nielsen
8th Grade Science Teacher/Science Fair Director, Todd County Middle School
Mission, South Dakota

Jacqueline Ann Plourde
Media Specialist, Madison Junior High
Naperville, Illinois

Jan Toth-Chernin
Media Specialist, Greenhills School
Ann Arbor, Michigan

Dedication and Special Thanks

The author dedicates this work to her husband, William Shea, and her son, Ryan Patrick Shea, for their patience, love, and support. Special thanks to Jan Toth-Chernin for her guidance.

Comments and Suggestions

We welcome your comments on this work as well as your suggestions for topics to be featured in future editions of *Astronomy & Space: From the Big Bang to the Big Crunch*. Please write: Editors, *Astronomy & Space*, U•X•L, 835 Penobscot Bldg., Detroit, Michigan 48226-4094; call toll-free: 1-800-877-4253; or fax: (313) 877-6348.

Timeline

15–20 billion B.C.: "Big bang" marks the beginning of the universe.

10 billion B.C.: Galaxies are formed.

4.5 billion B.C.: The solar system is formed.

4 billion B.C.: Amino acids, the building blocks of life, are formed on Earth.

248 million B.C.: Dinosaurs roam the Earth.

65 million B.C.: Dinosaurs become extinct.

100,000 B.C.: First modern humans inhabit the Earth.

10,000 B.C.: Ice Age ends.

8000 B.C.: Archaic Age begins.

c. 3100 B.C.: Construction begins on Stonehenge.

c. 3000 B.C.: Egyptians create the first 365-day calendar.

c. 1500 B.C.: Chinese astronomers create the first star chart.

1300 B.C.: Chinese astronomers note a nova in the constellation Scorpius.

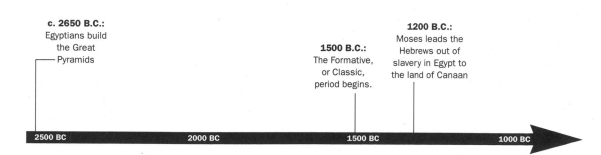

c. 2650 B.C.: Egyptians build the Great Pyramids

1500 B.C.: The Formative, or Classic, period begins.

1200 B.C.: Moses leads the Hebrews out of slavery in Egypt to the land of Canaan

2500 BC   2000 BC   1500 BC   1000 BC

585 B.C.: Greek philosopher Thales correctly predicts a total eclipse of the sun.

c. 330 B.C.: Aristotle writes *De caelo* (*On the Heavens*).

c. 260 B.C.: Greek astronomer Aristarchus proposes that the Earth revolves around the sun.

c. 130 B.C.: Greek astronomer Hipparchus creates a star chart.

46 B.C.: Julius Caesar adds leap year days to the calendar, creating the Julian calendar.

c. A.D. 140: Alexandrian astronomer Ptolemy publishes his Earth-centered theory of the universe.

927: Muslim instrument-maker Nastulus creates the first astrolabe.

1006: Egyptian astrologer Ali ibn Ridwan observes what is considered to be the brightest supernova in history.

1408: Chinese observers note supernova in the constellation Cygnus the Swan, today believed to be a black hole.

1572: Danish astronomer Tycho Brahe observes supernova in the constellation Cassiopeia.

1608: Dutch optometrist Hans Lippershey creates the first telescope.

1609: German astronomer Johannes Kepler publishes his first two laws of planetary motion.

1616: The Catholic Church bans Copernicus' *De Revolutionibus Orbium Coelestium.*

1633: Galileo is placed under house arrest for advocating the sun-centered model of solar system.

1675: Danish astronomer Olaus Roemer measures the speed of light at 76 percent its actual value.

1682: English astronomer Edmond Halley first views the famous comet that is later named after him.

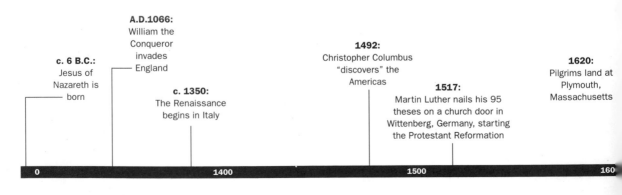

c. 6 B.C.: Jesus of Nazareth is born

A.D.1066: William the Conqueror invades England

c. 1350: The Renaissance begins in Italy

1492: Christopher Columbus "discovers" the Americas

1517: Martin Luther nails his 95 theses on a church door in Wittenberg, Germany, starting the Protestant Reformation

1620: Pilgrims land at Plymouth, Massachusetts

0   1400   1500   160

1728: English astronomer James Bradley calculates speed of light to be 185,000 miles per second.

1758: French astronomer Charles Messier begins his catalogue of non-star celestial objects.

1772: German astronomer Johann Elert Bode publishes his law of interplanetary distances.

1781: German astronomer William Herschel discovers Uranus.

1783: English geologist John Michell suggests the existence of black holes.

1800: William Herschel discovers infrared radiation.

1845: English astronomer John Couch Adams and French astronomer Urbain Leverrier co-discover Neptune.

1847: American astronomer Maria Mitchell makes the first discovery of a comet not visible to the naked eye.

1852: French physicist Jean Bernard Léon Foucault proves that the Earth rotates with his famous pendulum experiment.

1877: American astronomer Asaph Hall discovers moons of Mars.

1877: Italian astronomer Giovanni Schiaparelli describes markings called *canali* on surface of Mars, which is erroneously translated to "canals," fueling speculation of life on Mars.

1889: American astronomer George Hale invents the spectrohelioscope.

1895: German physicist Wilhelm Röntgen discovers X-rays.

1905: Albert Einstein publishes his special theory of relativity.

1912: American astronomer Henrietta Swan Leavitt discovers how to use cepheid variable stars as "astronomical yardsticks."

1914: Einstein publishes his general theory of relativity.

1917: Dutch astronomer Willem de Sitter proposes that the universe is expanding.

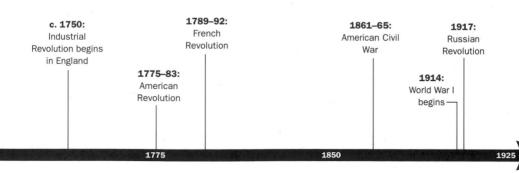

c. 1750: Industrial Revolution begins in England

1775–83: American Revolution

1789–92: French Revolution

1861–65: American Civil War

1914: World War I begins

1917: Russian Revolution

700   1775   1850   1925

1919: Star observations during a solar eclipse prove Einstein's theory (that gravity bends light) correct.

1923: American astronomer Edwin Hubble discovers that the Andromeda nebula is actually a separate galaxy, establishing the existence of galaxies beyond our own.

1926: American physicist Robert Goddard launches the world's first liquid-propelled rocket.

1929: Hubble pens Hubble's Law, which describes the rate of universal expansion.

1930: American amateur astronomer Clyde Tombaugh discovers Pluto.

1932: American physicist Carl Anderson discovers anti-matter.

1932: American radio engineer Karl Jansky discovers radio waves coming from space.

1939: Ham radio operator Grete Rober builds the first radio telescope in his backyard and maps radio waves coming from throughout the Milky Way.

1943: American astronomer Carl Seyfert discovers bright, violent, spiral galaxies that now bear his name.

1947: The 200-inch Hale Telescope, which for the next thirty years remains the world's largest, becomes operational at Palomar Observatory.

1950: Dutch astronomer Jan Oort suggests comets lie dormant in an "Oort cloud" that surrounds the solar system.

October 4, 1957: Soviets launch *Sputnik 1*, initiating the space race with the United States.

1958: National Aeronautics and Space Administration (NASA) created.

January 31, 1958: *Explorer 1*, the first U.S. satellite, is launched into orbit.

October 4, 1959: Soviet satellite *Luna 3* takes the first photographs of the far side of the moon.

1960: United States launches the *Echo* communications satellite.

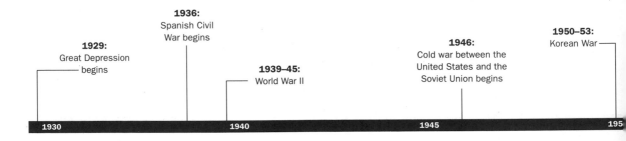

1929:
Great Depression
begins

1936:
Spanish Civil
War begins

1939–45:
World War II

1946:
Cold war between the
United States and the
Soviet Union begins

1950–53:
Korean War

1930   1940   1945   195

April 12, 1961: Soviet pilot Yuri Gagarin orbits Earth aboard *Vostok 1*, becoming the first human in space.

May 5, 1961: Alan Shepard takes a sub-orbital flight aboard *Mercury 3*, becoming the first American in space.

August 27, 1962: *Mariner 2* is launched into orbit, becoming the first interplanetary space probe.

1963: Construction completed on the world's largest radio telescope, at Arecibo Observatory in Puerto Rico.

June 16, 1963: Soviet cosmonaut Valentina Tereshkova rides aboard *Vostok 6*, becoming the first woman in space.

1967: Irish graduate student Jocelyn Bell Burnell discovers pulsars.

1967: Mauna Kea Observatory, which has the world's largest concentration of optical telescopes, opens in Hawaii.

July 20, 1969: American astronauts Neil Armstrong and Buzz Aldrin become the first humans to walk on the moon.

April 13, 1970: Explosion occurs aboard *Apollo 13* when it is over halfway to the moon.

December 15, 1970: Soviet probe *Venera 7* arrives at Venus, making the first-ever successful landing on another planet.

April 19, 1971: Soviet Union launches *Salyut 1*, the world's first space station.

December 2, 1971: Soviet probe *Mars 3* makes first-ever successful landing on Mars.

March 3, 1972: U.S. probe *Pioneer 10* is launched.

December 7, 1972: Launch of *Apollo 17*, the final mission landing humans on the moon.

April 5, 1973: U.S. probe *Pioneer 11* is launched.

May 26, 1973: *Skylab*, the first and only U.S. space station, is launched.

December 4, 1973: U.S. probe *Pioneer 10* flies by Jupiter.

1961: The Berlin Wall is built

1963: President John F. Kennedy is assassinated

1965: Malcolm X is assassinated

1968: Martin Luther King Jr., is assassinated

1973: Americans pull out of Vietnam

1974: Richard M. Nixon resigns the U.S. presidency

1960   1965   1970   1975

1975: European Space Agency founded.

July 15, 1975: *Apollo 18* docks with *Soyuz 19*; Americans and Soviets unite for historic "handshake in space."

August 20, 1977: U.S. probe *Voyager 2* launched.

September 5, 1977: U.S. probe *Voyager 1* is launched.

June 22, 1978: American astronomer James W. Christy discovers Pluto's moon, Charon.

September 1, 1979: *Pioneer 11* becomes the first spacecraft to reach Saturn.

December 6, 1979: American astronomer Alan Guth develops the "inflationary theory" describing the rapid inflation of the universe immediately following the big bang.

1980: The Very Large Array, an interferometer consisting of 27 radio telescopes, becomes operational in Socorro, New Mexico.

April 12, 1981: First launch of a space shuttle: *Columbia.*

June 13, 1983: *Pioneer 10* becomes the first spacecraft to leave the solar system.

June 18, 1983: Sally Ride becomes the first U.S. woman in space, aboard the space shuttle *Challenger.*

August 30, 1983: Guion Bluford becomes the first African American in space, aboard *Challenger.*

November 28, 1983: First Spacelab launched.

January 24, 1986: *Voyager 2* flies by Uranus.

January 28, 1986: Space shuttle *Challenger* explodes just after lift-off, killing all seven crew members.

February 20, 1986: Launch of the Russian space station *Mir,* currently the only space station in operation.

March 13, 1986: First crew arrives at *Mir.*

March 14, 1986: European probe *Giotto* flies in to the nucleus of Halley's comet.

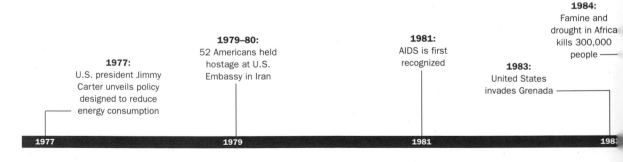

1984:
Famine and drought in Africa kills 300,000 people —

1979–80:
52 Americans held hostage at U.S. Embassy in Iran

1981:
AIDS is first recognized

1977:
U.S. president Jimmy Carter unveils policy designed to reduce energy consumption

1983:
United States invades Grenada —

1977   1979   1981   198

May 4, 1989: U.S. Venus probe *Magellan* is launched.

August 24, 1989: *Voyager 2* flies past Neptune and heads out of the solar system.

October 18, 1989: U.S. Jupiter probe *Galileo* is launched.

November 18, 1989: NASA launches the *Cosmic Background Explorer*.

April 24, 1990: The Hubble Space Telescope is deployed from the space shuttle *Discovery*.

August 10, 1990: *Magellan* arrives at Venus and begins mapping surface.

April 5, 1991: Compton Gamma Ray Observatory is launched by NASA to produce an all-sky map of cosmic gamma-ray emissions.

September 12, 1992: Mae Jemison becomes first African American woman in space, aboard the space shuttle *Endeavour*.

December 1993: Astronauts aboard *Endeavour* repair the flawed Hubble Space Telescope.

December 7, 1995: *Galileo* reaches Jupiter and drops a mini-probe to the surface.

December 12, 1995: Solar and Heliospheric Observatory is launched to study the sun's internal structure.

January 1996: American astronomers Geoffrey Marcy and Paul Butler discover two new planets orbiting stars in the Big Dipper and Virgo constellations.

January 16, 1996: A team of astronomers led by David Bennett of the Lawrence Livermore National Laboratory announce their discovery that white dwarfs make up at least half of all dark matter.

March 25, 1996: Comet Hyakutake reaches its closest point to Earth in about 20,000 years.

August 7, 1996: Discovery of possible evidence of primitive Martian life, found in a 4.5-billion-year-old meteorite.

September 26, 1996: Astronaut Shannon Lucid returns to Earth after 188 days in space aboard *Mir*.

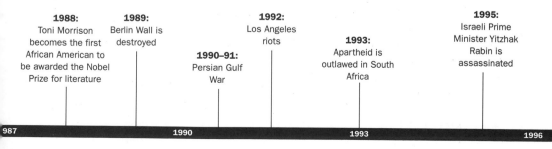

1988: Toni Morrison becomes the first African American to be awarded the Nobel Prize for literature

1989: Berlin Wall is destroyed

1990–91: Persian Gulf War

1992: Los Angeles riots

1993: Apartheid is outlawed in South Africa

1995: Israeli Prime Minister Yitzhak Rabin is assassinated

987   1990   1993   1996

Words to Know

A

Aberration of light: the apparent movement of stars due to Earth's motion forward into starlight.

Absolute magnitude: a star's brightness at a constant distance from Earth.

Absolute zero: the lowest possible temperature at which matter can exist; equal to -259 degrees Fahrenheit and -273 degrees Celsius.

Absorption lines: dark lines that appear in the **spectrum** of an object, indicating **wavelength**s at which light is absorbed.

Adaptive optics: a system that makes minute adjustments to the shape of a **reflector telescope**'s primary mirror to correct distortions that result from disturbances in the atmosphere.

Aphelion: the point along an orbit of a planet or **comet** that is farthest from the sun.

Apollo objects: the group of **asteroid**s that cross Earth's orbit.

Armillary sphere: an instrument made up of spheres and rings used to observe the stars.

Asteroid: a relatively small, rocky chunk of matter that orbits the sun.

Astrolabe: a primitive star map historically used for timekeeping, navigation, and surveying.

Astrology: the study of the supposed effect of celestial objects on the course of human affairs.

Astrometric binary star: a **binary star** system in which only one star can be seen, but its wobble implies that there is another star in orbit around it.

Astronomical unit: a standard measure of distance to celestial objects, equal to the average distance from Earth to the sun (87 million miles).

Astrophysics: the study of the physical properties and evolution of celestial bodies, particularly concerning the production and use of energy in stars and **galaxies.**

Aurora: a bright, colorful display of light in the night sky, better known as the Northern and Southern lights, that results when charged particles from the sun enter Earth's atmosphere.

B

Big bang theory: the theory that explains the beginning of the universe as a tremendous explosion from a single point that occurred fifteen to twenty billion years ago.

Big crunch theory: the catastrophic prediction that there will come a point, very far in the future, in which matter will reverse direction and crunch back into the single point from which it began.

Binary star: a double star system in which two stars orbit one another around a central point of **gravity.**

Black dwarf: the cooling remnants of a **white dwarf** star that has ceased to glow.

Black hole: the remains of a massive star that has burned out its nuclear fuel and collapsed under tremendous gravitational force into a single point of infinite **mass** and **gravity.**

Blue-shift: the shift of **wavelength**s of an object's light **spectrum** into the blue (shorter wavelength) end of the range of visible light—an indication that the object is approaching the observer.

Bode's Law: the simple yet flawed mathematical formula published by eighteenth-century German astronomer Johann Elert Bode dictating the distances of planets from the sun.

Bolometer: an instrument that can detect **electromagnetic radiation** entering Earth's atmosphere, used in particular to measure **radiation** and **microwave**s from the sun and stars.

Brown dwarf: a small, cool, dark ball of matter that never completes the process of becoming a star.

C

Calendar: any system for organizing time into days, months, and years.

Celestial sphere: the sky, or imaginary sphere, that surrounds Earth and provides a visual surface on which we can plot celestial objects and chart their apparent movement due to Earth's rotation.

Cepheid variable: a pulsating yellow **supergiant** star that can be used to measure distance in space.

Chandrasekhar's limit: the theory that any star with a **mass** greater than one and one-half times that of the sun will be crushed at the end of its lifetime by its own **gravity,** so that it will become either a **neutron star** or a **black hole.** A star below this limit will end up as a **white dwarf** star.

Charged coupling device (CCD): a light-capturing device placed at the end of a telescope that is the modern, computerized version of old photographic plates.

Chromosphere: the glowing layer of gas that makes up the middle atmospheric layer of the sun.

Cold war: the period of tense relations, from 1945–1990, between the former **Soviet Union** (and its Eastern allies) and the United States (and its Western European allies).

Comet: a small body of rocky material, dust, and ice in orbit around the sun.

Command module: the section of the Apollo spacecraft in which astronauts traveled.

Constellation: one of eighty-eight groups of stars in the sky named for mythological beings. Each constellation is bordered by an imaginary line running north-south and east-west across the **celestial sphere,** so that every point in the sky belongs to one constellation or another.

Convection: the process by which heat is transferred from the core of the sun toward the surface via slow-moving gas currents.

Copernican model. *See* **Heliocentric model**

Corona: the outermost atmospheric layer of the sun.

Coronagraph: a modified telescope that uses a black disc to block out most of the sunlight entering its chamber, leaving only the image of the sun's **corona.**

Cosmic dust: solid, microscopic particles found in the **interstellar medium.**

Cosmic rays: invisible, high-energy particles that constantly bombard Earth from all directions. Most are high-speed protons (hydrogen atoms that have lost a electron) although they also include the nuclei of all known elements.

Cosmic string: a giant vibrating strand with tremendous gravitational pull containing trapped **spacetime** from a much earlier period.

Cosmology: the study of the origin, evolution, and structure of the universe.

Cosmonaut: a Russian astronaut.

Cosmos: the universe regarded as an orderly system.

Coudé telescope: a modified **reflector telescope** that has the eyepiece angled so that it keeps the image of an object in view, even as that object moves across the sky.

D

Dark matter: virtually undetectable matter that is thought to account for 90 percent of the **mass** in the universe and acts as the "cosmic glue" that holds together **galaxies** and clusters of galaxies.

Diffraction: deflection of a beam of light.

Dwarf galaxy: an unusually small, faint **galaxy.**

E

Earth's meridian: an imaginary circle on the surface of Earth passing through the North and South poles.

Eclipsing binary star: a **binary star** system in which the orbital plane is nearly edgewise to our line of sight, meaning that each star is eclipsed (partially or totally hidden) by the other as they revolve around a common point of **gravity.**

Electromagnetic radiation: radiation that transmits energy through the interaction of electricity and **magnetism.**

Electromagnetic spectrum: the complete array of **electromagnetic radiation,** including **radio waves** (at the longest-**wavelength** end), **infrared radiation,** visible light, **ultraviolet radiation, X-rays,** and **gamma rays** (at the shortest-wavelength end).

Electroscope: an instrument used to detect electrons.

Elliptical galaxy: the most common type of **galaxy** in the universe; elliptical galaxies vary in shape from circles to narrow, elongated ellipses (ovals) and may be spherical or flat.

Emission lines: bright lines that appear in the **spectrum** of an object, indicating **wavelength**s at which light is emitted.

Epicycle: a small secondary orbit erroneously added to the planetary orbits by pre-Copernican astronomers to account for periods in which the planets appeared to move backwards with respect to Earth.

Equinoxes: the days marking the start of spring and fall and the only two days of the year in which day and night are of equal length.

Event horizon: the surface of a collapsed massive star or **black hole.**

Exosphere: the outer layer of Earth's atmosphere, starting about 250 miles above ground, in which molecules of gas break down into atoms and become ionized (electrically charged) by the sun's rays (also called the "ionosphere").

Extravehicular activity (EVA): an activity performed in space by an astronaut attached to the outside of a spacecraft (also called "space walk").

F

Faculae: bright hydrogen clouds often found near **sunspot**s on the sun's surface.

Flare: a temporary bright spot that explodes on the sun's surface.

G

Galaxy: a huge region of space that contains hundreds of billions of stars, **nebulae** (clouds), gas, dust, empty space, and possibly a **black hole.**

Gamma ray: short-**wavelength,** high-energy **radiation** formed either by the decay of radioactive elements or by nuclear reactions.

Gamma ray astronomy: the study of objects in space by observing the **gamma rays** they emit.

General theory of relativity: the theory in which Albert Einstein demonstrated that **gravity** is the result of curved **spacetime.**

Geocentric model: the flawed theory of the **solar system** placing Earth at the center, with the sun, moon, and planets revolving around it.

Geodesy: the study of Earth's external shape, internal construction, and gravitational field.

Geostationary orbit: a special kind of geosynchronous orbit, in which a satellite travels in the same plane as Earth's equator. A geostationary satellite remains more or less stationary over the same point on Earth.

Geosynchronous orbit: an orbit around Earth that takes twenty-four hours to complete.

Globular cluster: a tight grouping of stars found near the edges of the Milky Way.

Globules: small dark patches of concentrated particles found in the **interstellar medium.**

Granules: Earth-sized cells covering the sun's surface that transfer hot gas from the sun's interior to its outer atmospheric layers.

Gravity: the force of attraction between objects, the strength of which depends on the **mass** of each object and the distance between them.

Gravity assist: a technique used by a spacecraft journeying to distant planets, in which it uses the gravitational field of one planet to propel it toward another, eliminating the need for additional **rocket** motors.

Greenhouse effect: the warming of an environment that occurs when **infrared radiation** enters the atmosphere and becomes trapped inside.

Gyroscope: a navigational instrument consisting of a wheel that spins around a rod through its center. The wheel continues spinning in the same direction, even when the direction of the instrument is changed.

H

Heliocentric model: the theory that the sun is at the center of the **solar system** with the planets revolving around it.

Helioseismology: the study of the sun's interior structure and dynamics, determined by measuring the vibrations of sound waves deep within the sun's core.

Heliosphere: the vast region permeated by charged particles flowing out from the sun that surrounds the sun and extends throughout the **solar system.**

Heliostat: a flat, rotating mirror that collects light at the top of a solar telescope tower.

Heliotrope: an instrument that reflects sunlight over great distances to mark the positions of participants in a land survey.

Hertzsprung-Russell diagram: the graph showing the relationship between the color, brightness, and temperature of stars. It places **absolute magnitude** (or brightness) on the vertical axis and color (or temperature) on the horizontal axis.

Homogeneity: uniformity; the state of being the same everywhere.

Hubble's Law: the distance-to-speed relationship showing that the more distant a **galaxy,** the faster it is receding; it describes the expansion of the universe.

I

Inertia: the property of matter that requires a force to act on it to change its state of motion.

Inflationary theory: the theory that the universe underwent a period of rapid expansion immediately following the **big bang.**

Infrared astronomy: the study of objects in space by the **infrared radiation** they emit.

Infrared radiation: electromagnetic radiation of a **wavelength** shorter than **radio wave**s but longer than visible light that takes the form of heat.

Interferometry: the process of splitting a beam of light (or other form of **electromagnetic radiation**) in two, bouncing it off a series of mirrors, and examining its pattern when it comes back together.

Interstellar medium: the space between the stars, consisting mainly of empty space with a very small concentration of gas atoms and tiny solid particles.

Ionosphere. *See* **Exosphere**

K

Kirkwood gaps: areas separating distinct asteroid belts that lie between the orbits of Mars and Jupiter.

Kuiper belt: the proposed cometary reservoir, located just beyond the edge of the orbit of Pluto, containing an estimated ten million to one billion inactive **comet**s.

L

Latitude: an imaginary line circling Earth, parallel to the equator, that tells one's north-south position on the globe.

Launch vehicle: a **rocket** system used to launch satellites and piloted spacecraft into space.

Light-year: the distance light travels in one year, about 5.9 trillion miles.

Longitude: an imaginary line circling Earth, perpendicular to the equator, that tells one's east-west position on the globe.

Lunar eclipse: the complete or partial blocking of the moon by Earth's shadow that occurs when Earth passes between the sun and moon.

Lunar module: the section of Apollo spacecraft that detached to land on the moon.

M

Magnetic axis: the imaginary line connecting Earth's, and other planet's, magnetic poles.

Magnetic field: the area of a planet affected by magnetic force.

Magnetism: the property of a body to produce an electrical current around itself.

Magnetosphere: the region around a planet occupied by its magnetic field.

Mass: the measure of the total amount of matter in an object.

Mass-luminosity law: the law describing the relationship between a star's **mass** and brightness; the more massive a star, the greater the interior pressure and temperature, and therefore the greater the brightness.

Mesosphere: the middle layer of Earth's atmosphere, existing between 40 and 50 miles above ground.

Meteor: also known as a "shooting star," a meteor is a small particle of dust or a small rock left behind by a **comet**'s tail.

Meteor shower: periods of increased **meteor** activity from a common point in the sky, caused by Earth's passage through the orbit of a **comet** or the debris left behind by a comet.

Meteorite: a large chunk of rock, metal, or rock-and-metal that breaks off an **asteroid** or a **comet** and survives passage through Earth's atmosphere to hit the ground.

Meteoroid: the term that collectively describes all forms of meteoric material, including **meteor**s and **meteorite**s.

Micrometer: a device used to measure minute distances or angles.

Microwave: a subset of **radio wave**s, those with the shortest **wavelength**s (less than three feet across).

Milky Way: our home **galaxy,** which contains the sun and billions of other stars, possibly one or more **black hole**s, star clusters, planets, glowing **nebula**e, dust, and empty space. It is approximately 100,000 light-years in diameter and 2,000 light-years thick.

Molecular cloud: a cool area in the **interstellar medium** in which molecules are formed.

N

Nebula: a cloud of interstellar gas and dust.

Neutrino: a high-energy subatomic particle with no **mass,** or such a small mass as to be undetectable, and no electrical charge.

Neutron star: the extremely dense, compact, neutron-filled remains of a star following a **supernova.**

Nova: a sudden, intense, temporary brightening of a star.

Nuclear fusion: the merging of two hydrogen nuclei into one helium nucleus, accompanied by a tremendous release of energy.

Nutation: the slight shift in the angle of tilt of Earth's axis due to the gravitational tug of the moon as it orbits Earth.

O

Oort cloud: a region of space beyond the **solar system,** about one light-year from the sun, theoretically containing trillions of inactive **comet**s.

Open cluster: a loose grouping of stars found toward the center of the **Milky Way.**

Optical interferometer: a series of two or more optical telescopes that are linked together electronically, with a viewing power far greater than the sum of the individual telescopes.

Ozone layer: the layer of Earth's atmosphere, between 25 and 40 miles above ground, that filters out the sun's harmful rays.

P

Parallax: the observed change of a star's position due to Earth's motion around the sun.

Payload: the passengers, instruments, or equipment carried by a spacecraft.

Penumbra: the lighter region surrounding the dark, central part of the moon's shadow that sweeps across Earth during a **solar eclipse.**

Perihelion: the point along an orbit (of a planet or **comet**) that's closest to the sun.

Period-luminosity curve: the graph that enables one to find the distance to a **cepheid variable.** It places **absolute magnitude** (brightness) on the vertical axis and period (days to complete a cycle) on the horizontal axis.

Photometry: the measurement of the properties of a light source. In astronomy, it pertains to the measurement of the brightness and colors of stars that, in turn, are indicators of stellar surface temperature.

Photosphere: the few-hundred-mile thick innermost layer of solar atmosphere that constitutes the sun's surface.

Planetesimals: ancient chunks of matter that originated with the formation of the **solar system** but never came together to form a planet.

Plasma: a substance made of ions (electrically charged atoms) and electrons that exists at extremely hot temperatures.

Plasma theory: the theory that the universe was born out of electrical and magnetic phenomena involving **plasma.**

Probe. *See* **Space probe**

Prominence: a high-density cloud of gas projecting outward from the sun's surface.

Propellant: an energy source for **rocket**s that consists of fuel and an oxidizer. Types of fuel include alcohol, kerosene, liquid hydrogen, and hydrazine. The oxidizer may be nitrogen tetroxide or liquid oxygen.

Proper motion: the apparent motion of a star resulting from both its actual movement in space and the shift in its position relative to Earth.

Protoplanet: the earliest form of a planet, plus its moons, formed by the combination of **planetesimals.**

Ptolemaic model. *See* **Geocentric model**

Pulsar: a rapidly spinning, blinking **neutron star.**

Q

Quadrant: an ancient instrument used for measuring the positions of stars.

Quantum mechanics: the study of the behavior of subatomic particles.

Quasars: extremely bright, star-like sources of **radio wave**s that are the oldest known objects in the universe.

R

Radiation: energy emitted in the form of waves or particles.

Radio astronomy: the study of objects in space by observing the **radio wave**s they emit.

Radio interferometer: a system of multiple **radio telescope**s linked electronically that act as a single telescope with a diameter equal to the area separating them. Powerful computers combine their information and create detailed pictures of objects in space.

Radio telescope: an instrument consisting of a large concave dish with an antenna at the center, tuned to a certain **wavelength**. It receives and processes **radio wave**s and produces a picture of the source emitting the radio waves.

Radio wave: the longest form of **electromagnetic radiation,** measuring up to six miles from peak to peak.

Red dwarf: a star that is 10 to 70 percent smaller in mass and much cooler than the sun.

Red giant: the stage in which an average-sized star (like our sun) spends the final 10 percent of its lifetime. Its surface temperature drops and its diameter expands to ten to one thousand times that of the sun.

Red-shift: the shift of an object's light **spectrum** toward the red-end of the visible light range—an indication that the object is moving away from the observer.

Reflector telescope: a telescope that uses mirrors to bring light rays into focus. It works by directing light from an opening at one end of a tube to a mirror at the far end. The light is then reflected back to a smaller mirror and directed to an eyepiece on the side of the tube.

Refractor telescope: the simplest type of telescope; light enters through one end of a tube and passes through a glass lens, which bends the light rays and brings them into focus. The light then strikes an eyepiece, which acts as a magnifying glass.

Retrograde motion: the perceived backward motion of the outer planets (those farther from the sun than Earth) as Earth overtakes them along their respective orbits around the sun.

Rocket: a tube-like device containing explosive material which, on being ignited, releases gases that propel the device through the air.

S

Schmidt telescope: a combined refractor-reflector telescope that has a specially shaped thin glass lens at one end of a tube and a mirror at the other.

Service module: the section of Apollo spacecraft in which supplies and equipment are carried.

Sextant: an early navigational instrument used to measure the angle from the horizon to a celestial body.

Seyfert galaxy: a fast-moving, spiral-shaped **galaxy** characterized by an exceptionally bright nucleus.

Singularity: the single point at which pressure and density are infinite.

Solar eclipse: the complete or partial blocking of the sun that occurs when the moon's orbit takes it in front of Earth.

Solar system: the sun plus all its orbiting bodies, including the planets, moons, **comet**s, **asteroid**s, **meteoroid**s, and particles of dust and debris.

Solar telescope: a modified reflecting or refracting telescope capable of directly observing the sun.

Solar wind: electrically charged subatomic particles that flow out from the sun.

Solstices: the two days each year when the sun is at its highest and its lowest points in the sky.

Soviet Union: the former country in Northern Asia and Eastern Europe that in 1991 broke up into the independent states of Armenia, Azerbaijan, Belarus, Estonia, Georgia, Kazakhstan, Kyrgyzstan, Latvia, Lithuania, Moldova, Russia, Tajikistan, Turkmenistan, Ukraine, and Uzbekistan.

Space age: the modern historical period beginning with the launch of *Sputnik 1* in 1957 and continuing to the present, characterized by space travel and exploration.

Space probe: an unpiloted spacecraft that leaves Earth's orbit to explore the moon, other bodies, or outer space.

Space race: the twenty-year-long contest, from the mid-1950s to the mid-1970s, for superiority in space travel and exploration, between the United States and the **Soviet Union.**

Space shuttle: a reusable winged space plane that transports astronauts and equipment into space and back.

Space station: an orbiting spacecraft designed to sustain humans for periods of up to several months.

Space telescope: a telescope placed on board a satellite that can make observations free from interference of Earth's atmosphere.

Space walk. *See* **Extravehicular activity (EVA)**

Spacetime: a four-dimensional construct that unites the three dimensions of space (length, width, and height) and a fourth dimension, time.

Special theory of relativity: Albert Einstein's theory—applicable to situations in which the rate of motion is constant—that space and time are not fixed, but change depending on how fast and in what direction the observer is moving.

Spectrograph: an instrument that photographs light **spectra** of celestial objects, making it possible to learn their temperature and chemical composition.

Spectrohelioscope: a combined telescope and **spectroscope** that breaks down sunlight into a colorful display of the sun's chemical components.

Spectroscope: an instrument used to break down **radiation** into its component **wavelength**s.

Spectroscopic binary star: a **binary star** system that appears as one star that produces two different light **spectra.**

Spectroscopy: the process of separating the light of an object (generally, a star) into its component colors so that the various elements present within that object can be identified.

Spectra. *See* **Spectrum**

Spectrum: the range of individual **wavelength**s of **radiation** produced when light is broken down by the process of **spectroscopy.**

Speed of light: the speed at which light travels in a vacuum—186,282.397 miles per second.

Spicules: narrow gas jets that characterize the outer edge of the sun's **chromosphere.**

Spiral galaxy: a **galaxy** with old stars at the center, surrounded by a band of star clusters and an invisible cloud of **dark matter,** with arms spiraling out like a pinwheel.

Steady-state theory: the theory of the origin of the universe stating that all matter in the universe has been created continuously, at a constant rate throughout time.

Stellar nurseries: areas within glowing clouds of gas and dust where new stars are in formation.

Stellar spectrophotometry: the study of the intensity of a particular spectral line or series of spectral lines in a star's absorption or emission **spectrum.**

Stratosphere: the second-lowest layer of Earth's atmosphere, from about 9 to 40 miles above ground.

Sundial: a primitive instrument used to keep time by following the sun's passage across the sky.

Sunspot: a cool area of magnetic disturbance that forms a dark blemish on the surface of the sun.

Supergiant: the largest and brightest type of star, which has over fifteen times the **mass** of the sun and shines over one million times more brightly than the sun.

Supernova: the explosion of a massive star at the end of its lifetime, causing it to shine more brightly than the rest of the stars in the **galaxy** put together.

T

Thermosphere: the layer of Earth's atmosphere, between 50 and 200 miles above ground, in which temperatures reach 1800 degrees Fahrenheit.

Transit: the passage of an inner planet (Mercury or Venus) between the sun and Earth.

Tropical year: the time it takes Earth to complete an orbit around the sun.

Troposphere: the lowest layer of Earth's atmosphere, in which weather patterns are formed.

U

Ultraviolet radiation: electromagnetic radiation of a **wavelength** just shorter than the violet (shortest wavelength) end of visible light **spectrum.**

Umbra: the dark, central part of the moon's shadow that sweeps across Earth during a **solar eclipse.**

V

Van Allen belts: doughnut-shaped regions of charged particles encircling Earth.

Variable star: a star that varies in brightness over periods of time ranging from hours to years.

Visual binary star: a **binary star** system in which each star can be seen distinctly.

W

Wavelength: the distance between one peak of a wave of light, heat, or energy and the next corresponding peak.

White dwarf: the cooling, shrunken core remaining after a medium-sized star ceases to burn.

X

X-ray: electromagnetic radiation of a **wavelength** shorter than **ultraviolet radiation** but longer than **gamma rays** that can penetrate solids and produce an electrical charge in gases.

Picture Credits

The photographs and illustrations appearing in *Astronomy & Space: From the Big Bang to the Big Crunch* were received from the following sources:

On the cover: Hans Bethe (**AP/Wide World Photos. Reproduced by permission.**); Annie Jump Cannon (**UPI/Corbis-Bettmann. Reproduced by permission.**); Percival Lowell (**Lowell Observatory. Reproduced by permission.**); *Atlantis* space shuttle (**Corbis-Bettmann. Reproduced by permission.**).

Corbis-Bettmann. Reproduced by permission.: pp. 1, 18, 27, 28, 32, 34, 39, 41, 43, 48, 52, 69, 74, 80, 84, 111, 142, 154, 157, 178, 181, 215, 217, 262, 265, 295, 297, 309, 310, 325, 385, 413, 436, 459; **UPI/Corbis-Bettmann. Reproduced by permission.:** pp. 3, 30, 82, 91, 95, 139, 141, 162, 163, 168, 170, 186, 189, 243, 244, 251, 255, 284, 286, 301, 320, 330, 381, 392, 429, 508, 517, 533, 540, 547, 551, 559, 601, 610, 618, 658; **AP/Wide World Photos. Reproduced by permission.:** pp. 5, 24, 45, 54, 57, 93, 103, 129, 175, 176, 191, 202, 205, 208, 213, 269, 303, 322, 327, 352, 360, 408, 420, 424, 492, 497, 500, 505, 510, 519, 585, 588, 637, 645, 664, 669, 675, 677, 689, 697, 700, 704; **Frank Rossotto/Stocktrek Photo Agency. Reproduced by permission.:** pp. 37, 64, 88, 97, 126, 135, 148, 150, 173, 375, 383, 388, 405, 457, 488, 529, 570, 615, 625, 655, 672, 684, 691; **Mullard Radio Astronomy Laboratory/Science Photo Library, National Audubon Society/Photo Researchers, Inc. Reproduced by permission.:** p. 62; **Courtesy of the Library of Congress:** pp. 68, 514, 648; **Archive Photos. Reproduced by permission.:** pp. 71, 166, 258, 307, 315, 343, 394, 398, 544, 634; **Chris Butler/Science Photo Library, National Audubon Society/Photo Researchers, Inc. Reproduced**

by permission.: pp. 77, 502; **Frank Rossotto. Reproduced by permission.:** pp. 101, 346, 350, 354; **Stav Birnbaum Collection/Corbis-Bettmann. Reproduced by permission.:** p. 109; **Tommaso Guicciardini/INFN/Science Photo Library, National Audubon Society/Photo Researchers, Inc. Reproduced by permission.:** pp. 116, 410; **Dr. Charles Alcock, Macho Collaboration/Science Photo Library, National Audubon Society/Photo Researchers, Inc. Reproduced by permission.:** p. 124; **Illustrations reprinted by permission of Robert L. Wolke:** p. 146; **SETI Institute/Science Photo Library, National Audubon Society/Photo Researchers, Inc. Reproduced by permission.:** p. 158; **Courtesy of U.S. National Aeronautics and Space Administration (NASA):** p. 194; **Hans & Cassidy. Courtesy of Gale Research.:** pp. 196, 537; **Mehau Kulyk/Science Photo Library, National Audubon Society/Photo Researchers, Inc. Reproduced by permission.:** p. 219; **Science Photo Library, National Audubon Society/Photo Researchers, Inc. Reproduced by permission.:** pp. 260, 552, 567; **© NASA, National Audubon Society Collection/Photo Researchers, Inc. Reproduced with permission.:** p. 275; **JLM Visuals. Reproduced by permission.:** pp. 289, 640, 641; **Courtesy of National Optical Astronomy Observatories:** p. 299; **Royal Observatory, Edinburgh/Science Photo Library, National Audubon Society/Photo Researchers, Inc. Reproduced by permission.:** p. 312; **Lowell Observatory. Reproduced by permission.:** p. 332; **Sovfoto/Eastfoto. Reproduced by permission.:** p. 339; **Reuters/Corbis-Bettmann. Reproduced by permission.:** p. 341; **The Bettmann Archive. Reproduced by permission.:** pp. 363, 416; **UPI/Bettmann. Reproduced by permission.:** pp. 367, 370, 378, 438, 441, 462, 522, 549, 599, 613, 616, 630, 662, 681; **NASA. Reproduced with permission.:** pp. 454, 581; **Julian Baum/Science Photo Library, National Audubon Society/Photo Researchers, Inc. Reproduced by permission.:** pp. 564, 628; **Reuters/Bettmann. Reproduced by permission.:** p. 577; **Finley Holiday Film/U.S. National Aeronautics and Space Administration. Reproduced by permission.:** p. 595; **David A. Hardy/Science Photo Library, National Audubon Society/Photo Researchers, Inc. Reproduced by permission.:** p. 621; **Courtesy of the University of Wyoming:** p. 693.

Quasars

Quasars are compact objects beyond our **galaxy,** so distant that their light takes several billion years to reach us, and so bright that they shine more intensely than one hundred galaxies combined. Through a telescope, a quasar appears to be a relatively close, faint star. However, beginning in the 1960s, astronomers learned the truth about these unusual phenomena in space.

The word quasar is a combined form of "quasi-stellar radio sources." It is so-named because some quasars have been observed through **radio telescope**s. However, only about 10 percent of all quasars emit **radio waves**. The energy coming from quasars also includes visible light, **infrared** and **ultraviolet radiation, X-ray**s, and possibly even **gamma ray**s.

In the early 1960s, astronomer Allan Sandage photographed an area of the sky and noticed that one star had a very unusual **spectrum,** the diagram of wavelengths at which the star emits radiation. Most stars emit radiation consistent with the spectrum of ionized hydrogen, the most abundant element on the surface of stars, but this object had a spectrum that was at first thought to be of an unknown element. The wavelengths at which it emitted radiation were heavily skewed toward the red-end range of visible light.

Such a skewed spectrum is known as a **red-shift** and is indicative of an object moving away from the point of observation. The greater the red-shift, the faster the object is moving. And as an object moves farther away, it picks up speed, increasing its red-shift.

Quasars

In late 1962, Maarten Schmidt was working at the California Institute of Technology where he viewed a quasar through the 200-inch (508-centimeter) Hale telescope at Palomar Observatory. Schmidt correctly identified the object's strange spectrum as that of a normal star with a high red-shift. His calculations, however, placed it at an amazing two billion **light-year**s away. At that distance, in order to be observable from Earth, the object couldn't be a star at all, but had to be something larger, like a galaxy.

Schmidt measured the diameter of the object and learned that although it was emitting as much energy as 1 trillion suns, it was only about the size of the **solar system.** The brightest quasar to date, located in the **constellation** Draco, shines with the light of 1.5 quadrillion suns!

Astronomers now believe that a quasar is formed during the collision between two distant galaxies. When this happens, one galaxy creates a **black hole** in the other with the **mass** of about one hundred million suns.

Image of a "quasi-stellar radio source," or quasar.

Gas, dust, and stars are continually pulled into the black hole. The temperature in the black hole then rises to hundreds of millions of degrees, and it spews out tremendous quantities of radiation.

Quasars are particularly fascinating objects because they give us a glimpse of the early universe. Remember that looking at an object a billion light-years away is really like looking a billion years back in time. The reason is that it takes a billion years for light from the object to reach us. Thus, when we look at a quasar, we do not see it as it is now, but as it was when the light left its surface. Some quasars arc so distant that they are virtually at the edge of time. They are relics from the period following the **big bang.**

See also **Schmidt, Maarten**

Radio astronomy

Prior to the 1930s, our knowledge of the **cosmos** was limited to those areas that give off visible light. Matter in space, however, emits radiation from all parts of the **electromagnetic spectrum,** the range of wavelengths produced by the interaction of electricity and magnetism. In addition to light waves, the electromagnetic spectrum includes **radio waves, infrared radiation, ultraviolet radiation, X-ray**s, and **gamma ray**s.

Radio astronomy is the study of objects in space by observing the radio waves they create. Radio waves are the longest form of **electromagnetic radiation,** some measuring up to 6 miles (more than 9 kilometers) from peak to peak. Objects that appear very dim or invisible to our eye, may shine brightly in radio wavelengths. Thus, with the arrival of radio astronomy, a much more complicated picture of the universe has emerged.

A basic **radio telescope** consists of an antenna and a receiver tuned to some appropriate frequency. The frequency of radiation is inversely proportional to its wavelength. The shorter the wavelength, the greater the number of waves produced in a given time period, and vice versa. The first radio telescope was constructed, quite by accident, in the late 1920s by radio engineer Karl Jansky. An employee of Bell Telephone Laboratories, Jansky was assigned the task of locating the source of interference that was disrupting radio-calls across the Atlantic Ocean.

Jansky constructed an antenna from wood and brass to detect radio signals at a specific frequency. He found signals coming from three places but could identify only two, which were due to thunderstorms. The third, an unknown source, produced a steady hiss. Jansky eventually learned that the signal was coming from interstellar gas and dust.

Jansky then sought funds for the construction of a larger receiver, with which he could make more complete observations. Bell Laboratories, however, was not interested in the project since astronomy was not related to their line of work. Nor could Jansky convince any university to provide the needed resources.

Development of Radio Telescopes

It was not until amateur astronomer Grote Reber built his own radio dish in 1937 that the world learned more about the new field of radio astronomy. When Reber heard of Jansky's findings, he took rafters, galvanized sheet metal, and auto parts, and built a 31-foot-diameter (9.4-meter-diameter) dish antenna with a receiver mounted above it—all for thirteen hundred dollars. Reber alone charted radio sources in the sky for the next

The mounted aluminum reflector on this 84-foot (26-meter) antenna can track celestial objects at any point in the sky.

decade. Then at the end of World War II, professional scientists began entering the field.

In 1947, construction began on what was then the world's largest radio telescope with a dish 250 feet (76 meters) across at Jodrell Bank, England. Ten years later, the telescope went into operation.

British astronomer Martin Ryle used the Jodrell Bank telescope to study radio waves in the **constellation**s Cassiopeia and Cygnus. He discovered signals too strong to be individual stars and found that they were entire radio **galaxies.**

Ryle then learned how to multiply the power of individual radio telescopes. He found that two or more telescopes placed a distance apart from each other acted as a single telescope with a diameter equal to the area separating them. In 1955, he used twelve telescopes to create the first **radio interferometer.** The signals collected by the twelve individual telescopes were sent to a single receiver, where a computer processed the information.

Perhaps the most famous radio interferometer today is the Very Large Array, constructed in 1977 in Socorro, New Mexico. This instrument consists of twenty-seven radio telescopes, each one about 75 feet (23 meters) in diameter. The telescopes are set on railroad tracks and arranged in a "Y" shape. The telescope dishes are linked to each other by powerful computers that combine their information and create detailed pictures of objects in space.

While the Jodrell Bank radio **reflector** was still under construction, the field of radio science was also being pursued at the atomic level. In a Harvard University laboratory, American physicist Edward Purcell was using radio signals to assess the magnetic strength of elements. Nuclear magnetic resonance (NMR), an indication of atomic magnetic strength of an element, could be determined by its response to a particular radio frequency.

In 1951, Purcell found that NMR also had applications in astronomy. He measured radio waves coming from space to determine the frequency of interstellar hydrogen's emission spectrum, Purcell and astronomy graduate student Harold Ewen thus created a radio telescope capable of examining dark patches of hydrogen invisible to optical telescopes.

The late 1950s witnessed the construction of the world's largest steerable radio telescope. The National Radio Astronomy Observatory was established in Green Bank, West Virginia, as home to this 300-foot (91-meter) telescope with an 85-foot-diameter (26-meter-diameter) dish. Unfortunately, this magnificent piece of equipment gave way under its own weight in 1982. The largest single radio telescope dish in operation today, with a diameter of 1,000 feet (305 meters), is in Arecibo, Puerto Rico.

Developments Since the 1950s

The post-1950 development of stronger radio telescopes paved the way for many important discoveries. For instance, in 1955, American astrophysicists Bernard Burke and Kenneth Franklin found that Jupiter is second only to the sun as the strongest source of radio waves in the **solar system.** Around this time, Dutch astronomer Jan Oort used a radio telescope to map the spiral structure of the **Milky Way** galaxy. And in the late 1960s, British astronomers Antony Hewish and Jocelyn Bell Burnell detected the first **pulsar,** a strong radio source in the core of the Crab **nebula.**

In 1963, radio astronomers turned up some very compelling evidence in support of the **big bang theory** of how the universe began. Arno Penzias and Robert Wilson were attempting to use Bell Telephone Laboratories' long, horn-shaped radio antenna to chart cosmic sources of radio waves. However, they were unable to eliminate a constant background noise that seemed to come from every direction. They finally learned that what they were detecting matched the pattern of an object radiating at 3 degrees above **absolute zero** (-465 degrees Fahrenheit, or -276 degrees Celsius), the predicted temperature to which radiation left over from the big bang should have cooled by the present.

Today astronomers use radio astronomy and other sophisticated methods including gamma ray, infrared, and X-ray astronomy to examine the cosmos. Until fairly recently, due to dense clouds and dust that block visible light, scientists did not have a picture of the galactic core. Now they can map the radio waves and infrared light which shine through these obstacles. With modern technology, scientists have come closer to answering many questions that have puzzled astronomers for centuries, such as how stars are born and how galaxies are formed.

See also **Arecibo Observatory; Electromagnetic waves; Interferometry;** and **Very Large Array**

Radio interferometer

Radio interferometers work on a simple but ingenious principle: two telescopes are better than one. And, by extension, a large number of telescopes is best of all. A radio interferometer is a series of two or more **radio telescope**s, all trained on the same celestial object. They are linked electronically so that the information collected by each one is transmitted to a central computer, which combines the data. The string of telescopes acts as a single telescope with a diameter equal to the distance separating them. The result is a radio "picture" with much finer detail than could be produced by any one telescope.

The field of radio **interferometry** originated in the mid-1950s, about a decade after the birth of **radio astronomy,** the study of objects in space by observing the **radio wave**s they create. Radio telescopes were first constructed in a number of locations around the world in the mid-1940s, shortly after the end of World War II. Radio observatories are now as plentiful as optical observatories (those with telescopes that detect visible light).

While certain functions are better fulfilled by single radio telescopes (such as general surveys of broad regions of the sky), much modern radio astronomy relies on interferometers. Perhaps the most famous radio interferometer in use today is the Very Large Array (VLA), constructed in 1977 in Socorro, New Mexico. This instrument consists of twenty-seven radio telescopes, each about 75 feet (23 meters) in diameter. They are set on railroad tracks, arranged in a "Y" shape.

The European counterpart to VLA is MERLIN, the Multi-Element Radio-Linked Interferometer Network. This network consists of seven radio telescopes throughout England, constructed in 1980.

Very Long Baseline Interferometry

The 1980s also saw the advent of Very Long Baseline Interferometry (VLBI). VLBI involves a series of telescopes placed huge distances apart, such as between the two coasts of the United States. The advantage of VLBI is that finer details of distant objects, such as **quasar**s can be brought into focus. A disadvantage of VLBI is that with such long interferometers, only narrow slices of the sky can be examined at one time.

Some examples of VLBI consist of dedicated telescopes, that is, telescopes that are used exclusively in the interferometer. Others utilize general-purpose radio telescopes at observatories. In the latter cases, each telescope focuses on the same object for periods of time. The signals they receive are stored on magnetic tape and sent to a central facility for processing.

The only dedicated VLBI array in the United States, the Very Long Baseline Array (VLB), was constructed in 1993. This series of ten identical radio telescopes stretches across the United States from the Virgin Islands to Hawaii. Information collected by telescopes around the world can be linked in a process called intercontinental VLBI.

And in a science where, literally, "the sky's the limit," there are now two projects in the planning stages in which one telescope of an interferometer would be placed on a satellite in space. Both are international projects supported by the National Aeronautics and Space Administration (NASA). The first, called VSOP (VLBI Space Observatory Program), was launched in September 1996. The second, dubbed RadioAstron, should lift off in 1997 or 1998. These space-based interferometers will study galactic nuclei, **pulsar**s, and other distant objects.

See also **Interferometry**; **Radio astronomy**; **Radio telescope**; and **Very Large Array**

Radio telescope

A **radio telescope** is the basic tool of **radio astronomy,** the study of objects in space by observing the **radio wave**s they emit. An optical telescope, the kind with which most people are familiar, detects visible light. Visible light, however, represents just one of the many types of radiation on the **electromagnetic spectrum.**

Radio waves are the longest form of **electromagnetic radiation.** They have wavelengths that cover a huge range, from a fraction of an inch up to 6 miles (9.7 kilometers) from peak to peak. Objects that appear very dim in visible light may shine brightly in radio wavelengths. Thus, by combining the images captured by radio telescopes with what we see through optical telescopes, a much more complicated picture of the universe emerges.

A basic radio telescope consists of a large concave dish with a small antenna at the center, tuned to a certain wavelength. The incoming signal is magnified by amplifiers and transmitted through cables to receivers in the control room. There the information is passed on to a computer, which analyzes it and produces a picture.

As with all telescopes, bigger is better. The reason is that larger dishes result in sharper radio images. Most modern radio telescope dishes

*This radio telescope
at the National
Radio Astronomy
Observatory near
Green Bank, West
Virginia, reaches an
elevation of about
4,000 feet (1,219
meters).*

are very large indeed. They are typically over 100 feet (30 meters) in diameter—about the size of two city lots—while most are two to three times that size. The largest radio telescope in existence today is the 1,000-foot-diameter (305-meter-diameter) dish at the Arecibo Observatory in Puerto Rico. The dish there is larger than three football fields across.

Radio waves have been found to come from almost every object in the sky, including the sun, planets, stars, and **galaxies.** Radio telescopes have been used to map the spiral structure of the **Milky Way** galaxy; to detect **pulsar**s; and to see right through the Venusian cloud cover to the planet's surface. They have even picked up background radiation present throughout the universe that is believed to be left over from the **big bang,** from which the universe is believed to have been created around fifteen billion years ago.

History of Radio Telescopes

The first radio telescope was constructed in the late 1920s by radio engineer Karl Jansky, an employee of Bell Telephone Laboratories. At the time, Jansky was looking for the source of interference commonly experienced in trans-Atlantic radio calls. He constructed an antenna from wood and brass and, in addition to detecting signals from thunderstorms, found radio waves coming from interstellar gas and dust. At the time, Jansky's discovery was largely ignored by the scientific community.

Jansky's work, however, did not go unnoticed by amateur astronomer Grote Reber. In 1937, Reber constructed a backyard radio dish from rafters, galvanized sheet metal, and auto parts. He then used this telescope to make the first radio map of the Milky Way. Reber's map, coupled with the end of World War II, finally caused astronomers to pay attention to this promising new field. They took radar equipment left over from the war and began putting up radio telescopes all around the world.

In 1947, construction began on what was then to be the world's largest radio telescope, at Jodrell Bank, England. The dish used in this telescope was to be 250 feet (76 meters) in diameter. Ten years later, the telescope was placed into operation.

The late 1950s witnessed the construction of the world's largest steerable radio telescope. A steerable telescope is one capable of moving to compensate for the Earth's rotation. The National Radio Astronomy Observatory (NRAO) was established in Green Bank, West Virginia, as home to this telescope with a 300-foot-diameter (91-meter-diameter) dish. Unfortunately, this magnificent piece of equipment collapsed under its own weight in 1982. Since that time, the NRAO has constructed and put into use a number of modernized radio telescopes around the country.

The modern age of radio astronomy is largely focused on **radio interferometer**s. Radio **interferometry** is a system of multiple radio dishes connected to a computer, which act as a single telescope with a diameter equal to the area separating them. In short, the combination of telescopes produces images of a much higher quality than could any one telescope. Single large radio telescopes, however, remain the most effective means of mapping large areas of thc sky and studying rapidly changing objects, such as pulsars.

See also **Arecibo Observatory**; **Interferometry**; **Radio astronomy**; **Radio interferometer**; and **Very Large Array**

Reber, Grote (1911–)
American radio engineer

Grote Reber is a pioneer in the field of **radio astronomy,** the study of objects in space by observing the **radio wave**s they emit. Radio waves are the longest form of **electromagnetic radiation,** measuring up to 6 miles (10 kilometers) from peak to peak, and have been detected coming from the sun, planets, stars, **galaxies, pulsar**s, and other matter in space. Then an amateur astronomer, Reber's life was forever changed by the 1932 announcement that radio waves had been found in space. Reber followed up on this finding with his homemade backyard telescope, and as it turned out, he was the only one to do so for the next decade.

Reber was born in 1911 in Wheaton, Illinois. He first became a ham (amateur) radio operator during his youth. He then went to college at the Illinois Institute of Technology to study radio engineering. After completing his degree, Reber took a job as an electronics engineer with a radio manufacturer in Chicago.

In 1932, Reber read in the *Proceedings of the Institute of Radio Engineers* about the findings of Bell Telephone Laboratories employee Karl Jansky. Jansky had constructed an antenna from wood and brass to look for the source of the interference in trans-Atlantic radio-calls. He found signals coming from three places but could identify only two, both of which were thunderstorms. The third, a mystery source, produced a steady hiss. Jansky eventually learned that this signal was coming from interstellar gas and dust in the direction of the **constellation** Sagittarius. This discovery led Jansky to conclude that celestial objects emit radiation in the form of radio waves.

Jansky then sought funds for the construction of a larger receiver with which he could make more complete observations, but could find no university or industry to provide financial support. So when Reber took thirteen hundred dollars of his own money (a considerable sum in the 1930s) and built his **radio telescope,** he became the sole investor in the future of radio astronomy.

Reber's Discovery of Radio Sources

Reber's telescope consisted of a 31-foot-diameter (9.4-meter-diameter) dish made of wooden beams and galvanized sheet metal, with a re-

Grote Reber holds a scale model of his first radio telescope.

ceiver mounted above it. He installed a Model-T engine to rotate the dish. At first Reber had no luck detecting signals from space. He soon realized, however, that this failure was caused by being tuned to a higher frequency than Jansky's. After re-tuning the receiver to intercept waves of a longer wavelength (wavelength is inversely proportional to frequency), Reber began to detect radio noise.

Reber created a map of the radio signals coming from our **galaxy.** He found that these signals often coincide with the positions of stars, but not always. For instance, some of the brightest stars are barely detectable by the radio telescope. Conversely, he found dark patches in the sky that are strong radio sources. Thus, Reber showed that visual brightness of objects bears no relation to the strength of the radio waves those objects emit. He also concluded that some radio waves are coming from interstellar neutral hydrogen that occupied seemingly "empty" space. During this time, Reber was working full-time days at the radio factory, after which he spent nights at his backyard dish.

In 1940, Reber's findings were published under the title "Cosmic Static" in the *Astrophysical Journal*. The decision to publish this article was made by the journal's editor, Otto Struve, despite the editorial board's having voted against it. Struve felt that Reber had presented findings too important to ignore.

Reber's article was published at an auspicious time. World War II had kept scientists busy from 1939–1945. The end of the war and Reber's article had finally caused astronomers to pay attention to this promising new field. They took radar equipment left over from the war and began putting up radio telescopes all over the world. It at about this time that Reber was finally able to quit his day job and support himself solely as a radio astronomer.

In order to avoid most of the human-made radio interference he was encountering in his observations, Reber moved to Hawaii in 1951. Three years later he moved to an even more remote location, Tasmania. There he worked with a large, unusual-looking radio telescope. It consisted of a huge circle outlined by several eight-story poles connected by 57 miles (91 kilometers) of wire. Using this monstrosity, Reber made a radio map of the entire portion of the universe visible from the Southern Hemisphere.

See also **Radio astronomy** and **Radio telescope**

Red giant star

An average-sized star like our sun will spend the final 10 percent of its life as a **red giant.** In this phase a star's surface temperature drops to between -918,800 and -1,837,600 degrees Fahrenheit (-510,427 and -1,020,871 degrees Celsius) and its diameter expands to ten to one thousand times that of the sun. The star takes on a reddish color, which is what gives it its name.

The process of becoming a red giant begins when the hydrogen at the core is all used up. However, there is still hydrogen in the areas of the star surrounding the core. With nothing left to fuel the nuclear reaction at the core, the core begins to contract. This releases gravitational energy into the surrounding regions of the star, causing it to expand. The outer layers, consequently, cool down, and the color (which is a function of temperature) becomes red. The star may slowly shrink and expand more than once as it evolves into a red giant.

Artwork representing the red giant variable star Mira Ceti as seen from a nearby small planet.

This change marks the start of a dynamic process in which the object becomes a **variable star.** It becomes alternately brighter and dimmer, generally spending about one year in each phase. The star continues in a variable state until it completely runs out of fuel.

While the star is in its puffed-up state, helium continues to accumulate at its core. Since it is not hot enough initially to undergo fusion (the process by which two atoms combine, releasing a vast amount of energy), the helium becomes denser and denser. Finally, pressure alone forces the atoms to fuse, forming carbon and oxygen. At the same time, the core shrinks and the star becomes bluer and smaller.

Using helium as fuel, the star's core continues to burn normally for a while, although the star shines less brightly than it did in its expanded state. At the same time, hydrogen fuses into helium in regions of the star farther out from the core. The core becomes so hot that it may pulsate (vary in brightness). This stage doesn't last long, however, because the helium burns quickly and is soon all used up.

As the helium runs out, the star again puffs up—this time to about five hundred times the size of the sun, with about five thousand times the brightness of the sun. Buried deep inside the star's unstable atmosphere is a hot core, around the size of the Earth, but with about 60 percent the sun's **mass.** As a final act, the atmosphere dislodges from the core and floats off as a planetary **nebula.** The glowing core, called a **white dwarf,** is left to cool for eternity.

More massive stars exit the red giant stage with a bang, transformed by a **supernova** into a **neutron star** or a **black hole.** The fate described in this essay, however, awaits our sun billions of years in the future.

See also **Stellar evolution**

Red-shift

When matter, such as a **galaxy,** moves away from an observation point, such as Earth, its light **spectrum** displays a **red-shift.** A red-shift is one type of Doppler effect. Named for nineteenth-century physicist Christian Johann Doppler, this principle states that if a light (or sound) source is moving away from given point, its wavelengths will be lengthened. Conversely, if an object emitting light or sound is moving toward that point, its wavelengths will be shortened. With light, longer wavelengths stretch to the red end of the color spectrum while shorter wavelengths bunch up at the blue end. The shortening of wavelengths of an approaching object is called a **blue-shift.**

The first astronomer to observe a space object's Doppler shift was Vesto Melvin Slipher in 1912. His subject was the Andromeda galaxy, which was then believed to be a **nebula,** or cloud of gas and dust (at that time it was not known there were other galaxies beyond the **Milky Way**). He discovered that the spectrum of the Andromeda was shifted toward the blue end, meaning that the Andromeda was approaching Earth.

Two years later he analyzed the **spectra** of fourteen other spiral nebula and found that while twelve were red-shifted, only two were blue-shifted. It was only due to the influence of the Milky Way's gravitational field on these small galaxies that they were approaching us, causing them to exhibit blue-shifts.

An extremely important finding relating to red-shifts was made in 1929 by Edwin Hubble, the American astronomer who first proved the existence of other galaxies. Together with his colleague Milton Humason, he photographed distant galaxies and learned that their spectra were all shifted toward the red wavelengths of light. Further study showed a relationship between the degree of red-shift and that object's distance from Earth. In other words, the greater an object's red-shift, the more distant it is, and the faster it's moving away from us.

This finding suggested that, due to the large degree to which these galaxies' spectra were red-shifted, they were receding at a phenomenal rate. Humason found some galaxies moving at one-seventh the **speed of light.**

Hubble and Humason's research on red-shifts led to two important conclusions: that every galaxy is moving away from every other galaxy and, therefore, that the universe is expanding.

See also **Hubble, Edwin**; **Humason, Milton**; and **Slipher, Vesto Melvin**

Resnik, Judith (1949–1986)

American astronaut

Judith Resnik was the second American woman and the first Jewish person in space, although that may not be the reason that most people remember her. Resnik is better remembered as one of the seven astronauts who died in the **space shuttle** *Challenger* disaster on January 28, 1986.

Challenger exploded seventy-two seconds after lift-off on a cold morning at Kennedy Space Center in Cape Canaveral, Florida. A few puffs of smoke first appeared and soon the entire vessel burst into flames. All seven people on board were killed. The cause of the accident was later found to be a faulty rubberized seal called an O-ring, which created a leak in one of the two solid **rocket** boosters that ignite the main fuel tank.

The *Challenger* flight would have been Resnik's second space flight. She first flew on the maiden voyage of the space shuttle *Discovery,* a flight that also suffered initial setbacks. On June 26, 1984, lift-off of *Discovery* was stopped after a hydrogen leak caused the main engines to shut down after firing briefly. The problem was fixed, and two months later, on August 30, the ship was successfully launched. Over the next seven days, *Discovery* circled the Earth ninety-six times. The six-person crew placed

Judith Resnik returns to Houston after the launch of the Discovery *space shuttle was aborted when the main engines shut down with four seconds to liftoff.*

three communications satellites into orbit, constructed a 100-foot-long (30-meter-long) experimental solar panel in the cargo bay, and conducted biomedical research.

Judith Arlene Resnik was born in 1949 in Akron, Ohio. Her father was an optometrist. Resnik, who excelled at her studies and at playing the piano, graduated from high school in 1966 and went on to Carnegie-Mellon University in Pittsburgh, Pennsylvania. There she earned a bachelor's degree in electrical engineering in 1970. Next, Resnik attended the University of Maryland, where she earned a Ph.D. in electrical engineering in 1977.

While a doctoral student, Resnik worked as an engineer for RCA designing radar systems and rocket telemetry (data transmission) systems. From 1974 to 1977, she was a biomedical engineer at the Laboratory of Neurophysiology at the National Institutes of Health in Bethesda, Maryland.

Resnik's Enters the Astronaut Program

In 1978, Resnik was in El Segundo, California, working for the Xerox Corporation, when she was accepted into the National Aeronautics and Space Administration (NASA) astronaut training program. Along with Sally Ride and four other women, she was among the first women selected to become astronauts.

In August 1979, upon completion of her training, Resnik became a qualified space shuttle mission specialist. For the next four years leading up to her *Discovery* mission, Resnik worked on the remote arm used by the shuttle crews to retrieve satellites in space and bring them into the cargo area. She also designed computer software.

Resnik always considered herself more a scientist than an adventurer. "Progress in science is as exciting to me as sitting in a rocket is to some people,"she said. "I feel less like Columbus and more like Galileo."

Resnik, who was thirty-six at the time of her death, was not married. In her honor, an **asteroid** and a crater on Venus bear her name.

See also Challenger

Ride, Sally (1951–)

American astronaut

Sally Ride became the first American woman in space on June 18, 1983, when she flew aboard the **space shuttle** *Challenger.* She was not the first woman in space, however. That honor belongs to Soviet **cosmonaut** Valentina Tereshkova, who traveled in space two full decades before Ride. Nevertheless, to a generation of American girls, the name Sally Ride has become synonymous with opportunity and adventure.

Sally Kristen Ride was born in 1951 in Encino, California. At age fourteen, while still in high school, she became nationally ranked at number eighteen on the junior tennis circuit. After graduation in 1968, she entered Stanford University. Five years later, she had completed bachelor's degrees in English and in physics. She continued her studies in physics, earning a master's degree in 1975 and a Ph.D in 1978.

The same year she received her Ph.D, Ride was selected by the National Aeronautics and Space Administration (NASA) to become an astronaut, something she called a "once-in-a-lifetime opportunity." Of the eight thousand people who had applied, only thirty-five were accepted, six of whom were women. A year later, Ride had completed her training and was qualified as a space shuttle mission specialist (the crew member responsible for equipment and cargo).

For the next three years, Ride worked at the Shuttle Avionics Integration Laboratory, working on a support team for two flights of *Columbia*. Ride established herself as a skilled and resourceful scientist, capable of solving almost any problem. Her own opportunity to join a shuttle mission came in April 1982, on the *Challenger* mission scheduled for the following year.

Ride, who was not only the first woman but also the youngest American astronaut in space, served as the mission's flight engineer. During the six-day journey, the *Challenger* crew transported two communications satellites into space. They also released and then retrieved the German-built Shuttle Pallet Satellite.

Ride's second and final mission came a year later, in October 1984. She had a female crewmate on that mission, Kathryn Sullivan. In a remarkable coincidence, Sullivan had been a classmate of Ride's in first grade. The purpose of that flight was to deploy the *Earth Radiation Budget Satellite,* a satellite that studies global climate changes, and to make scientific observations of the Earth with a specialized camera.

Ride was preparing for a third space flight scheduled for the summer of 1986 when *Challenger* exploded, killing all seven astronauts on board. That accident led to the grounding of the entire shuttle fleet for the next

Sally Ride, the first American woman to travel into space, arrives at Kennedy Space Center to prepare for her historic journey aboard the Challenger space shuttle.

two years and eight months, while NASA investigated the cause of the explosion. Ride served as the astronaut office representative on the investigative commission.

Ride next moved to Washington D.C., where she worked for NASA on long-range planning. In that capacity, she founded NASA's Office of Exploration and authored a report entitled "Leadership and America's Future in Space."

In 1987, Ride retired from NASA and returned to Stanford University as a Science Fellow at the Center for International Security and Arms Control. Two years later, she assumed her present posts as Director of the California Space Institute and Professor of Physics at the University of California, San Diego.

Rockets

Around A.D. 160, Greek mathematician Hero of Alexandria created a spinning, spherical steam-powered device. Although this device does not qualify as a real **rocket,** it did demonstrate propulsion. Since then, humans have maintained a steady fascination with rocketry. Larger and more sophisticated rockets and missiles have been constructed, primarily for use in warfare. And in this century, rocket development has taken on a new spin: space travel.

With the invention of gunpowder in the ninth century by the Chinese, the field of rocketry advanced rapidly. In thirteenth-century China, simple hand-held rockets described as "arrows of flying fire" were set off during religious ceremonies and celebration. These inaccurate, short-range devices were fueled by a mixture of saltpeter (potassium nitrate), charcoal, and sulfur. Their use eventually spread throughout Asia and Europe, where they were used as weapons during the wars of the Middle Ages. Then, for a period, rocketry was all but ignored, as military personnel turned their attention to the development of guns and other weapons.

In the late eighteenth century, when Indian forces used rockets to defeat the British in a number of battles, interest in rocketry was rekindled. The Indian rockets weighed 6 to 12 pounds (2.2 to 2.5 kilograms) and could travel between 1 and 1.5 miles (1.6 and 2.4 kilometers). Whereas a single rocket seldom hit its target, rockets in large numbers caused a lot of damage.

The Centaur rocket rises from its launch pad about fifty seconds before it blew apart in a fiery explosion.

In 1804, British army officer William Congreve developed a metal-cased, stick-guided rocket that could travel 2,000 to 3,000 yards (1,829 and 2,743 meters). His later rockets, weighing 30 pounds (11 kilograms), were made more accurate by the addition of a three-finned tail. They carried warheads that would start fires or explode on impact. These "Congreve" rockets were widely used throughout the 1800s in Asia, Africa, and the Americas by colonial powers (foreign governments that had taken control of the land and the population).

Rockets and Early Space Travel

Not until the 1900s were rockets considered in the context of space travel. This use of rockets was first suggested by Russian physicist Konstantin Tsiolkovsky. Tsiolkovsky was ahead of his time, publishing articles about liquid fuels, methods of cooling fuel-burning chambers, navigation, and even plans for multi-stage rockets. He suggested that rockets could function outside of the Earth's atmosphere because they have a self-contained propulsion system that does not rely on oxygen.

Shortly thereafter, Robert Goddard, the father of American rocketry, developed systems for the various stages of a rocket's flight, from ignition and fuel systems, to guidance controls, to parachute recovery.

In 1926, Goddard came to the conclusion that gasoline and liquid oxygen would make an effective rocket fuel. That same year he launched the world's first liquid-propelled rocket. The small rocket (weighing 10 pounds, or 3.7 kilograms) reached a height of 41 feet (12.5 meters) and a distance of 184 feet (56 meters). Some of his later flights, at his test site in Roswell, New Mexico, went as high as 1.25 miles (2 kilometers).

Goddard made an extremely valuable contribution to the field with his liquid-propellant models. In fact, most of the rockets used in space flight have been liquid-**propellant** rockets. They contain a mixture of liquid fuel and liquid oxidizer. The liquid oxidizer replaces gaseous oxygen and allows the fuel to burn. Types of liquid fuel include alcohol, kerosene, liquid hydrogen, and hydrazine. Two common liquid oxidizers are nitrogen tetroxide and liquid oxygen.

While Goddard was conducting experiments in the United States, schoolteacher Hermann Oberth launched the field of rocketry bound for space in Germany. In 1923, he published the basic mathematical formulas fundamental to rocket space flight. He also drew up plans for piloted spacecraft, research rockets, and even conceived of a **space station** for re-fueling.

Rocket Research During World War II

The next generation of work by German rocket scientists was devoted mostly to the Nazi war effort in World War II. Among the most famous individuals in this field was engineer Wernher von Braun, who headed rocket research and development throughout the war.

Von Braun was central to the development of long range missiles, in particular the A-4, the forerunner of all later rockets and ballistic missiles. Later renamed the V-2 (Vengeance Weapon 2), the rocket weighed 29,000 pounds (10,817 kilograms), carried 2,000 pounds (746 kilograms) of high explosives, and traveled at a speed of 3,000 miles (4,827 kilometers) per hour and to a height of about 50 miles (80 kilometers). First successfully launched in 1942, the V-2 proved to be a terrifying weapon.

After the war, von Braun and several of his associates were captured and came to work for the U.S. government. At the White Sands Proving Grounds in New Mexico, von Braun continued conducting rocket research and test flights. Years later, as director of NASA's George C. Marshall Space Flight Center in Huntsville, Alabama, von Braun presided over the construction of a new long-range ballistic missile called the Redstone. It was 70 feet (21 meters) tall, twice the size of the V-2.

Anxious to develop a rocket that could launch a satellite into orbit, von Braun produced the Jupiter-C, a rocket capable of flying at a height of 680 miles (1,094 kilometers)and covering a distance of 3,300 miles (5,310 kilometers).

Meanwhile, scientists in the former **Soviet Union** were also working on a rocket that could launch a vessel into space. Under the leadership of engineer Sergei Korolëv they designed and built the first Soviet liquid-propellant rockets and winged engines, and later, the first Soviet intercontinental ballistic missile (ICBM).

In 1957, a rocket based on the ICBM was used to launch *Sputnik 1,* the first human-made satellite to orbit the Earth. This rocket, which was 100 feet (30.5 meters) long and weighed about 300 tons (272 metric tons), became the most widely used rocket in the world. More significantly, it pushed the **space race** between the United States and the Soviet Union into high gear.

A few months after the launch of *Sputnik,* von Braun's Juno 1 (a modified Jupiter-C) was used to launch the *Explorer 1* satellite into orbit. Then in 1961 and 1962 his Redstone was used to launch two short piloted flights.

The most celebrated of von Braun's rockets was the Saturn V, which in 1969 launched *Apollo 8,* the first manned mission to the moon. This giant rocket stood 363 feet (111 meters) tall and weighed 3,000 tons (2,721 metric tons).

Bigger and more powerful rockets were developed at a rapid pace by both nations over the next two decades, only to come to a virtual standstill in the late 1980s. In the United States this halt was due to the explosion of the **space shuttle** *Challenger,* resulting in the deaths of the entire crew. And political problems leading to the breakup of the Soviet Union put that country's space program on hold.

The 1990s have seen a resurgence in space exploration, primarily by re-usable space shuttles and unpiloted spacecraft that travel throughout the **solar system** conducting research. However, with the **cold war** over, and the space race a notion of the past, rocket development has become less of a priority for both the United States and Russia.

See also **Braun, Wernher von**; **Goddard, Robert**; **Oberth, Hermann**; and **Tsiolkovsky, Konstantin**

Roemer, Olaus (1644–1710)

Danish astronomer

Olaus Roemer was a man to whom precision mattered a great deal. He was preoccupied with all sorts of measurements, including measurements of time, weight, distance, volume, and temperature. He is most famous for his measurement of the **speed of light,** an experiment which he did with greater accuracy than anyone before him.

Roemer was born in Jutland, Denmark. He studied astronomy at the University of Copenhagen, after which he moved to Paris, France. There he began to observe the motion of Jupiter's largest moons.

Roemer relied on the notes of his colleague Gian Dominico Cassini, who had kept careful records of the times that each of Jupiter's moons passed behind Jupiter and thus was eclipsed (hidden from view) by the planet.

Roemer, however, found that his own observations did not always agree with Cassini's predicted times. He discovered that the eclipses came a bit sooner than expected when the Earth's orbit brought it closer to Jupiter, and later than expected when the Earth and Jupiter were farther apart. He assumed, correctly, that the differences were due to the time it took light to travel from Jupiter to Earth.

In 1675, Roemer made calculations based on information taken from two eclipses, one when Earth and Jupiter were closest and the other when they were farthest apart. By measuring the differences of distance between the planets and time of the eclipses, Roemer computed that light travels at 141,000 miles (226,870 kilometers) per second. He came within 76 percent of the value accepted today at 186,282.397 miles (299,728.377 kilometers) per second. At this speed, a particle of light can travel around the Earth's equator about 7.5 times in just one second. More important than the accuracy of his estimation, Roemer showed that light travels at a finite speed. Previously, astronomers had assumed that the speed of light knew no limits.

This figure went unchallenged until the mid-1700s, when English astronomer James Bradley came up with the much more precise measurement of 185,000 miles (297,665 kilometers) per second. To obtain this measurement, Bradley tilted a telescope at various angles to observe the **aberration of light,** or the Earth's motion forward into the starlight. The amount he angled his telescope allowed Bradley to determine the ratio between the speed of light and the speed at which the Earth moves. He calculated first that light moves ten thousand times faster than the Earth, then that the Earth travels at 18.5 miles (29.8 kilometers) per second.

After Roemer completed his study of Jupiter's moons, he returned to Copenhagen. There he helped reform the Danish system of weights and measures and argued for the adoption of the Gregorian **calendar** (the calendar we use today). He also assisted Gabriel Daniel Fahrenheit in formulating a new system of temperature.

Roemer is further known for crafting a variety of mechanical devices, including clocks, a thermometer, a **micrometer** (an instrument that measures minute distances), and astronomical instruments.

See also **Speed of light**

Olaus Roemer.

Rubin, Vera (1928–)

American astronomer

Vera Cooper Rubin set the stage for women astronomers. She burst onto the astronomy scene with her 1954 doctoral dissertation on the distribution of **galaxies** and a decade later became the first female observer ever appointed to the Palomar Observatory in southern California. In her current tenure at the Carnegie Institution, Rubin has investigated the motion of galaxies, as well as the existence of large amounts of the invisible substance called **dark matter** in our area of the universe. By example, as well as through outspoken advocacy, Rubin continues to widen opportunities for women and girls in all fields of science.

Vera Cooper Rubin was born on July 23, 1928, in Philadelphia, Pennsylvania, to electrical engineer Philip Cooper and the former Rose Applebaum. At the age of ten, Rubin's family moved to Washington, D.C., where she attended public high school. As a teenager Rubin informed her father that she wanted to be an astronomer. He helped her build a telescope and took her to meetings of the local amateur astronomers club. He also offered advice that she take up something more practical, such as mathematics. Following her graduation from high school, Rubin received a scholarship to Vassar College, which was then a women's school.

Rubin studied science and mathematics at Vassar and graduated in 1948. The same year, she married physicist Robert Rubin, who was at the time a graduate student at Cornell University. Rubin subsequently went through a master's program at Cornell. She claims to have found the atmosphere there rather discouraging to women and noted that, had she stayed at Cornell, she "would have been too intimidated to become an astronomer."

After graduating in 1951, Rubin moved with her husband to Washington, D.C., where their first child was born. Rather than studying astronomy, as she had planned, she suddenly found herself at home, changing diapers. Before long, however, Rubin enrolled in a Ph.D. program in astronomy at Georgetown University. There she studied under the influential Russian-American physicist and **big bang** theorist George Gamow. Her dissertation, which pointed out how galaxies tend to be clumped together throughout space, was initially ignored, although its importance was finally acknowledged in the 1970s.

By 1954, the Rubins had two children and two doctoral degrees between them. They eventually had a total of four children, three of whom are now scientists, and one, a mathematician. Rubin's daughter, Judy Young, is a professor of astronomy at the University of Massachusetts.

Rubin's Career at DTM

Rubin next taught for one year at a junior college before being hired at Georgetown. She accepted a position there in 1955 as a research associate and in 1962 was promoted to assistant professor. In 1965, she left Georgetown to join the staff of Palomar Observatory. Her next career move was to the Washington, D.C.-based Carnegie Institution's Department of Terrestrial Magnetism (DTM), where she remains to this day.

The Carnegie Institution is a private foundation, begun in 1902 by multimillionaire Andrew Carnegie, to support scientific research. The DTM was founded in 1904 to study the Earth's magnetic properties. Over the last several decades, astronomical research has dominated this department's agenda.

Rubin's research at the DTM has focused primarily on two areas: galactic dynamics (the motion of galaxies) and dark matter. In the first area, Rubin has studied the mutual attraction of stars within a galaxy, the forces that hold a galaxy together. She has also studied the formation of **spiral galaxies** out of moving clouds of gas and dust.

The realization that both bright and dark parts of a galaxy contain equal amounts of matter led Rubin to conclude that invisible, or "dark" matter, is present. She built on the observations of Swiss astronomer Fritz Zwicky, who first speculated that dark matter exists. Astronomers now believe that dark matter is a "cosmic glue," holding together rapidly spinning galaxies and controlling the rate at which the universe expands.

Rubin's career has hardly been limited to her post at the Carnegie Institution. In fact, she has to her credit a long list of publications, editorial appointments, organizational posts, and visiting professorships. She was elected to the National Academy of Sciences in 1981 and has sat on Harvard University's astronomical committee.

Rubin has also devoted much time and energy to encouraging women and girls in scientific pursuits. To this end, Rubin is a member of American Women in Science and has served as a visiting professor at Vassar College. Rubin has also written a children's book on astronomy entitled *My Grandmother Is an Astronomer,* in which she explains the role of an astronomer to a young girl.

See also **Dark matter** and **Spiral galaxy**

Russell, Henry (1877–1957)

American astronomer

Henry Norris Russell was born in Oyster Bay, New York. At the age of twenty-three he earned his Ph.D. from Princeton University. He then traveled to England and worked at laboratories in London and Cambridge. At the Cambridge Observatory, Russell photographed stars to determine their **parallax,** the apparent shift in the position of stars, due to observing them from different places. In 1905, he returned to Princeton, where seven years later he was appointed director of Princeton's observatory.

There, Russell's main interest continued to be stars. He established that there was a connection between a star's color, brightness, and spectral class. A star's spectral class is determined by a its light **spectrum,** which, in turn, is a function of its temperature. Russell found that blue stars were hottest, red stars were coolest, and the temperature of yellow-white stars was somewhere in between. Similarly, blue stars were the brightest and red stars the dimmest.

Russell found some exceptions, however. For example, some red stars were very bright, which meant they either had to be very close or very large. This type of star is called a **red giant.** A red giant is a once-average-sized star that, towards the end of its lifetime, expands to many times its original size and turns a reddish color. Small red stars, in contrast, are called **red dwarf**s.

Russell then drew a graph with luminosity (brightness) on the vertical axis and temperature (as well as spectral class) on the horizontal axis. He plotted numerous stars and found that, with few exceptions, they fell on a diagonal line with

Henry Russell.

hot, blue-white stars on the upper left, continuing down to cool, red stars on the lower right. Red giants, however, being both bright and cool, formed a cluster in the upper right of the diagram. The stars along the diagonal line are called main sequence stars.

A star spends most of its lifetime at one position (determined by its brightness and temperature) on the diagonal line. If, however, a star becomes a red giant and then later a **white dwarf** (or, if it's large enough, a **black hole**), it falls off the main line and occupies a place on the upper right or lower left of the diagram. Thus, the distribution of stars on the diagram tells us a lot about both the life cycle of an individual star and the characteristics of a population of stars.

Russell published his work in 1913 only to discover that ten years earlier Danish astronomer Ejnar Hertzsprung had come to the same conclusion. The chart, therefore, was given the name **Hertzsprung-Russell diagram,** in honor of both of its creators. It is still considered one of the most famous diagrams in astronomy.

See also **Hertzsprung, Ejnar** and **Stellar evolution**

Ryle, Martin (1918–)
English astronomer

When Martin Ryle entered the field of **radio astronomy** (the study of objects in space by observing the **radio wave**s they emit), it was still brand new. In 1932, radio engineer Karl Jansky had created the first, simple radio antenna that picked up signals from space. The next step was taken five years later by amateur astronomer Grote Reber, who built a 31-foot-diameter (9.4-meter-diameter) radio dish in his backyard. Ryle greatly enhanced the power of **radio telescope**s so that they could detect many, fainter sources, with greatly enhanced detail.

Matter in space emits radiation from all across the **electromagnetic spectrum** (the range of wavelengths produced by the interaction of electricity and magnetism). In addition to light waves, the electromagnetic spectrum includes **radio wave**s, **infrared radiation, ultraviolet radiation, X-ray**s, and **gamma ray**s. For centuries, astronomers knew only about objects in space that shine with visible light. Since the development of radio astronomy,

infrared astronomy, and **gamma ray astronomy,** scientists have learned about many other parts of the **cosmos** that were previously invisible.

During World War II, Ryle was assigned to a government post at the Telecommunications Research Establishment (later renamed the Royal Radar Establishment) where he developed methods of counteracting the effects of enemy radar. He then studied radio astronomy at Cambridge University. Next he went to Jodrell Bank, England, to use what was then the world's largest radio telescope with a dish 250 feet (76 meters) across. While scanning the **constellation**s Cassiopeia and Cygnus, Ryle discovered signals too strong to be coming from individual stars and found that they were entire radio **galaxies.**

Ryle Designs Radio Telescope Systems

Ryle then learned how to multiply the power of individual radio telescopes and thus produce a sharper image. Radio waves are hard to focus because they are so long and stretched out. Some measure up to 6 miles (9.7 kilometers) from peak to peak. Ryle found that two or more telescopes placed a distance apart acted as a single telescope with a diameter equal to the area separating them. He spaced them up to 140 wavelengths from one another and found that the farther apart they were, the clearer the picture was that they produced.

Martin Ryle.

In 1955, he used twelve telescopes to create the first **radio interferometer,** a system of multiple radio telescopes linked electronically. The radio waves detected by each telescope were sent to a single receiver where a computer processed the information, creating a much more detailed picture than could ever come from a single radio telescope. In the following decade, astronomers around the world copied this technique.

Ryle's task was made more difficult because he had to work with the primitive computers available at the time. He compensated for this by developing his own technology, a "phase-switching" receiver. Phase-switching technology is something used to "clean-up" the radio signal. It gets rid of unwanted noise and interference. Phase-switching adds half a wavelength to the path of the signal from the second antennae in a pair, every other half-cycle. It therefore modifies the "phase" (one complete up-and-down motion of a wave) of incoming radio waves from each antenna, to produce a clean pattern. With this device, Ryle discovered fifty new astronomical sources of radio waves.

Ryle and his colleague Antony Hewish used a form of the radio interferometer in the 1960s when they, along with graduate student Jocelyn Bell Burnell discovered **pulsars**, rapidly spinning **neutron star**s that produce a blinking on-and-off signal. For this achievement, Ryle and Hewish shared the Nobel Prize for physics in 1974.

Ryle's development of radio **interferometry** thrust the new field of radio astronomy into the cutting edge of astronomical discovery. In honor of his achievements, Ryle was made a knight in 1966.

See also **Radio astronomy**

Sagan, Carl (1934–1996)

American astronomer

The name Carl Sagan is nearly synonymous with popular astronomy today. No one has done more than he to introduce so many people to the wonders of space. Among his works are a 1980 Pulitzer Prize-winning public television series and companion book, both called *Cosmos*. Sagan, who has extensively studied the Earth's atmosphere and the beginnings of life, also believes that humans have a responsibility to protect our planet. For this reason he is an outspoken advocate against nuclear war.

Carl Sagan was born in New York City. He first earned a bachelor's degree, followed by a doctoral degree in 1960, from the University of Chicago. He next taught and conducted research at the University of California, Berkeley, and then at Harvard University. In 1968, he accepted a faculty position at Cornell University in Ithaca, New York, where he remains a professor of astronomy and space science. Sagan is also the director of Cornell's Laboratory for Planetary Studies.

Sagan's first research topic was the surface and atmosphere of Venus. In the early 1960s, he studied the planet using radar, as well as an optical telescope, to explore why the planet has such a high temperature. The **radio wave**s given off by Venus were measured at 621 degrees Fahrenheit (327 degrees Celsius), well over ten times the temperature of the Earth's surface. Sagan calculated the height and composition of Venus' dense clouds. He learned that they trap heat, creating a **"greenhouse effect,"** the warming that occurs when a planet's atmosphere allows heat from the sun to enter, but not leave.

Carl Sagan uses a giant model of the solar system to explain why the orbits of the planets are stable.

Sagan then moved on to what has become his primary area of study, the beginnings of life on Earth. He mixed together and shone radiation through a mixture of methane, ammonia, water, and hydrogen sulfide to recreate, as closely as possible, the conditions that produced early life. In this melting pot formed amino acids, the building blocks of DNA (deoxyribonucleic acid). Sagan also detected simple sugars that can combine to form nucleic acids, glucose, and fructose (all essential to sustaining life), and adenosine triphosphate (ATP), which stores energy in living cells. This experiment was based on the earlier work of scientist Stanley Lloyd Miller, who studied the production of organic molecules from non-living matter and concluded that life arose on Earth when discharges from lightning sparked the formation of complex nucleic acids and proteins in the oceans.

Sagan is also been a strong proponent of space research. He has held important scientific positions in a series of planetary missions launched by

the National Aeronautics and Space Administration (NASA). These include the Viking program, the Mariner program, the Pioneer program, and the Voyager program.

In 1966, Sagan used reflecting radar to map mountains and cliffs on the surface of Mars. He also collected information about a dust storm on Mars, which blocked out the sun for a period of time. He hypothesized that a similar situation would occur on Earth in the case of a nuclear war, coining the phrase nuclear winter. Thus began Sagan's long-term quest to reverse the arms race and prevent nuclear war, a consequence of which, he believes, would be to wipe out most forms of life on our planet.

Sagan has authored or co-authored over a dozen books, including three with his wife and science writer Anna Druyan. He has also published over four hundred scientific articles and is editor of the astronomical journal *Icarus.* Many of Sagan's writings support his view that life exists on other planets.

Sagan, who is currently president of the Planetary Society, has received honors and awards too numerous to list in the areas of writing, education, and space exploration. He is currently conducting research on ways in which atmospheric temperature is affected by volcanic activity, as well as studying the chemical composition of planetary atmospheres.

At a 1994 astronomy conference at Cornell, held in honor of his sixtieth birthday, Sagan spoke about a photograph of Earth taken by one of the two *Voyager* spacecraft, in reference to his most recent book *Pale Blue Dot.* "There is perhaps no better demonstration of the folly of human conceits than this distant image of our tiny world," he said. "To me, it underscores our responsibility to deal more kindly with one another, and to preserve and cherish the pale blue dot, the only home we've ever known."

In 1995, Sagan underwent a bone marrow transplant in an attempt to treat a rare but curable bone marrow disease called myelodysplasia. He died on December 20, 1996.

Salyut program

On April 19, 1971, the Soviets launched *Salyut 1,* the world's first **space station.** A space station is an orbiting craft in space that can be boarded by astronauts and in which they can be housed for extended periods of time. The Salyut series was a diversion of sorts from the **space race,** the contest to achieve superiority in space flight between the United States and the former **Soviet Union.** At the end of the 1960s, the Soviets quietly gave up their quest to land a human on the moon and shifted their focus to other types of space exploration.

Salyut 1 was a small station that could accommodate three **cosmonaut**s for three to four weeks. The station was intended to be used multiple times, but as fate was to have it, it was only used once.

Salyut 1 was shaped like a tube that was skinnier in some parts than others. It was 47 feet (14 meters) long and 13 feet (4 meters) across at its widest point. It weighed over 25 tons (23 metric tons). Four solar panels extended from its body like propellers, providing the station's power. It contained a work compartment and control center, a propulsion system, sanitation facilities, and a room for experiments. At one end was a dock through which astronauts could enter.

Soyuz 10, launched on April 22, 1971, was the first mission to *Salyut 1*. The spacecraft, carrying three cosmonauts, reached *Salyut* the next day. The spacecraft was unable to dock with *Salyut,* however, for an as-yet-unexplained reason and returned to Earth. Another attempt to dock was made by *Soyuz 11,* launched June 6, 1971. This crew succeeded in docking and entering the station. They remained on board for twenty-four days, but their mission ended in tragedy. During the descent to Earth, a valve in the spacecraft opened unexpectedly, allowing all the air in the cabin to escape. As a result, the crew suffocated.

After this mishap, the Soviets decided to end the Salyut program. They programmed *Salyut 1* to re-enter the Earth's atmosphere on October 11, 1971. Six months after it was lifted into space, the space station was incinerated.

Military Missions

Over the next twenty years, the Soviets operated six more Salyut space stations, which met with mixed success. Three of these—*Salyut 2, Salyut 3* and *Salyut 5*—were military missions. These stations were similar to the civilian Salyuts in design, but somewhat smaller, with only two solar panels. They also contained an unmanned capsule that could return material such as film or other sensitive information to Earth. All members of these crews were military pilots.

Salyut 2 was launched on April 3, 1973. Eleven days later, however, something went wrong, and the space station exploded. No attempt had been made to send a crew to that station. *Salyut 3* was launched on June 25, 1974. It received only one crew, which spent two weeks on board that July. The next mission to *Salyut 3* was unable to dock. The station burned up on re-entering the Earth's atmosphere in January 1975. The final military space station, *Salyut 5*, was launched on June 22, 1976. This station received two crews during its fourteen months in orbit. Little is known about the activities of the crews during these military missions.

Civilian Missions

After two unsuccessful attempts in July 1972 and May 1973 to put civilian stations into orbit, *Salyut 4* was launched on December 26, 1974. The design of this station was essentially the same as the first civilian station, *Salyut 1*, but with a different distribution of solar panels. The purpose of *Salyut 4* was to carry out scientific experiments. To this end, it contained a large **solar telescope.**

The first visitors to *Salyut 4* arrived on January 10, 1975, and stayed for a month, setting a Soviet space endurance record. The second crew headed for the station but never made it. Their spacecraft malfunctioned, and they were forced to make an emergency landing in Siberia. The third and final mission to *Salyut 4* took off on May 24, 1975. This crew again set an endurance record, remaining on board for sixty-three days.

The last two stations—*Salyut 6* and *7*—were equipped with two docking ports, which made it easier to transfer supplies. This change meant that astronauts could remain on board for longer periods of time. The crews of those stations, including a number of people from other countries, performed astronomical research, plant growth experiments, and Earth observations.

Salyut 6 was launched on September 29, 1977, and remained in orbit until July 1982. During this time it, received numerous sets of astronauts, as well as supplies carried by unpiloted *Progress* spaceships. The longest stay on *Salyut 6* by any crew was 185 days.

The final station in the series, *Salyut 7*, was launched on April 19, 1982. During its decade in space, *Salyut 7* also hosted numerous delegations. The longest visit lasted was 237 days. The last time the space station was occupied was in March 1986, by cosmonauts who had already begun their stay at the new *Mir* space station. This group spent six weeks on *Salyut 7* before returning to *Mir. Salyut 7* burned up in the Earth's atmosphere on February 7, 1991.

The Russians are still considered world leaders in space station technology. They are currently operating *Mir,* the only functioning space station in existence today. For the past eleven years, *Mir* has continuously hosted a series of Russian cosmonauts and international space travelers. *Mir* is being looked to as a model for the International Space Station, scheduled for completion early in the next century.

See also **International Space Station**; *Mir* **space station**; *Skylab* **space station**; and **Space station**

Sandage, Allan (1926–)
American astronomer

In 1991, Allan Sandage was the recipient of the Royal Swedish Academy of Sciences' Crafoord Prize. Sandage was recognized, in the words of the academy, for "his very important contributions to the study of **galaxies,** their populations of stars, clusters and **nebula**e, their evolution, the velocity-distance relation and its evolution with time." The Crafoord Prize is the highest honor that can be bestowed on an astronomer. It is considered the equivalent of the Nobel Prize, since astronomy is not a category considered by the Nobel Prize committee.

Sandage started out as an assistant to pioneering astronomer, Edwin Hubble. He has had a long and distinguished career at the Mount Wilson and Palomar observatories in California. He was the first person to detect and try to explain the nature of **quasar**s, the brightest known objects in the universe. He is also recognized for his work in attempting to determine the age and size of the universe.

Allan Rex Sandage was born in 1926 in Iowa City, Iowa. He had just begun attending classes at Miami University in Ohio when he was drafted into the Navy in 1945. Shortly thereafter he went back to school, this time at the University of Illinois, where he completed a bachelor's degree in 1948. He then entered the new graduate program in astronomy at the California Institute of Technology. Sandage wrote his dissertation on the composition of stars in a **globular cluster** called "M3," referring to its position as the third non-star object to be catalogued by French astronomer Charles Messier.

By 1953, when Sandage completed his Ph.D., he had already been working for a year at Mount Wilson Observatory as Hubble's research assistant. Shortly thereafter he was made a permanent staff observer at both Mount Wilson and Palomar observatories (collectively known as the Hale Observatories), a position that he continues to hold. Over the years, Sandage has also served as a visiting fellow at numerous universities. These include Cambridge, Harvard, Haverford, the University of South Africa, Australian National University, the University of Basel (Switzerland), the University of California at San Diego, the University of Hawaii, and Johns Hopkins.

Sandage's Research On Quasars

Sandage's greatest claim to fame is the discovery of quasars. Quasars are compact objects beyond our galaxy, so distant that their light takes several billion years to reach us, yet so bright that they shine more intensely than one hundred galaxies combined. Through a telescope, a quasar appears to be a relatively close, faint star.

Sandage spotted a quasar in the course of analyzing the **spectra** of stars present in an area of the sky where **radio wave**s had been detected. Along with radio astronomer Thomas Matthews, Sandage located one particularly strong source of radio waves that coincided with the position of a star-like object in another galaxy. Never before had an individual star been identified as a source of radio waves, so Sandage and Matthews did not know what to make of this object. They called it a "quasi-stellar radio source," which was later shortened to "quasar."

This discovery attracted the attention and curiosity of many other astronomers. The first to have any success at describing quasars, in late 1962, was a Dutch astronomer named Maarten Schmidt. Schmidt's calculations placed the quasar at an amazing two billion **light-year**s away. He then measured the diameter of the object and learned that although it was emitting as much energy as one trillion suns, it was only about the size of the **solar system.**

Sandage's other research has mainly been in determining the location and age of globular clusters. His work begins where that of his mentor, Edwin Hubble, left off. In the 1920s, Hubble and his colleague Milton Humason had photographed globular clusters in distant galaxies and found that their light **spectra** were shifted toward the red end of the visible light range. This phenomenon, called **red-shift,** indicates movement away from the observer. Hubble and Humason found that, within their sample, all galaxies were moving away from all other galaxies, implying that the universe is expanding. Hubble then derived an equation (**Hubble's Law**) that describes a distance-to-speed relationship of galaxies and, ultimately, the expansion of the universe. It states that the farther away a galaxy is from us, the faster it is receding.

Sandage measured the distance to globular clusters in the **Milky Way,** information that he then used to estimate their age at ten billion years old. By extension, he reasoned that the universe must be at least that old. Sandage combined his data with Hubble's to come up with the theory that the universe is expanding at a decreasing rate. He carried that logic one step further to predict that at some point in the future the universe will stop expanding altogether and will enter a period of contraction.

Sandage has received numerous awards in addition to the Craoord Prize, from groups including England's Royal Astronomical Society, the American Astronomical Society, the Swiss Physics Society, and others. He is married to Mary Lois Connelly and has two sons. When he is not immersed in globular clusters, Sandage relaxes by gardening, cooking, and listening to opera music.

See also **Hubble, Edwin**; **Quasars**; and **Schmidt, Maarten**

Saturn

In 1980 and 1981 the world watched with wonder as the *Voyager 1* and *Voyager 2* spacecraft sent back the first detailed photos of Saturn and its spectacular rings. The two **space probe**s also transmitted images of Saturn's moons, revealing new details about many of them and even discovering a few new ones. This elaborate system of planet, rings, and moons still holds many mysteries, most of which will probably remain unsolved until the next scheduled spacecraft reaches Saturn in the year 2004.

Saturn is the sixth planet from the sun and the second largest, after Jupiter. Saturn is also the only planet with a density less than water (about 30 percent less). This fact means that, if plopped into an ocean, Saturn would float. However, given that Saturn is about 9.4 times wider and 95 times more massive than Earth, it is unlikely that an ocean big enough could be found.

Saturn rotates very quickly on its axis. In fact, it takes this giant planet only ten hours and thirty-nine minutes—less than half the time it takes Earth—to complete a turn. As a result of all this spinning, Saturn has been flattened at its poles. It is wider by 10 percent at its equator than it is from pole to pole. In contrast to the length of its day, Saturn has a very long year. Because it is so far from the sun, it takes 29.5 Earth years to complete one orbit.

Saturn consists primarily of gas. Its hazy yellow clouds are made of crystallized ammonia, swept into bands by fierce, easterly winds, that have been clocked at up to 1,100 miles (1,770 kilometers) per hour at the equator. Winds near the poles, however, are much tamer near the poles. Covering Saturn's surface is a sea of liquid hydrogen and helium, that gradually becomes a metallic form of hydrogen. The liquid hydrogen and helium conducts strong electric currents that, in turn, generate the planet's powerful **magnetic field.** Saturn's core, which is several times the size of the Earth, is made of rock and ice. The planet's atmosphere is made up of

Saturn and her moons.

about 97 percent hydrogen, 3 percent helium, and trace amounts of methane and ammonia.

About every thirty years, following Saturn's summer, a massive storm occurs. Known as the "Great White Spot," it is visible for nearly a month, shining like a spotlight on the planet's face. The spot then dissipates and stretches around the planet as a thick white stripe. The storm is thought to be a result of the warming of the atmosphere, which causes ammonia to bubble up and solidify, and be whipped around by the planet's monstrous winds.

The Rings of Saturn

Saturn's most outstanding characteristic is its set of rings. The three other largest planets (Jupiter, Uranus, and Neptune) also have rings, but Saturn's are by far the most spectacular.

Centuries ago, astronomers saw the rings as bulges on either side of the planet, which they guessed were moons. For this reason Galileo Galilei hypothesized in the early 1600s that Saturn was a triple-planet. In 1658, Dutch astronomer Christiaan Huygens, equipped with a stronger telescope, first correctly identified the structure as a ring. In later years, astronomers discovered that the ring actually consisted of three distinct rings. The Voyager missions of 1980 and 1981 revealed a system of over one thousand ringlets encircling the planet at a distance of 50,000 miles (80,450 kilometers) from its surface. *Voyager 1* and *2* also detected markings like dark spokes radiating from the planet, through its brightest ring.

The rings, which are estimated to be about one mile thick, are divided into three main parts: the bright A and B rings and the dimmer C ring. The A and B rings are divided by a gap called the Cassini Division, named for its seventeenth-century discoverer Giovanni Domenico Cassini. The A ring itself also contains a gap, called the Encke Division, in honor of Johann Encke, who discovered it in 1837. Whereas the Encke Division really is a gap, meaning it contains no matter, the Voyager missions showed that the Cassini Division contains at least one hundred tiny ringlets, each composed of countless particles.

While the composition of the rings is not entirely known, scientists do know that they contain dust and a large quantity of water. The water is frozen in various forms, such as snowflakes, snowballs, hailstones, and icebergs, ranging in size from a 3 inches (7.6 centimeters) or so to 10 yards (9 meters) in diameter.

Nor are scientists sure how the rings were formed. One theory states that they were once larger moons that were smashed to tiny pieces by **comet**s or **meteorite**s. Another theory holds that the rings are pre-moon matter, cosmic fragments that never quite formed a moon.

The Moons of Saturn

Saturn has eighteen known moons, more than any other planet. And in 1995 the Hubble Space Telescope detected four more objects that appear to be moons, but which have yet to be confirmed. All of the moons are composed of about 30 to 40 percent rock and 60 to 70 percent ice. All but two have nearly circular orbits and travel around Saturn in the same plane.

Christiaan Huygens discovered Saturn's first moon, Titan, in 1655. It is the only moon in the **solar system** with a substantial atmosphere. Titan is composed mainly of nitrogen, with smaller quantities of methane and possibly argon. *Voyager 1* also revealed that Titan has seas of liquid nitrogen, which may be bordered with an organic tar-like matter. We have been prevented from taking a closer look by Titan's thick blanket of orange clouds.

Before the Voyager missions, Titan was thought to be the largest moon in the solar system. That distinction is now held by one of Jupiter's moons, Ganymede.

October 6, 1997, is the planned launch date for the *Cassini* orbiter, which will deliver much more complete information about Saturn and its moons. The *Cassini,* which will arrive at Saturn in June 2004, will carry with it a **probe**, called *Huygens,* that it will drop onto the surface of Titan for a detailed look at the moon's surface. Once it delivers *Huygens,* the spacecraft will orbit Saturn at least thirty times over a four year period.

National Aeronautics and Space Administration (NASA) engineers plan for *Cassini* and *Huygens* to collect information on the following features: the structure and behavior of Saturn's rings; the surface features and composition of each moon; Saturn's **magnetosphere** (magnetic field surrounding the planet); the gravitational field of the planet and each moon; and the atmosphere of Saturn and Titan.

See also **Voyager program**

Saturn V rocket

The Saturn V **rocket** stands out as the largest and most powerful rocket ever developed. This giant rocket stands 363 feet (111 meters) tall and weighs 3,000 tons (2,721 metric tons). It is nearly twice as tall as a **space shuttle** at launch. To get an idea of just how spectacular it was, think of a New York City skyscraper taller than the Statue of Liberty blasting off with a deafening roar and enough force to make the earth shake.

Saturn V was one of a series of Saturn rockets developed by German engineer Wernher von Braun and his colleagues. Von Braun came to work for the U.S. government at the end of World War II. Just prior to Saturn, von Braun had created the Redstone rocket, which was used in the earliest piloted space flights, the Mercury missions of 1961 and 1962.

The Saturn series included two rockets besides Saturn V. They were Saturn I and Saturn IB. The first Saturn rockets were about 150 feet (45 meters) tall and 21 feet (6.4 meters) thick at the base. Studies indicated that neither had sufficient thrust to send an Apollo spacecraft to the moon, which led to the development of the many-times-more-powerful Saturn V.

Saturn V proved remarkably successful. It was used as the **launch vehicle** for all piloted Apollo flights to the moon, beginning with the December 1968 launch of *Apollo 8*. And in July 1969, Saturn V was the force behind *Apollo 11,* the first lunar landing mission. In all, Saturn V propelled twenty-four astronauts toward the moon, twelve of whom set foot on the lunar surface. This rocket was capable of lifting an object weighing 285,000 pounds (129,273 kilograms) into orbit around the Earth and of sending 100,000 pounds (45,359 kilograms) to the moon.

Saturn V was comprised of three stages. The first (bottom) stage was 138 feet (42 meters) tall and 33 feet (10 meters) in diameter and was powered by five engines. It operated for just over two minutes, by which time the spacecraft had reached a height of 38 miles (61 kilometers) above Earth. This stage then fell away from the rest of the vehicle and dropped into the ocean.

The second stage then took over for the next six minutes. It was also 33 feet (10 meters) in diameter, but only 81 feet (25 meters) tall. It was propelled by five engines, with the combined power of thirty diesel locomotives. This stage fired for six minutes, driving the Apollo spacecraft to a speed of 14,000 miles (22,000 kilometers) per hour. It separated from the spacecraft at about 120 miles (190 kilometers) above ground.

*A Saturn V rocket
blasts off from
Kennedy Space
Center with the
Apollo 11 spacecraft
on its nose, July 16,
1969.*

The third and final stage of the rocket was nearly the same height as the second stage, but only about half as wide. Its single engine fired twice: the first time immediately after the second stage separated, to project the spacecraft into orbit around the Earth; and the second time, about ninety minutes later, to push the spacecraft out of its orbit, and in the direction of the moon.

Like most of the rockets used in space flight, Saturn V was fueled by liquid **propellant,** a mixture of liquid fuel and liquid oxidizer. These two substances are initially stored in separate tanks. When combined in the combustion chamber, they ignite and produce the energy that propels the vehicle. Types of liquid fuel include alcohol, kerosene, liquid hydrogen, and hydrazine. The liquid oxidizer may be nitrogen tetroxide or liquid oxygen. Liquid-propellant rockets have advantages over solid-propellant rockets in that they ignite with a much more powerful explosion and are capable of shutting down and restarting.

Fifteen Saturn V rockets were built in all. The first two were used on unpiloted Apollo test flights and the next ten on piloted Apollo missions. The thirteenth and final Saturn V flight came on May 14, 1973, when it placed the U.S. **space station** *Skylab* into orbit. Due to the cancellation of the last two Apollo missions, the two remaining Saturn V rockets were never used and are on display at space centers, one at Cape Canaveral and the other in Houston.

See also **Braun, Wernher von**; **Launch vehicle**; and **Rockets**

Schmidt, Maarten (1929–)

Dutch astronomer

Maarten Schmidt, currently a professor of astronomy at the California Institute of Technology (CalTech), was the first person to explain the nature of **quasar**s. Quasars are compact objects beyond our **galaxy,** so distant that their light takes several billion years to reach us, yet so bright that they shine more intensely than one hundred galaxies combined. The first of these objects—originally called "quasi-stellar radio sources"—was observed by Allan Sandage, an astronomer at the Hale Observatories in 1960. Two years later Schmidt uncovered the reason that quasars are truly remarkable.

Schmidt grew up in the city of Gröningen, in the Netherlands. He was thirteen years old when he first became interested in astronomy, an interest he traces to a particular night during World War II when the power was knocked out through the entire city. Schmidt looked up at the sky and noticed how brilliant the stars were against the black background. He constructed a small telescope from a cardboard tube, taping a magnifying glass to one end and an eyepiece to the other, and began to explore the stars.

Schmidt went on to study **astrophysics** at the University of Leiden under Jan Oort, who is known for his pioneering work on **comet**s. Schmidt's early area of research was the distribution of **mass** throughout the **Milky Way.**

Schmidt completed his Ph.D. in 1956, and three years later came to the United States to undertake a research project at Palomar Observatory in Southern California. He used the 200-inch (508-centimeter) Hale Telescope, at that time the world's largest, to complete a survey of radio galaxies that had been started by retiring astronomer Rudolph Minkowski. Night after night Schmidt sat in the telescope control room, photographing the **spectra** of objects within those galaxies.

Schmidt's Quasar Discoveries

One night in late 1962, Schmidt photographed a star-like object and found it had a **spectrum** unlike any he had seen before. Most stars emit radiation consistent with the spectrum of hydrogen, but this unusual object had wavelengths heavily skewed toward the range of red light.

Such a skewed spectrum is known as a **red-shift** and is indicative of an object moving away from the point of observation. The greater the redshift, the faster the object is moving. Schmidt determined that this particular object was moving at about 16 percent the **speed of light.**

Schmidt then calculated that the object was located at an amazing two billion **light-year**s away. In order to be observable from Earth at that distance, the object could not be a star at all, but had to be something larger, such as a galaxy. He then measured the diameter of the object and learned that although it was emitting as much energy as one trillion suns, it was only about the size of the **solar system.**

Schmidt immediately recognized the value of his discovery in terms of learning about the evolution of the universe. He had just observed the most distant, hence the oldest, object known to exist. He also determined that the galaxies located along the line of sight between the observer and the quasar provide a window into the evolutionary stages of the universe.

For his discovery, Schmidt, along with his colleague Jesse Greenstein, was named California Scientist of the Year in 1964. He was also given the Helen B. Warner Prize of the American Astronomical Society, which is granted for significant achievements made by astronomers under the age of thirty-six (Schmidt was thirty-three when he discovered the nature of quasars). As further testament to the importance of his discovery, Schmidt was featured on the cover of *Time* magazine. The design consisted of several overlapping images of Schmidt's head, floating in a sea of quasars and stars.

Since that time, Schmidt's research has largely focused on the evolution and distribution of quasars in space. His main finding has been that quasars were more prevalent in the earliest stages of the universe than in latter stages. This discovery means that the farther into space one looks, the greater the concentration of quasars one will encounter.

Schmidt served as Director of the Hale Observatories from 1978 to 1980 and as President of the American Astronomical Society from 1984 to 1986. In addition to his current teaching post at CalTech, Schmidt chairs the Board of the Associated Universities for Research in Astronomy (AURA), which is now involved in placing the twin giant Gemini telescopes at the Mauna Kea Observatory in Hawaii.

In 1992, Schmidt was given the Catherine Wolfe Bruce Medal, one of astronomy's highest honors. The Astronomical Society of the Pacific grants this prize for a lifetime of achievement in astronomy.

Even after residing in the United States for forty years, Schmidt is quick to point out that he is still a Dutch citizen. He proudly carries his "green card" identifying him as a resident alien and he still votes in Dutch elections.

See also **Quasars** and **Sandage, Allan**

Seasons

The change of seasons is a result of the Earth's yearly journey around the sun. Most places in the world have four seasons: winter, when the sun shines for the fewest hours per day and never gets very high in the sky;

spring, when there is roughly the same number of hours of daylight as night and the sun can be seen at a higher point in the sky; summer, when day is longer than night and the sun shines almost directly overhead; and fall, when the number of hours of day and night evens out again and the sun drops in the sky.

Many people believe that the seasons exist due to the changing distance of the Earth from the sun as the Earth completes its elliptical orbit. However, this explanation is incorrect. The difference of distance from the Earth to the sun, between any given points on the orbit, is not large enough to influence our seasons. In fact, the Northern Hemisphere of the Earth is closest to the sun on about January 4 (one of the coldest days) and is farthest away on about July 5 (one of the hottest).

What, then, is the explanation for the occurrence of seasons? Simply put, the seasons are caused by changes in the angle at which sunlight strikes any particular place on Earth. This angle changes throughout the year because the tilt of the Earth's axis is different than the angle of the plane of the Earth's orbit around the sun.

The best way to understand this phenomena is to try a simple experiment. Place a lamp on the desk in front of you. Now take a tennis ball or a ping pong ball and draw a line around its middle (representing the equa-

The seasons.

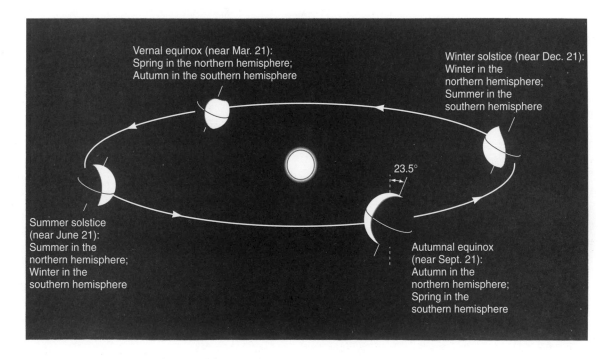

Vernal equinox (near Mar. 21):
Spring in the northern hemisphere;
Autumn in the southern hemisphere

Winter solstice (near Dec. 21):
Winter in the
northern hemisphere;
Summer in the
southern hemisphere

23.5°

Summer solstice
(near June 21):
Summer in the
northern hemisphere;
Winter in the
southern hemisphere

Autumnal equinox
(near Sept. 21):
Autumn in the
northern hemisphere;
Spring in the
southern hemisphere

tor). Mark an "N" on the top half (for the Northern Hemisphere) and an "S" on the bottom half (for the Southern Hemisphere).

First hold the ball with the "N" pointing straight up and the "S" pointing down. Now tilt the ball so the "N" is slightly to the right side of center (this represents the 23.5 degree-tilt of the Earth's axis away from the perpendicular). Hold the ball this way in front of the light and move it in a circle in this order: move it to the right of the light, swing it behind the light, then over to the left of the light, and finally to the front again. You will notice that when the ball is to the right of the light (similar to the Earth on December 22, the first day of winter in the Northern Hemisphere), the "S" half of the ball receives more light than the "N" half. When the ball is directly behind or in front of the light (representing March 21 and September 23, the start of spring and fall, respectively), both halves are equally illuminated. When the ball is to the left of the light, representing June 22—the start of summer—the "N" half is brighter.

If you'd like to more closely simulate the Earth's motion, you can spin the ball about its axis (keeping your fingers on the "N" and "S" while turning it) as you move it around the light. The area of the ball facing away from the light represents the part of the world experiencing nighttime.

The main point of this exercise is to understand that the Northern Hemisphere receives the greatest hours of, and most direct, sunlight in June, causing the long days and warm temperatures of summer. In contrast, we receive the fewest hours of, and least direct, sunlight in December, causing the cold temperatures and short days of winter. Fall and spring are "neutral" seasons, in a sense, because at those times both hemispheres are bathed in an approximately equal amount of sunlight.

Seasons in the Southern Hemisphere are opposite those in the Northern Hemisphere, so that, for instance, it is summer in Australia when it is winter in Illinois. The variation in seasons also depends on your **latitude.** The closer to the equator you get, the less seasonal change you will experience. The reason is that at the equator, the amount of sunlight remains relatively constant. The most extreme changes in season occur at the poles. In the polar summer, the sun shines most of the day, while at the same time the opposite pole is going through a winter of darkness.

See also **Equinox** and **Solstice**

Seyfert, Carl (1911–1960)

American astronomer and astrophysicist

Carl Seyfert is credited with the discovery of a whole class of **galaxies** that bear his name, the **Seyfert galaxies.** These spiral-shaped galaxies are characterized by having an exceptionally bright nucleus. Seyfert's general area of astronomical expertise was determining the **spectra** as well as brightness and color, of stars and galaxies.

Carl Keenan Seyfert was born on February 11, 1911, in Cleveland, Ohio. He was trained in astronomy at Harvard University and graduated with a bachelor's degree in 1933. Two years later he completed his master's degree and in 1936 he earned his Ph.D.

Seyfert then spent four years working in the Chicago, Illinois, branch of the McDonald Observatory. This observatory, which is headquartered in Texas, was then partly owned by the University of Chicago. Since 1962 it has been under the sole proprietorship of the University of Texas. Seyfert's research there centered on analyzing the spectra of stars in the **Milky Way.**

In 1940, Seyfert moved to the West Coast to work as a National Research Fellow at the Mount Wilson Observatory near Pasadena, California. It was there in 1943 that he discovered Seyfert galaxies. From 1946 to 1951 he served as the director of Barnard Observatory at Vanderbilt University in Nashville, Tennessee. In 1952, he was made a professor of astronomy at the university, where he remained until his death in an automobile accident in 1960.

Seyfert's work at Mount Wilson involved a study of twelve **spiral galaxies,** galaxies like the Milky Way that consist of a central disk of stars with starry arms that extend outward and wrap around the disk like a pinwheel. The galaxies in Seyfert's study had very faint arms and a very bright nucleus. He found that the nuclei, in addition to emitting radiation in visible light wavelengths, also gave off **infrared radiation, radio wave**s, and **X-ray**s. In analyzing their spectra, he concluded that they contained the following very hot gases: hydrogen, ionized oxygen, nitrogen, neon, sulphur, iron, and argon. These gases are prone to explosions, which cause the nucleus to rotate much faster and more violently than the rest of the galaxy.

Seyfert galaxies greatly outshine the other galaxies in a cluster. Some even approach the brightness of **quasar**s, the brightest and most distant objects from Earth. The nuclei of Seyfert galaxies are also similar to quasars in that both types of objects emit radiation from all across the **electromagnetic spectrum.** This pattern has led some astronomers to theorize that the nuclei of Seyfert galaxies may be faint quasars.

At present over 150 Seyfert galaxies have been discovered, accounting for roughly 10 percent of all known giant spiral galaxies. Another recent theory about Seyfert galaxies is that they are a stage of development through which all giant spirals pass. If this is true, our own galaxy may spend 10 percent of its existence as a Seyfert galaxy.

See also **Galaxy**; **Quasars**; **Spectroscopy**; and **Spiral galaxy**

Shapley, Harlow (1885–1972)

American astronomer

Harlow Shapley did not become an astronomer the usual way. When he was a teenager, with no more than a fifth-grade education, he landed a job as a journalist at the *Daily Sun* in Chanute, Kansas. Seeking to improve his writing skills, he made his way to the University of Missouri to enroll in journalism school. It turned out, though, that the school wasn't due to open for another year. So Shapley sat down with a catalogue of available courses and started with the letter "A." He couldn't pronounce the first course, archaeology, but he turned the page and saw one he could pronounce: astronomy. He signed up and soon left journalism behind.

Harlow Shapley.

Shapley grew up in rural Nashville, Missouri, the son of a hay farmer. His grandfather was an abolitionist (someone who worked to end slavery) whose house formed a link in the underground railroad, the network that helped slaves to freedom. The ideals of social justice were forever ingrained in young Shapley's mind, and he later became involved in human rights issues.

Shapley received a bachelor's degree from the University of Missouri in 1910 and a master's degree the following year, with honors in mathematics and physics. After graduation, he began a doctoral program at Princeton University. There he worked with astronomer Henry Russell on **eclipsing binary stars,** systems of two stars orbiting around a common point of **gravity,** that cross paths, often hiding one star from view. The two men studied ninety such pairs of stars, using new methods to measure their sizes.

Shapley earned his Ph.D. in 1914. That same year, he was hired to work at the Mount Wilson Observatory in Pasadena, California. There he studied **cepheid variable** stars, yellow **supergiant**s that become brighter and dimmer at regular intervals. Shapley discovered many new caught variables within **globular cluster**s of stars and attempted to calculate the distance to those clusters.

Leavitt's Discovery of the Period-Luminosity Relationship

In this task, Shapley relied on the work of Henrietta Swan Leavitt, the astronomer who first identified and explained the functions of cepheid variables. Leavitt had discovered that the longer it took one of these stars to complete a cycle, the brighter it was. This discovery provided a method by which cepheids could be used to measure distances to objects in space. She constructed a **period-luminosity curve,** on which the relationship between the time period and brightness of a caught can be used to come up with its distance from the Earth.

Shapley calculated the distance to cepheids in numerous globular clusters and determined a new value for the size of our **galaxy,** an enormous three hundred thousand **light-year**s across. This value was so drastically different from previous estimate of fifteen to twenty thousand light-years across that Shapley's colleagues had trouble believing it. Shapley further changed the picture of the galaxy by estimating that the sun was fifty thousand light-years from the galaxy's center, whereas scientists had always assumed that the sun was at the galactic center.

The estimate made by Shapley turned out to be about three times too large. The reason for his error was that the **variable star**s he used as "astronomical yardsticks" were really smaller and dimmer than he had thought, and hence not as far away as he believed. Accordingly, he positioned the sun too far from the center of the galaxy, but only by about twenty thousand light-years. Shapley's work, flawed as it was, was important for at least two reasons. First, it established the fact that our galaxy is much larger than previously thought. Second, it demonstrated that our sun (and therefore our planet) had no special position of prominence within the galaxy.

The Great Debate

At about this time, in 1920, Shapley entered into an historic argument—an event known as the Great Debate—with Heber Curtis, an astronomer from Lick Observatory. Shapley and Curtis had both been invited to a symposium held by the National Academy of Sciences on the topic of the size of the universe. The two men debated the dimensions of the **Milky Way** and whether the Andromeda **nebula,** as it was then known, was part of the Milky Way or a galaxy itself, beyond the Milky Way.

Shapley argued that the galaxy was enormous, at three hundred thousand light-years across and that it encompassed the stars of Andromeda. Curtis attacked Shapley's method of measurement using variable stars, and estimated the Milky Way was much smaller. And he placed the Andromeda well outside of our galaxy.

As testament to the fact that new discoveries in 1920 raised more questions than provided answers, both Shapley and Curtis were right—and both were wrong. The Milky Way is large, larger than anyone before Shapley had ever estimated. Yet the Andromeda is its own galaxy far away. All told, the universe is a much larger place than either man had imagined. The significance of this debate is that it addressed issues relevant to the research of the day, which was about to radically change our whole notion of the scope of the universe and our place within it.

The following year Shapley accepted the position of director of the Harvard College Observatory. Some colleagues felt the move was a mistake because most cutting-edge discoveries were being made with the massive telescopes at the California observatories. Nonetheless, Shapley continued in his work, shifting his attention to the Small and Large Magellanic Clouds. In 1924, he determined that the Small Magellanic Cloud was a separate galaxy, about one hundred thousand light-years away.

That same year, Shapley was contacted by astronomer Edwin Hubble, who had discovered two cepheid variables in the Andromeda nebula. Upon studying those stars, Shapley became convinced that he had taken the wrong side in his debate with Curtis and that the Andromeda really was a separate galaxy. Shapley went on to examine tens of thousands of other galaxies in the following years.

In the late 1930s, as Hitler's Nazi forces grew in power, Shapley became active in human rights work. He formed his own type of "underground railroad" by rescuing several European scientists who were in danger from Nazi persecution, and bringing them to the United States. At the conclusion of World War II, Shapley became one of the founders of the United Nations Educational, Scientific, and Cultural Organization (UNESCO).

In the late 1940s and early 1950s, at the beginning of the **cold war** between the United States and the former **Soviet Union,** Shapley hosted scientific and political conferences. These conferences often included Soviet delegates, something harshly scorned by U.S. authorities. For his actions, Shapley was brought before the House Un-American Activities Committee but the committee found no wrongdoing on Shapley's part.

Shapley remained in charge of the Harvard College Observatory until his retirement in 1952. For the next eighteen years he continued to travel and give lectures. When his heart began to fail, Shapley moved to Boulder, Colorado, to live out his final years. He died at the age of eighty-seven.

See also **Cepheid variables** and **Leavitt, Henrietta Swan**

Shepard, Alan (1923–)

American astronaut

In 1961, Alan Shepard made history with the first piloted American space flight. At that time, the **space race** between the United States and the former **Soviet Union** was in high gear. It had begun with the Soviets' launch of the first unmanned satellite, *Sputnik 1,* in 1957. Over the next decade scientists and engineers from the two countries worked at a frenzied pace to achieve various "firsts" in the realm of space travel.

On April 12, 1961, the Soviets also beat the United States to the task of sending a person into space. Yuri Gagarin rode aboard *Vostok 1* for 108 minutes, making a single orbit around the Earth. Gagarin's flight pressured U.S. officials at the National Aeronautics and Space Administration (NASA) to match the Soviet accomplishment. Just four weeks later, on May 5, 1961, Alan Shepard made the first space flight for the United States in the *Mercury 3* spacecraft. Shepard's suborbital (below the height necessary to orbit Earth) flight lasted fifteen minutes. It reached a maximum altitude of 116 miles (187 kilometers) and traveled a distance of 303 miles (488 kilometers), at a speed of 5,146 miles (8,280 kilometers) per hour. The spacecraft then parachuted safely into the Atlantic Ocean.

During his NASA career, Shepard saw the U.S. space program grow tremendously and far exceed Soviet accomplishments. Just ten years after his historic short flight, Shepard flew on the *Apollo 14* mission to the moon. In doing so, he became the fifth man to set foot on lunar soil. By this time the Soviets had given up any hopes they may have had of a lunar landing.

Alan Bartlett Shepard, Jr. was born in 1923 in East Derry, New Hampshire. Like his father, an Army officer who had attended West Point Military Academy, Shepard chose a military career. Shepard went to high school at the Pinkerton Academy in his hometown, then spent a year at the

*Alan Shephard,
commander of the
Apollo 14.*

Admiral Farragut Academy in New Jersey. He next enrolled in the U.S. Naval Academy in Maryland, earning a bachelor of science degree in 1944.

Shepard spent the final year of World War II on the naval destroyer ship *Cogswell* before beginning pilot training at Corpus Christi, Texas, and Pensacola, Florida. Next, from 1947 to 1950, Shepard was stationed at Navy bases in Virginia and Florida and served aboard ships in the Mediterranean Sea. He then attended the U.S. Navy Test Pilot School at Patuxent River, Maryland. He remained there as a flight instructor until 1958, except for a stint aboard a ship in the Pacific Ocean from 1953 to 1956. When NASA chose him to be an astronaut in 1959, Shepard was an assistant to the commander-in-chief of the Navy's Atlantic Fleet.

Shepard Serves As an Astronaut

Shepard immediately stood out among the small group of astronauts as an excellent pilot and engineer. The honor to be the first American in space was granted Shepard by a vote of both NASA officials and his fellow astronauts.

After his first mission, Shepard spent the next three years in support roles for further Mercury flights. In early 1964, he and astronaut Frank Borman were training to be the crew for the first piloted Gemini mission, *Gemini 3,* when Shepard began experiencing health problems. He was diagnosed with Meniere's syndrome, an inner ear illness that causes dizziness and impaired hearing. Unable to fly, Shepard was assigned the responsibility of running the astronaut program, in essence becoming supervisor of all other astronauts. During that time, he also invested successfully in the stock market, making his fortune in the process.

In 1969, Shepard underwent risky experimental surgery on his ear, an operation that was successful. Soon after the operation, he began to ready himself for his 1971 *Apollo 14* journey to the moon. During his nine hours and twenty-two minutes on the moon, Shepard found time to hit a golf ball. Using the moon's light **gravity** to his advantage, Shepard reported that the ball went "miles and miles and miles."

Shepard retired from NASA in 1974 and has since served as a corporate executive for a number of Texas-based companies. His life is featured in the book and movie *The Right Stuff.*

Shepard lives in Houston with his wife, Louise. They have two children, Laura and Julie. Shepard is still involved in business ventures and chairs the board of the Mercury Seven Foundation, the educational organization of the original seven astronauts.

See also **Mercury program** and **Space race**

Sitter, Willem de (1872–1934)
Dutch astronomer

In 1919, the **big bang theory** received a big boost from astronomer Willem de Sitter. De Sitter was the first to offer a compelling argument that the universe was expanding. This is a critical piece of evidence supporting the big bang theory, which states that everything started at one point that exploded and expanded outward. De Sitter also holds the distinction of being one of the few people to take on Albert Einstein over an intellectual point and win.

Willem de Sitter was born in the city of Sneek in the Netherlands. He studied astronomy under the guidance of Jacobus Cornelius Kapteyn at the University of Gröningen. De Sitter's research included a survey of the skies from northern Europe to Cape Town, South Africa. For several years after graduation, he served as assistant to Kapteyn and in 1908 moved to Leiden, the Netherlands.

One long-term project undertaken by de Sitter was an attempt to determine the **mass** of Jupiter's moons. He observed the satellites over the course of several years, noting any movement caused by the interactions of their gravitational fields. Analyzing his findings, de Sitter produced a wealth of information on the motion of Jupiter's moons, which he published in a 1925 article entitled "New Mathematical Theory of Jupiter's Satellites."

While noting irregularities in planetary and lunar orbits, de Sitter became very interested in the concept of **gravity.** He had discussions with Einstein on this matter and even assisted him in developing his **general theory of relativity** and establishing its relevance to astronomy.

Einstein believed that the universe was static (unchanging). This concept, however, was inconsistent with his observation that whereas gravity drew objects together, there was also a force pulling them apart. Unable to identify such a force, he made one up, and called it a cosmological constant. He included this figure in his equations to make them fit with what he observed, while retaining the model of a static universe.

Willem de Sitter looks at the Loomis Telescope at Yale University's observatory, October 31, 1931.

De Sitter had another idea. He suggested accepting the notion that space was expanding, which would account for the perceived repulsion between objects. He urged Einstein to just do away with the bothersome cosmological constant. Einstein disliked this immensely and refused to toss out the number that seemed to hold the universe in place. Years later, however, Einstein realized that his logic had been flawed. Looking back, he called it the "greatest blunder of my life."

De Sitter's expanding universe was later supported by astronomers Edwin Hubble and Vesto Melvin Slipher, who observed objects that were **red-shift**ed, indicating they were moving away from each other.

De Sitter died in Leiden at the age of sixty-two.

See also **Big bang theory** and **Einstein, Albert**

Skylab space station

Skylab was the only **space station** ever operated by the United States. It orbited the Earth from 1973 to 1979, during which time three different crews carried out a variety of scientific experiments for a total of 171 days.

A space station is a satellite that serves as living and work quarters to visiting astronauts. Since 1971, a handful of space stations have been deployed for various lengths of time. All but *Skylab* have been the property of the former **Soviet Union** or its modern counterpart, Russia. For the most part, they have been scientific laboratories, in which groups of **cosmonauts** carry out experiments and themselves act as subjects in tests of the long-term effects of space on the human body. Some space stations have also been used for military missions.

Skylab was launched on May 14, 1973. This two-story craft was 118 feet (36 meters) long and 21 feet (6.4 meters) in diameter and weighed nearly 100 tons (91 metric tons). It contained a workshop, living quarters for three people, a module with multiple docks, and a solar observatory called the Apollo Telescope Mount.

Conditions on the station were far more comfortable than those on Apollo spacecraft. The living area was larger and the sleeping accommodations private and more comfortable. The kitchen area included a freezer containing seventy-two different food selections and an oven of sorts. The dining room table was placed beside a window so diners could enjoy the view of space while they ate. *Skylab* was also outfitted with the first space shower and private toilet. The toilet had a seat belt to prevent the user from floating off.

Exercise equipment, including a stationary bicycle and a treadmill, was also provided. By working out, astronauts could combat the loss of muscle tone caused by an extended stay in space. An odd consequence of exercising, however, was that sweat floated off their bodies in slimy puddles. The person working out had to catch these puddles with a towel so that they would not land on a control panel or other piece of equipment, where they could possibly cause harm.

Problems With *Skylab*

Almost immediately after launch, *Skylab* encountered problems. Its **meteoroid** shield, thermal shield, and one solar panel were lost, while the second solar panel was jammed. In addition, the station's power system

Skylab **space station**

View of Skylab *space station from an Apollo command module, February 8, 1974.*

was damaged. The temperature inside _Skylab_ rose, endangering the sensitive scientific equipment.

Eleven days after _Skylab_'s launch, a crew arrived and repaired most of the damage. Initially the crew was unable to loosen the jammed solar panel. Instead, crew members entered the station and lowered the temperature by thrusting a sun shade through an airlock to replace the lost thermal shield. Two weeks later, during a three-and-a-half hour **space walk,** they managed to open the solar panel and restore power to the station. The crew then remained on board for twenty-eight days and carried out planned experiments.

The second crew arrived at _Skylab_ on July 28, 1973, and stayed for fifty-nine days. Crew members made additional repairs and constructed a larger sun shade. They then carried out a number of experiments in materials science and space medicine, as well as making a series of Earth and solar observations. And the effects of zero **gravity** were demonstrated by the crew during a videotaped "classroom in space" lecture that was made available to schools.

An endurance record for U.S. astronauts of eighty-four days in space was set by the third and final crew to _Skylab_. Following their November 16, 1973, launch, the three astronauts studied the effects of weightlessness; set a new record of seven hours for working outside the spacecraft; photographed the Earth; conducted biomedical experiments; studied the Comet Kohoutek and a giant solar **flare**; and greatly increased our knowledge of the sun and its effect on the Earth's environment.

In addition, this mission provided an opportunity to learn about the psychological, as well as the physical effects, on humans subjected to long durations in space. An important lesson learned by flight controllers was not to make excessive demands on the crew. At one point, members of the third _Skylab_ team briefly refused to carry out their duties until a new schedule was negotiated with mission control.

The space station was originally expected to function well into the 1980s. However, it was pulled into a lower orbit more quickly than anticipated by unexpectedly high atmospheric drag and, before a repair mission could be sent, had re-entered the Earth's atmosphere. On July 11, 1979, _Skylab_ fell back to Earth, scattering fragments across an area from the Indian Ocean to Australia.

The National Aeronautics and Space Administration (NASA) is now working with Russia, Canada, Italy, Japan, and the European Space

Agency (ESA) on the construction of an International Space Station. It is due to be completed early in the twenty-first century.

See also **International Space Station**; *Mir* **space station**; **Salyut program**; and **Space station**

Slipher, Vesto Melvin (1875–1969)
American astronomer

Vesto Melvin Slipher was born in an era when scientists still believed that the universe was composed of a single **galaxy,** the **Milky Way.** Slipher photographed and studied fuzzy patches believed to be gases within our galaxy. To the surprise of the world, he found that these patches were made of stars, so far away as to be galaxies unto themselves.

Slipher received his training in astronomy at Indiana University. There he learned how to measure periods of planetary rotation, by analyzing a planet's **spectrum.** He was also the first to use this technique in a study of Jupiter's moons.

Vesto Melvin Slipher.

In 1903, Slipher accepted a position at the Lowell Observatory in Flagstaff, Arizona. He was brought to Flaggstaff by astronomer Percival Lowell, famous for his studies of Mars, to investigate the mystery of **nebula**e. Lowell felt that the spiral types of these cloud-like structures were the beginnings of other **solar systems** within our galaxy. It was Slipher's job to study the **spectra** of the light from these spirals, beginning with one called Andromeda.

This was easier said than done. The project required taking photographs that needed twenty to forty hours of exposure each. As a result, it took several nights to produce just one photograph, and many, many photos had to be pieced together to complete the whole picture. By late 1912, Slipher had photographed the entire Andromeda four times.

Studying the spectrum, he discovered it did not match that of any known gas, but was more like the pattern made by starlight. In addition, the spectrum was **blue-shift**ed, meaning the wavelengths were shifted toward the blue (shorter wavelength) end of the range of visible light. A blue-shifted object is one that is approaching the observer. Slipher calculated that the Andromeda was moving toward Earth at a speed of 186 miles (299 kilometers) per second, a tremendous speed that was later revised downward to 31 miles (50 kilometers) per second.

Within two years Slipher, had analyzed the light spectra of twelve other so-called spiral nebulae and learned three things. First, only two of the nebulae showed a blue-shift whereas all the others were **red-shift**ed (moving away from Earth). Second, some of these objects were moving at incredible speeds—up to 683 miles (1,099 kilometers) per second. Third, the objects were not nebulae at all, but star systems so distant that they had to be separate galaxies.

By 1925, Slipher had studied over forty galaxies, two with blue-shifts and the rest with red-shifts. His pioneering work laid the foundation for Edwin Hubble's discovery that all matter is moving away from all other matter and that the universe is expanding.

See also **Red-shift**

Willebrord Snell.

Snell, Willebrord
(1580–1626)
Dutch physicist, astronomer, and mathematician

Very rarely does one find a twenty-year-old student, without even a master's degree, lecturing at a prestigious university. Yet this was the case with Willebrord Snell, who was a mathematical whiz ever since childhood. Perhaps it was in his genes. His father was also a professor of mathematics. Over his lifetime, Snell made significant advances in the fields of trigonometry, optics (the study of light), and map-making.

Snell was born in Leiden, the Netherlands. After a few years of study at the University of Leiden, Snell set out to travel across Europe. Along the way he met such important scientists as Tycho Brahe and Johannes Kepler. He then returned and in 1608 completed his graduate studies. Five years later, he was appointed to his father's post at the university, teaching mathematics, physics, and optics.

Snell next determined how to measure distances using trigonometry. This field was a new one, so Snell had to create its rules and techniques. He used a large **quadrant** (a circular arc divided into 90-degree angles) to measure angles of separation of two points, and in this way could calculate the distance between them. He even arrived at a figure for the radius of the Earth, a figure we know today to be very accurate.

Snell is best remembered today for Snell's law, which explains the angle of refraction (bending) of light. If you shine a flashlight through a glass of water, you will notice that the light beam bends slightly as it enters the water. Snell proved that the angle at which light bends is related to the angle at which it enters the water. The ratio of these angles is a constant, which is determined by the type of material through which the light is passed.

Snell never published his findings on refraction. The information was not widely circulated until 1637, when René Descartes published a law of refraction that was remarkably similar to Snell's law. It bore such a strong resemblance that many, including Christiaan Huygens accused Descartes of plagiarism.

Solar and Heliospheric Observatory

On December 2, 1995, the Solar and Heliospheric Observatory (SOHO) **probe,** was launched toward the sun. This billion-dollar project is a joint mission of the National Aeronautics and Space Administration (NASA) and the European Space Agency (ESA). SOHO is so named because in addition to the sun, it will study the **heliosphere,** the vast region permeated by charged particles flowing out from the **solar wind** that surrounds the sun and extends throughout the **solar system.**

SOHO's goals are to learn the structure of the solar interior, to chart movements in the sun's outer atmospheric layer (the **corona**), and to determine how the solar wind is created. In particular, SOHO aims to uncover the mechanism behind the production of the corona's intense 3.6 million-degree-Fahrenheit (2 million-degree-Celsius) temperature and the expansion of the corona into the solar wind.

SOHO contains a set of telescopes that study processes such as heat production and transfer that originate beneath the sun's surface and work their way through to the surface and solar atmosphere. Also on board SOHO are spectrometers that measure the wavelengths at which radiation is emitted and absorbed by ions in the various layers of the solar atmosphere. From this, scientists can determine density, temperature, and chemical composition of the solar atmosphere. In addition, the satellite contains particle detectors that sample the solar wind to find out its chemical composition and energy levels.

SOHO is the first satellite to probe beneath the sun's surface, where heat production takes place, and get a glimpse of its structure. For this purpose, SOHO contains helioseismological instruments that measure the vibrations of sound waves deep within the sun's core. These instruments are similar to seismographs that detect earthquakes. The areas where vibrations are felt most strongly imply the presence of cavities. Knowing where cavities are is important for coming up with a picture of the sun's interior.

SOHO is a 2-ton (1.8-metric ton) satellite consisting of a **payload** module, where the scientific instruments are kept, and a **service module,** which contains control systems and energy-producing solar panels. The spacecraft was built in Europe and the instruments were constructed by scientists in both the United States and Europe. NASA oversaw the launch and is responsible for mission operations. Keeping track of SOHO's location are the three large radio dishes of the Deep Space Network, located outside of the cities of Madrid, Spain; Goldstone, California; and Canberra, Australia. SOHO returns data to mission headquarters at the Goddard Space Flight Center (GSFC) in Greenbelt, Maryland.

After launch, SOHO traveled nearly a million miles from Earth over two-month period and then entered a "**halo** orbit" around the sun. A halo orbit, which takes 180 days to complete, is situated such that the gravitational fields of the sun and Earth are balanced. Within such an orbit, the satellite has a tendency to fall towards neither the sun nor the Earth.

Once in orbit, SOHO began returning data including television footage. According to a statement made by Goddard-SOHO scientist Joseph Gurman in *The Washington Post,* SOHO's footage showed that "there is continuous motion and action everywhere on the sun."

SOHO is expected to have a lifetime of at least two years and, depending on how the equipment fares, possibly up to six years.

See also **Solar atmosphere**; **Sun**; and *Ulysses*

Solar atmosphere

The sun is about 865,000 miles (1,391,785 kilometers) in diameter or about 109 times the diameter of Earth. The only part of this giant, gaseous body that we can view directly, however, is its atmosphere. The atmosphere consists of three general layers, the **photosphere,** the **chromosphere,** and the **corona.** No sharp boundaries mark the beginning of one layer and the end of another. Rather, transition regions exist in one layer which gradually fades into the next.

The Photosphere

The photosphere is the innermost layer of the sun's atmosphere. Since the sun has no solid component, it does not have a surface the way Earth does. However, the photosphere becomes opaque (solid looking) a few hundred miles into it. Therefore the sun's surface can be considered to be the boundary between transparent and opaque gases, in other words, the photosphere.

The photosphere (which means "light sphere") is a few hundred miles thick. Through it the sun's intense heat and light is given off through the atmosphere's outer layers and into space. In the photosphere, gas cools from about 10,800 degrees Fahrenheit (5,982 degrees Celsius) to about 7,200 degrees Fahrenheit (3,982 degrees Celsius).

The process by which the photosphere transfers heat outward from the sun is called **convection.** It works like this: hot gas flows from the sun's interior to the photosphere, gives off heat, and then is cycled back into the sun, where it is re-heated. (Just remember the principle that hot air rises and cool air falls.) The photosphere is covered with convective cells in which this heat transfer occurs. These cells, called **granules,** are Earth-sized chunks that constantly change in size and shape.

Another feature of the photosphere is the presence of **sunspot**s, dark areas that may exceed the Earth in size. Sunspots are caused by magnetic disturbances and are dark because of their low temperature, about 2,700 degrees Fahrenheit (1,482 degrees Celsius) less than the rest of the surface.

The Chromosphere

Beyond the photosphere lies the chromosphere, another region of transparent gas through which heat and light continue on their way out to space. The chromosphere is around 1,200 to 1,900 miles (1,931 to 3,057 kilometers) thick. It is difficult to determine the point at which the chromosphere ends because, at its outer limit, it breaks up into narrow gas jets called **spicules.**

Although the density of gas decreases from the inner to outer reaches of the chromosphere, the temperature increases tremendously. It goes from about 8,000 degrees Fahrenheit (4,427 degrees Celsius) near the photosphere to about 180,000 degrees Fahrenheit (99,982 degrees Celsius) near the corona.

The chromosphere, which can be viewed only through specialized instruments such as a **spectrohelioscope,** was first observed as a streak of red light during a total **solar eclipse.** This atmospheric layer is punctuated with **flare**s and plages. Flares are sudden, temporary outbursts of light that extend from the outer edge of the chromosphere into the corona. Plages are bright patches that are hotter than their surroundings.

The Corona

The chromosphere merges into the outermost part of the sun's atmosphere, the corona. The corona was also first discovered during a solar eclipse. The weak light emitted by the corona (about half the light of a full moon) is usually overpowered by the light of the photosphere and therefore not detectable. During a solar eclipse, however, the light from the photosphere is blocked by the moon, and the corona can be seen shining around the edges.

The corona is the thinnest part of the atmosphere. It consists of low-density gas and is peppered with **prominence**s. Prominences are high-density clouds of gas projecting outward from the sun's surface into the inner corona. They can be over 100,000 miles (161,000 kilometers) long and maintain their shape for several months before breaking down. The corona extends for millions of miles out into space. As the corona's distance from the sun increases, so does its temperature, to a whopping 3.6 million degrees Fahrenheit (2 million degrees Celsius). At its farthest reaches, the corona becomes the **solar wind,** a stream of charged particles that flows throughout the **solar system** and beyond.

See also **Solar wind**; **Sun**; and **Sunspot**

Solar eclipse

A total eclipse of the sun, also called totality, happens rarely—only about twice a decade and only in those parts of the world touched by the moon's shadow as it speeds across the Earth's surface. The most recent total **solar eclipse,** on November 3, 1994, was visible in the South American countries of Chile, Paraguay, Bolivia, Peru, and Argentina.

For dedicated eclipse-watchers who gathered in South America on that day, the eclipse took on spiritual significance. "Totality was very emotional," said one viewer in a report in *Astronomy* magazine. "I was trembling and crying. It was the best experience of my life."

"The eclipse was a spectacular sight," remarked another observer. "At our altitude of 12,000 feet (19,308 kilometers) the planets were silhouetted against a black sky."

The term eclipse refers to the complete or partial blocking of a celestial body by another body and can be used to describe a wide range of phenomena. Solar and **lunar eclipse**s—occur any time the sun, moon, and Earth are all positioned in a straight line. This arrangement is uncommon because the plane of the Earth's orbit around the sun lies at an angle different than the angle of the plane of the moon's orbit around the Earth. Thus, the moon is usually located just above or below the imaginary plane of the Earth's orbit.

An eclipse may be partial, total, or annular (where one object covers all but the outer rim of another); and it may be barely noticeable or quite spectacular. Only twice a year, do the planes of the Earth's orbit and the moon's orbit coincide, signaling an eclipse season. And only during a small percentage of eclipse seasons do total eclipses occur.

A solar eclipse takes place when the moon's orbit takes it in front of the Earth, blocking the sun from view. A lunar eclipse is different in that the Earth passes between the sun and moon, casting a shadow on the moon. Another way to remember the difference between the two kinds of eclipses is that you can witness a solar eclipse only during the day and a lunar eclipse only at night. While the moon is often visible during the day, an eclipse requires the sun, moon, and the Earth to be lined up, which is only possible at night.

Partial and Total Eclipses

During a solar eclipse, the moon's shadow sweeps across the Earth. The shadow has two parts: the dark, central part called the **umbra,** and the lighter region surrounding the umbra called the **penumbra.** If you are standing in a place covered by the umbra, the sun will be completely blocked from your view, meaning that you will experience a total eclipse. If you happen to be in the penumbra, you will be able to see only part of the sun, a partial eclipse.

The type of solar eclipse also depends on the distance of the moon from Earth. The moon's orbit, like the Earth's, is elongated (stretched out). Thus, at some points along its orbit, the moon is closer to Earth than at others. In order for the umbra to reach Earth and block out the sun, the moon must be at a close point on its orbit. If the moon is too far away, meaning that it appears smaller than the sun, one of two things may happen. First, only the penumbra may reach Earth, creating a partial eclipse. The other possibility is that the moon appears to be centered within the sun. In this case, called an annular eclipse, the sun is seen as a ring of light around the silhouette of the moon.

You may wonder how the moon, a relatively small object, can block out something as massive as the sun. The reason is that, although the sun is four hundred times larger than the moon, the moon is four hundred times closer. Thus, to people on Earth, the sun and moon appear to be the same size.

The first stage of a solar eclipse is called first contact. At that point in time, the moon just begins to cover one edge of the sun. As the moon shifts moves across the sun's face, the sky begins to darken. At the same time, bands of light and dark called shadow bands race across the ground. Just before second contact, when the moon completely blocks out the sun, a final flash of light can be seen at the edge of the sun. This effect is called the diamond ring.

Then, at totality, all sunlight is blocked, the sky turns dark, and the planets and brighter stars are visible. During this period, the sun's **corona** is also visible. The weak light emitted by the corona (about half the light

Opposite page: An eclipse of the sun captured over Detroit, Michigan, in a series of multiple exposures.

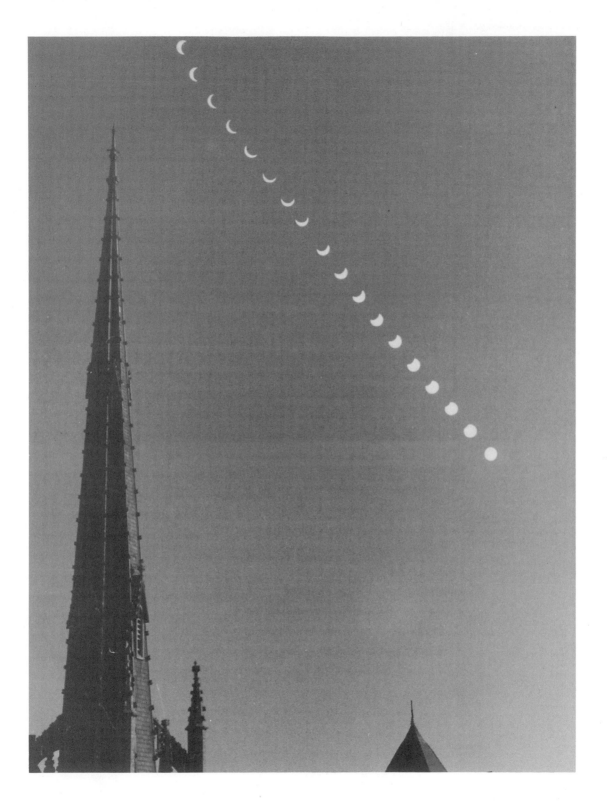

Observing a Solar Eclipse

Never look directly at the sun—even during an eclipse! Many people are tempted to stare at the thin crescent of sunlight visible during an eclipse, but even that level of radiation can cause permanent eye damage. Unless you have a special filter for viewing the sun (improper filters have also resulted in eye damage), you can safely watch an eclipse using the method described here.

All you need are two cards (about the thickness of index cards)—at least one of them with a white surface. Make a small hole in one card by piercing it with a pin and wiggling the pin around a little to enlarge the hole. Hold this card up so the sunlight enters the hole. Hold the other card (with the white surface facing up) below the first, so the image of the sun falls on it. Adjust the distance between the two cards to bring the image into focus. Watch the bottom card to follow the progression of the eclipse.

of a full moon) is normally not visible because it is overpowered by the light of the sun's surface. During a solar eclipse, however, the corona can be seen shining around the edges of the sun. A few short minutes later the moon passes to the other side of the sun and the eclipse is over.

See also **Lunar eclipse**

Solar energy transport

Energy in the form of heat and light is produced by a reaction called **nuclear fusion** in the sun's core. The pressure at the core (312,000 miles, or 502,000 kilometers, below the sun's surface) is great enough to squeeze gas molecules into a material ten times as dense as gold. And the temperature is 27 million degrees Fahrenheit (15 million degrees Celsius). In that intensely hot, pressurized environment, two hydrogen nuclei combine into one helium nucleus, releasing a tremendous amount of energy in the process.

The energy produced in this reaction is bundled into units called photons. Almost immediately after being produced, photons are absorbed by atoms of gas. The photons then begin their one million-year journey from the sun's core to its surface. Once a photon leaves the core (an area about the size of Jupiter), it enters the radiative zone. This is the region of the sun in which energy is "radiated" to the surrounding hot **plasma** (a substance made up of ions and electrons). As photons cross this zone, they spread out and heat greater numbers of gas atoms. As the energy becomes less concentrated, the temperature drops.

The radiative zone varies in size within the sun, from 0.25 to 0.9 solar radii (this means it covers anywhere from a 25 to 90 percent of the distance from the sun's core to the surface). Where a photon crosses from the core into the radiative zone the temperature is about 18 million degrees Fahrenheit (10 million degrees Celsius). The temperature continues to fall throughout the zone, until it reaches about 3.6 million degrees Fahrenheit (2 million degrees Celsius) at the zone's outer edge.

Eventually a photon comes to the inner edge of the convection zone. In this zone heat is carried toward the surface (in a process called **convection**) by slow-moving gas currents called giant cells. The hot gas moves through the long and narrow giant cells toward the surface. There the gas cools off and sinks back down in the direction of the radiative zone, where it picks up more heat and heads for the surface again. (Just remember the principle that hot air rises and cool air falls.)

The convective zone is the layer of sun between the radiative zone and the surface. It generally extends 25 percent of the way down from the surface to the core, although at certain points around the sun it is shallower or deeper. From its inner edge to its outer edge, the convective zone cools off dramatically. At the zone's outer limit, where it meets the **photosphere,** the temperature is about 10,800 degrees Fahrenheit (6,000 degrees Celsius) down from 3.6 million degrees Fahrenheit (2,000 degrees Celsius) at the inner limit.

Convection continues in the surface layer of the sun—the photosphere. This few-hundred-mile-thick layer, in which energy is cycled away from the sun, only accounts for about 1 percent of the sun's depth. Gas is opaque (solid-looking) as it enters the photosphere and becomes transparent by the time it exits. In the process, it cools to about 7,200 degrees Fahrenheit (4,000 degrees Celsius).

The photosphere is covered with Earth-sized convective cells called **granules.** Granules are constantly changing in size and shape, forming and reforming. Any particular granule lasts only about twenty minutes. Within a granule, hot gas rises through the center, cools, and sinks back down around the edges. There it is reheated and rises again. With each cycle, energy is released into the sun's outer atmospheric layers.

Ultimately, energy from the sun dissipates (leaks out) into space. It travels throughout the **solar system,** illuminating and heating the planets, moons, **asteroid**s, and any other object it encounters.

See also **Solar atmosphere** and **Sun**

Solar rotation

The sun, like the planets, rotates about its axis. Unlike most of the planets, the sun rotates from west to east, the same direction that the planets travel around the sun. Seventeenth-century Italian astronomer Galileo Galilei was the first person to track the sun's rotation by noting the movement of **sunspot**s, dark areas on the sun's surface. He calculated that it takes the sun a little less than a month to complete one rotation.

Astronomers in later years found that while the sun rotates in about twenty-five days near its equator, it takes over thirty days near the poles. The sun's rotation also varies with depth. That is, its rate of rotation is different at the surface than in lower layers. This variation in rotational period for different parts of the sun is called differential rotation. The effect is possible only because the sun is made completely of gas. The same phenomenon could not happen on Earth, for instance, because our planet is mostly solid.

Differential rotation results from the interaction of two different types of motion. The first is the rotation of the entire sun and the second is the flow of gas in the convection zone, the layer below the sun's surface. In the convection zone, heat is transported toward the surface by slow-moving gas currents called giant cells. The sun's rotation stretches out the giant cells from north to south, into long, banana-shaped units that are narrowest near the sun's poles. When closest to the sun's equator, gas in a giant cell flows to the east, which is the same direction in which the sun rotates. This effect causes the rotation of the sun's equator to speed up. Near the poles, however, gas in the giant cells cycles toward the west, which runs counter to the sun's rotational direction. This effect causes the polar gases to rotate more slowly.

Differential rotation also affects the sun's **magnetic field** and leads to the production of sunspots. Think of the magnetic field as a series of lines of magnetic force. The varying speeds of rotation cause these lines to become stretched out and twisted. The lines eventually break through the sun's surface and loop back down again. There they stop the flow of heat and form a cool, dark swirl called a sunspot.

See also **Solar energy transport**

Solar sail

Since the 1920s, scientists have considered the idea of harnessing energy from sunlight to propel spacecraft. The concept of a solar sail is similar to that of a wind sail on a sailboat. The sail consists of a large sheet (or sheets), the angle of which can be altered to change the direction of the vessel. In the case of a solar sail, however, it is photons of light rather than wind that acts on the sail.

Engineers from several countries were hard at work in the late 1980s, designing solar sail-powered spacecraft for a planned 1992 solar sail race to Mars. Funds ran out, however, and the race never took place. At present, solar sail use is still in the planning stages.

Using sunlight for spaceship fuel sounds like a great idea. After all, sunlight is free, it never runs out, and it saves carrying the weight of fuel and canisters into space. There are, however, some serious drawbacks. First, to be at all effective, a solar sail would require literally miles of material. Second, the energy of photons is relatively weak compared to rocket propellant. This fact means a spacecraft operating on sunlight would reach its destination at a much later date than one running on conventional chemical-based fuel. And third, the development and use of new technology is always costly and presents inevitable problems.

The most likely approach to the use of solar sails may be to combine fuel sources, essentially using sunlight to add to the ship's own propulsion system. Once in orbit, the ship would unfurl a sail to capture photons. In this way, a spacecraft would be able to operate for much longer than before, continuing even after its fuel packs were empty.

To study the possibility of solar sailing, scientists from the National Aeronautics and Space Administration (NASA) launched small metal needles high into the Earth's atmosphere and observed that sunlight altered the needles' orbit. Next they incorporated small-scale solar panels into the *Mariner 10* spacecraft which in 1974 traveled to Venus and Mercury. These panels, designed to tilt at certain angles to the sun, helped steer the spacecraft. NASA then planned to use solar sails to guide a spacecraft to Halley's **comet** when it passed through the inner **solar system** in 1985–86. These plans never materialized because NASA decided there wasn't enough time to develop and test the technology.

Solar Sail Design

The design and construction of a solar sail is relatively simple. It consists of a sheet made of plastic or some other polymer, coated with a thin layer of aluminum (to reflect the photons). The sail can be one of three shapes: square, disk, or heliogyro. The square design is similar to a kite; the disk is a solid, spinning circle; and the heliogyro consists of several strips radiating outward, like the spinning blades of a helicopter.

The size of a solar sail, however, is quite daunting. In order to reflect enough photon-energy to be effective, a massive surface is required. A square sail would have to have an area of 1 square mile (2.6 square kilometers), whereas the heliogyro would need strips 20 miles (32 kilometers) long by 30 feet (9 meters) wide.

Artist's rendition of a laser light-sail starship with a 621-mile-diameter (1,000-kilometer-diameter) light sail.

A solar sail becomes more effective the longer it is in operation because its rate of acceleration continues to increase. For instance, if a ship headed to Mars were to shut down its thrusters and unfurl a sail the size of one described above, it would initially travel at a speed of only 13 miles (21 kilometers) per hour. One day later it would be moving at 200 miles (322 kilometers) per hour; and after eighteen days its speed would reach 1 mile (1.6 kilometers) per second while still picking up speed. At that rate of acceleration, it would take about four hundred days to reach Mars.

A traditional spacecraft could reach Mars more quickly, but it would have to carry a lot of fuel to do so. About 95 percent of the **mass** of a **space shuttle** or **rocket** in use today is taken up by fuel. And for a round-trip to Mars, a ship would have to be huge, with fuel taking up about 99 percent of its mass. In contrast, a solar sail would account for only about 50 percent of a ship's mass. This frees up quite a bit of space, enabling a ship to carry a much greater cargo, even something the size of an early Apollo **command module.** In addition, a solar sail is re-usable and could power a ship on both its trip to Mars and its return home, and possibly even be used on another mission.

Solar system

Our **solar system** consists of the sun and all of its orbiting objects. These objects belong to various classes, including planets and their moons and rings; **asteroid**s; **comet**s; **meteor**s and **meteorite**s; and particles of dust and debris.

The sun, which keeps the other objects in orbit with its immense gravitational field, alone accounts for 99.8 percent of the **mass** of the solar system. Jupiter, the largest planet, represents another 0.1 percent of the mass, and everything else together makes up the remaining 0.1 percent.

Just how large is the solar system? The average distance between the sun and Pluto, the farthest planet, is about 3.65 billion miles (5.87 billion kilometers). And if we consider the solar system to incorporate the entire space within the orbit of the furthermost planet, that area would be a whopping 41.85 billion square miles (108.4 billion square kilometers). However, our solar system seems quite insignificant when considered in the context of the more than one hundred billion stars in our **galaxy** and the estimated fifty billion galaxies in the universe.

Planets

A planet is defined as a body that orbits the sun (or another star) and produces no light of its own, but reflects the light of the sun. At present, scientists know of nine planets in the solar system. They are grouped into three categories: the solid, terrestrial planets; the giant, gaseous (also known as "Jovian") planets; and Pluto. The first group of planets consists of Mercury, Venus, Earth, and Mars, the planets closest to the sun. The next group, farther from the sun, consists of Jupiter, Saturn, Uranus, and Neptune. The third group consists of a single planet, Pluto, the smallest planet, farther away even than the string of gas giants.

Astronomers have speculated about the existence of two other planets in our solar system: Vulcan, between Mercury and the sun, and Planet X, beyond Pluto. However, despite exhaustive efforts, neither planet has as yet been found.

Moons

A moon is any natural body (as opposed to a human-made satellite) that orbits a planet. Seven of the planets are accompanied on their journeys around the sun by moons. In total, these planets have sixty-one moons. This number is probably higher as a result of the recent unconfirmed sighting of four additional moons around Saturn. Although moons do not orbit the sun independently, they are still considered members of the solar system.

Asteroids

Asteroids are relatively small chunks of rock that orbit the sun. Except for their small size, they are similar to planets. For this reason they are often referred to as minor planets. The most widely accepted theory of the origin of asteroids is that they are ancient pieces of matter that were created with the formation of our solar system, but that never came together to form a planet. An estimated one million asteroids may exist in the solar system, about one hundred thousand of them bright enough to be photographed from Earth. About 95 percent of all asteroids occupy a band of space between the orbits of Mars and Jupiter. The largest of the asteroids, named Ceres, is 584 miles (940 kilometers) in diameter, while the smallest asteroids are no larger than particles of dust.

Comets

Comets are perhaps the most unique members of the solar system. They are made of dust and rocky material mixed with frozen methane, ammonia, and water. For this reason, they are often referred to as "dirty snowballs." A comet speeds within an elongated orbit around the sun. It consists of a nucleus, a head, and a gaseous tail. The tail is formed when some of the comet melts as it nears the sun and the resulting gas is pushed away by the **solar wind.** This causes the tail to always point away from the sun.

Where do comets come from? The most commonly accepted theory is that they originate on the edge of the solar system, in an area called the **Oort cloud.** This space is occupied by trillions of inactive comets, which remain there until a passing gas cloud or star jolts one into orbit around the sun.

Geocentric and Heliocentric Models

Early models of the solar system were **geocentric,** placing the Earth at the center, with the sun, moon, and planets revolving around it. One of the principle architects of this model was the early Alexandrian astronomer Ptolemy, which is the reason this model is also called the **Ptolemaic model.**

The geocentric model presented a troublesome situation, however, when observing the positions of the other planets relative to Earth. It appeared that Mars, Jupiter, and Saturn (the as yet undiscovered outer planets) moved backwards from time to time, but Mercury and Venus did not.

Depiction of our solar system.

To account for this **retrograde motion,** Ptolemy added small secondary orbits called **epicycles,** to the planetary paths.

The Ptolemaic system was accepted as true until Nicholas Copernicus proposed a new **heliocentric model** in 1543, placing the sun at the center of the planets.

Copernicus demonstrated that it was not necessary to make use of epicycles if the sun was placed at the center of the solar system. He explained that retrograde motion was merely an illusion that occurs because the planets' orbits are at different distances from the sun. Since the orbits of Mars, Jupiter, and Saturn were outside the Earth's orbit, the Earth's orbit was smaller and thus the Earth overtook the other planets as it circled the sun. By the same token, Mercury and Venus, because they're closer to the sun, have smaller orbits and thus race around the sun several times during an Earth year. Copernicus mistakenly assumed, however, that planetary orbits were perfectly circular. It was only discovered a century later by Johannes Kepler that planetary orbits are elliptical.

Copernicus was placed under house arrest by church officials for promoting his theories, which were in direct contradiction to church teachings and beliefs, and his publications were banned. Before long, however, the **Copernican model** of the solar system became accepted within the scientific community.

How It All Began

Over time, there have been various theories put forth as to the origin of the solar system. Most of these have since been disproved and discarded. Today the theory considered most likely to be correct is a modified version of the eighteenth-century nebular hypothesis, in which 4.56 billion years ago the sun and planets formed from the solar **nebula**—a cloud of interstellar gas and dust. Due to the mutual gravitational attraction of the material in the nebula, and possibly triggered by shock waves from a nearby **supernova,** the nebula eventually collapsed in on itself.

As the nebula contracted, it spun increasingly rapidly, leading to frequent collisions between dust grains. These grains stuck together to form ever larger objects, first pebbles, then boulders, and then **planetesimals.** These planetesimals continued to stick to solid particles as well as gas (in what's known as the accretion theory) and eventually gave way to **proto-planets,** planets in their early stages.

As the nebula continued to condense, the temperature at its core rose to the point where **nuclear fusion** could begin. It then became a star (our sun) and the bodies farther from the core became the planets.

The original nebular hypothesis was first suggested in 1755 by philosopher Immanuel Kant and later advanced by French mathematician Pierre-Simon Laplace. It is similar to the current theory in that it also states that the sun and planets were formed from a solar nebula. It differs, however, in the way the planets came to be.

The old nebular hypothesis theorized that as the nebula contracted, and spun more and more rapidly, it spewed off rings of material. The central portion of the nebula became the sun, while the rings came together to form the planets. This theory did not recognize the role of the sticking together of particles in the formation of the planets. The main reason why the notion of rings has been supplanted by the accretion theory is that accretion provides a much better explanation for the motion of the planets around the sun. According to the accretion theory, the planets began as part of the rotating nebula, in which case one would expect the fully formed planets to continue rotating. If the planets formed from cast-off rings, there is no reason to expect they would revolve around the sun.

While the nebular hypothesis was popular in the 1800s and the modified nebular theory is preferred today, there was a period in the early 1900s when another group of theories were in fashion—the encounter theories. These theories all stated, in one way or another, that the planets were created by a collision between a foreign object (such as another star) and the sun. This resulted in the ejection of material from the sun, which cooled to form the planets.

This theory has been rejected for two main reasons. One is that such material would have likely remained very close to the sun and not scattered at the distances of the planets, and the other is that solar material would be more likely to dissipate than to come together.

Other Solar Systems?

Recently, evidence has come to light suggesting that ours may not be the only solar system in the galaxy. In late 1995 and early 1996, three new planets were found, ranging in distance from thirty-five to forty **light-year**s from Earth. The first planet, discovered by Swiss astronomers Michael Mayor and Didier Queloz, orbits a star in the **constellation** Pegasus. The next two planets were discovered by American astronomers Geoffrey Marcy and Paul Butler. One is in the constellation Virgo and the other is in the Big Dipper. These new discoveries give astronomers and science-fiction enthusiasts hope that on some yet-to-be-discovered planet, in some yet-to-be-discovered solar system, scientists may yet find intelligent life.

Solar telescope

Only in the last century, with the invention of **solar telescope**s, has it been possible to conduct thorough studies of the sun. Prior to that scientists had to wait for a **solar eclipse** to observe the sun, since the sun's rays are much too intense to view through a regular telescope.

These solar telescopes, constructed by scientists beginning in the late 1800s, took the form of modified **reflecting** or **refracting telescope**s, that

Image of the sun taken by a solar X-ray telescope.

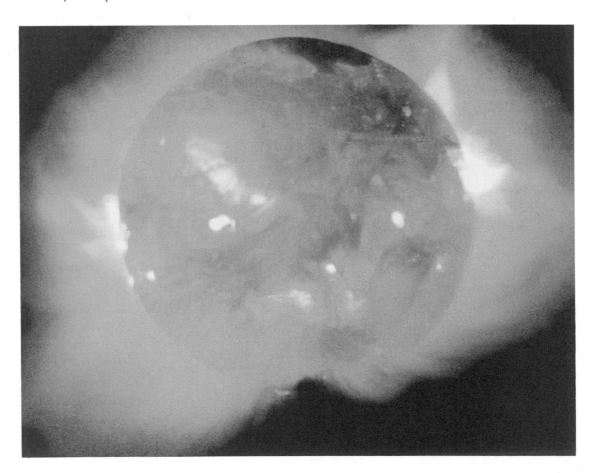

could record details of the outermost layers of the sun's atmosphere, the **chromosphere** and the **corona.** Some of the activities and conditions that occur in this area of the sun include **sunspot**s, **prominence**s, **spicules,** and **flare**s.

The first solar telescopes were developed simultaneously by astronomer George Hale in the United States and astrophysicist Henri-Alexandre Deslandres in France. In 1889, Hale began work on a **spectro-helioscope**—a combined telescope and **spectroscope.** A spectroscope is an instrument that separates light into its component wavelengths. With this kind of telescope, the sun's chemical components would show up as colors. For instance, hydrogen appears red and ionized calcium appears ultraviolet.

Deslandres, meanwhile, built a spectroheliograph, an improvement on Hale's instrument in that it could not only display, but also photograph, the **spectra** produced by solar activity.

These instruments were still limited, however, in their usefulness at times other than during an eclipse. This limitation led French astronomer Bernard Lyot to construct a **coronagraph** in 1930. This device contained a black disk that would create artificially the conditions of an eclipse by blocking out most of the sunlight entering its chamber. An image of just the corona, therefore, would appear on a black screen. With his invention, Lyot obtained the most precise measurements of the sun to date, including its temperature and brightness.

Over the next several years, Lyot continued to improve on his invention, eventually devising a piece of equipment capable of taking moving pictures of prominences across the sun's surface.

Most solar telescopes today are large stationary objects. The sunlight strikes an elevated **heliostat,** a flat, rotating mirror, which reflects light to a mirror at the end of a long shaft. The light is then bounced back to its ultimate destination, a **spectrograph,** which breaks light down into its component wavelengths and photographs the resulting image.

One consideration in designing a solar telescope is that the sunlight entering the instrument is very hot and must be cooled, or it will destroy the instruments. One way to reduce the temperature is to send the light to an underground chamber before it reaches the instruments. In addition, many solar telescope structures are air-conditioned.

Most modern solar telescopes are some form of tower telescope, meaning they consist of a tower through which sunlight enters and is reflected down into underground rooms. A variation of this is a vacuum tower, which is completely empty of air, creating a natural cooling system.

A number of large, sophisticated solar telescopes are in use today at observatories around the world. Most of these are located at high elevations in order to minimize interference from the Earth's atmosphere. The U.S. National Solar Observatory operates a vacuum tower telescope at Sacramento Peak, New Mexico, that is 134 feet (41 meters) high and extends 219 feet (67 meters) underground. The Swedish government operates a similar telescope at the La Palma Observatory in the Canary Islands. Their instrument, however, is more compact, rising only 52 feet (16 meters) above the ground. Both telescopes produce very detailed pictures.

Perhaps the most famous solar telescope is the McMath-Pierce Solar Telescope at Kitt Peak National Observatory near Flagstaff, Arizona. In this instrument, light first strikes a heliostat atop a 100-foot (30-meter) tower, then travels down a diagonal shaft to a depth of 164 feet (50 meters) underground, and finally reflects back to an observation room.

See also **Kitt Peak National Observatory** and **National Solar Observatory**

Solar wind

Solar wind is the outflow of charged particles from the sun's **corona,** its outermost atmosphere. The name "solar wind" makes one think of the blowing, gusting air that people on Earth call "wind." But make no mistake: solar and terrestrial (Earth-based) wind have nothing in common.

Solar wind is not air, but **plasma,** a substance made of ions and electrons that exist at extremely hot temperatures. It is not a solid, a liquid, or a gas, but a completely different state of matter. The particles within plasma appear to move at random and are affected by electric and **magnetic field**s.

The sun's corona extends millions of miles above the surface of the sun, where gravitational forces are very weak. Plasma, which possesses very high thermal (heat) energy, is thus able to escape. It flows out, into interplanetary space, and enters planetary **magnetosphere**s, the regions surrounding planets in which charged particles from the sun are controlled by a planet's magnetic field. Solar wind travels so far that it has been detected even beyond the limits of our **solar system,** in the **interstellar medium.**

One of the best-known examples of the effects of solar wind is the tail of a **comet.** The tail is formed when a comet nears the sun, causing some portion of its nucleus to evaporate. The gas thus formed is swept back by the solar wind into a tail, which always points away from the sun.

Another example is the **aurora**e (Northern and Southern Lights). These beautiful displays of light in the night sky are caused by the interaction of the solar wind and the Earth's magnetic field. As the plasma approaches Earth, its ions are drawn toward the north and south magnetic poles. The plasma ionizes (breaks apart) the oxygen and nitrogen atoms it encounters in the Earth's atmosphere, causing it to glow. Similar aurorae on the planet Jupiter were photographed by the *Voyager 2* spacecraft as it flew by that planet in 1980.

Another effect of the solar wind is to create an interplanetary magnetic field. This happens because the lines of the sun's magnetic field become intertwined with the plasma, and the two effectively "freeze" together. As the plasma expands, the sun's magnetic field flows with it.

The flow of plasma out from the sun is generally continuous in all directions, ranging in speed from 185 to 435 miles (298 to 700 kilometers) per second. It occasionally "gusts" out of holes in the corona at speeds of up to 621 miles (998 kilometers) per second. As the solar wind travels farther from the sun, it picks up speed while losing density. Once it reaches the Earth's orbit, its density is only a handful of particles per cubic inch.

Massive ejections of plasma have been shown to accompany **flare**s, **prominence**s, and **sunspot**s.

See also **Plasma**

Solstice

The **solstice** occurs twice a year, when the sun is at its highest and lowest points in the sky. The summer solstice occurs on about June 22, the longest day of the year. This is when greatest portion of the Earth's Northern Hemisphere is bathed in sunlight. The winter solstice occurs six months later, on about December 22, the shortest day of the year. This is when the smallest portion of the Northern Hemisphere (and the greatest portion of the Southern Hemisphere) is exposed to the sun.

The solstices usher in summer and winter, marking the turning points in the cycle of seasonal changes. The different seasons are due to the amount and intensity of sunlight that a given place on Earth receives at any particular time. The angle at which sunlight strikes a certain place changes throughout the year because the tilt of the Earth's axis is different from the angle of the plane of the Earth's orbit around the sun. Thus, as the Earth moves around the sun, its northern and southern halves are exposed to varying amounts of sunlight.

At noon on the summer solstice, the sun shines directly overhead at a **latitude** of 23.5 degrees north of the equator. This latitude is called the Tropic of Cancer. The closer a person is to this latitude, the more directly overhead the sun appears to be. (The Tropic of Cancer runs through central Mexico, about 10 degrees south of Dallas, Texas, and 20 degrees south of Detroit, Michigan).

Also on this date, the sun completely covers the North Pole. Anyone close to the North Pole on the summer solstice will see the sun approach the horizon around midnight only to rise again, staying up for a full twenty-four-hour period.

On about December 22, the winter solstice, the opposite occurs. At noon on this date the sun is directly above the Tropic of Capricorn (at a latitude of 23.5 degrees south of the equator), making it the longest day of the year for the Southern Hemisphere and the shortest day of the year for the Northern Hemisphere. On the winter solstice, the South Pole becomes the land of the midnight sun.

The Solstice and Mythology

For many cultures past and present, solstice has been an event of great spiritual significance. Some, such as one ancient Irish civilization, have connected it with death and the afterlife. This group in Newgrange, Ireland, constructed a burial tomb around 3300 B.C., the inner chamber of which was illuminated with only sunlight during the week of the winter solstice.

Another ancient group, from Brittany (a region in the northwest of France), built huge bonfires on the summer solstice, on which they would sacrifice cattle. The people of this region believed that the ceremony would prevent the rest of the herd from becoming diseased.

Other cultures have created entire mythologies around the heavens, in which stories about the solstice figure prominently. One such group was the Chumash people, who flourished in what is now California in the 1500s through the 1800s. The entire tribe participated in activities during the week before the winter solstice. One activity was a game in which one team representing the sun played ball against another team representing the North Star (which they called Sky Coyote). The North Star was always victorious over the sun. Next came a ceremony in which the sun rose again.

In many parts of the world, the solstices are still observed. Two groups for whom the solstices hold special meaning are the modern druids (originally an ancient order of Celtic priests) and followers of new-age religions. And, across the United States, one can find all-night dances called "dawn dances," held in celebration of the summer solstice.

See also **Equinox** and **Seasons**

Soyuz program

"Soyuz," which means "union" in Russian, is the longest-running Russian space program to date. Dozens of Soyuz spacecraft have been flown in piloted missions since 1967. A modified version of the original Soyuz vehicles are still used today to transport crews to and from the Russian **space station** *Mir.*

A fleet of **launch vehicle**s also bear the name Soyuz. The initial Soyuz **rocket,** launched in 1957, sent the world's first artificial satellite, *Sputnik,* into orbit. These launch vehicles stand 163 feet (50 meters) tall and are capable of lifting 7.5 tons (6.8 metric tons) into orbit around the Earth. Soyuz launch vehicles have been used for virtually all piloted Russian space flights, right up to the present.

The Soyuz program was originally intended for missions to the moon. The engineer behind this and most other facets of the Soviet space program, Sergei Korolëv, designed a series of three Soyuz spacecraft for this purpose in the early 1960s. In 1964, however, the Soviets decided to use a more powerful Proton rocket for moon flights. They scaled back the Soyuz program to a single series of spacecrafts that would be used for Earth-orbiting missions.

The first of the series, *Soyuz 1,* was comprised of three sections: an orbital module; a descent module; and a compartment containing instruments, engines, and fuel. For most of the mission, the crew remained in the orbital module. This could be depressurized to form an airlock, so **cosmonaut**s could exit to perform **space walk**s. For the ride back to Earth, the crew occupied the descent module, which had a heat shield. This was the only part of the spacecraft to re-enter the Earth's atmosphere intact.

Soyuz 1, launched in April 1967, was plagued with problems and ended in tragedy. Although scanty details of the mission were released by the Soviet authorities, the information we do have indicates that *Soyuz 1* was troubled from the start. It is likely that, due to the failure of at least one of the two solar panels, the spacecraft did not have electrical power. It has also been reported that the ship's thrusters were damaged, making it difficult to control. Soviet mission controllers made one desperate attempt after another to correct the troubled vehicle throughout its flight. They finally maneuvered it through a return sequence, only to have its parachutes fail to open just before landing. *Soyuz 1* crashed to Earth, killing cosmonaut Vladimir Komarov.

Soyuz 2 had been scheduled to launch shortly after *Soyuz 1* so that the two could dock in space. Given the former's problems, however, the latter's mission was delayed. When *Soyuz 2* finally did launch in October 1968, it was as an unpiloted test mission. The next day, the third *Soyuz* took off with one cosmonaut, Georgi Beregovoy, on board. It headed toward *Soyuz 2* and came within 650 feet (198 meters) of it, as a practice run for future docking missions. The two vehicles then returned to Earth.

The next pair of *Soyuz* spacecraft, *4* and *5,* did succeed in docking. In January 1969, cosmonauts Aleksei Yeliseyev and Evgeni Khrunov performed space walks and switched vehicles, accomplishing the first crew transfer in space.

Within a space of two days in October 1969, *Soyuz 6, 7,* and *8* were launched. *Soyuz 6* carried out experiments while *7* and *8* approached one another but did not dock. On the next *Soyuz* flight, in June 1970, the crew set a space endurance record of eighteen days.

Further Problems With Soyuz Program

Soyuz 10, launched on April 22, 1971, was the first mission to the space station *Salyut 1*. The spacecraft docked briefly with *Salyut* the next day, but for some reason that was never disclosed, the crew was unable to enter the station. Instead they undocked and returned to Earth. The crew of *Soyuz 11,* launched June 6, 1971, did succeed in docking with the space station. They then entered the station and remained on board for twenty-

*Soviet Soyuz TM-11
blasts off the
launch pad
December 2, 1990,
carrying a joint
Soviet-Japanese
crew.*

four days. During the crew's descent to Earth, however, a valve opened unexpectedly, allowing all the air in the cabin to escape. As a result, the crew—consisting of cosmonauts Georgi Dobrovolsky, Vladislav Volkov, and Viktor Patsayev—suffocated. The capsule landed in its designated location and members of the helicopter rescue crew were horrified to find the dead cosmonauts inside.

After this mishap, the Soviets made a number of modifications to the Soyuz crafts. They removed a seat in the cabin and reduced the number of cosmonauts on any mission to two. This change made it possible for each occupant to wear a pressurized spacesuit during launch, docking, and re-entry. If the *Soyuz 11* crew had been wearing spacesuits, their deaths probably would have been averted. Adjustments to the solar panels were also made, providing the spacecraft with more electrical power.

It was over two years before the Soviets attempted another Soyuz mission. *Soyuz 12* was launched in September 1973, during which two cosmonauts tested out the new systems. On the next few missions, cosmonauts conducted astronomical research, tested new flight technology, and prepared for the *Apollo-Soyuz* Test Project, the unprecedented U.S.-Soviet link-up in space.

This U.S.-Soviet joint venture came to symbolize a new era of cooperation between the two nations. *Soyuz 19* was launched on July 15, 1975, followed seven hours later by *Apollo 18*. That evening, the two spacecraft rendezvoused for the historic "handshake in space." The two spacecraft remained docked for two days, during which time the astronauts and cosmonauts carried out joint astronomical experiments. After separating from *Apollo, Soyuz* returned directly to Earth, landing on July 21.

Every Soyuz mission beginning with *17* (except *Soyuz 19*) has shuttled cosmonauts to a space station. Most flights have been to one of the *Salyut* stations, although more recently they have been to *Mir*.

The fifteen missions between December 1979 and March 1986 were part of the Soyuz T series. These ships were somewhat bigger and could accommodate three space-suit-clad cosmonauts. They were designed especially for docking with the Salyut space stations.

A series of modified Soyuz T, called the Soyuz TM, went into operation in February 1987. This spacecraft, which is more powerful than its predecessor and has an enlarged cargo bay, is the type used today for flights to and from *Mir*.

See also **Apollo-Soyuz** **Test Project**; **Korolëv, Sergei**; **Launch vehicle**; *Mir* **space station**; **Salyut program**; and **Spacecraft, piloted**

Space probe

Space probe

A **space probe** is an unpiloted spacecraft that leaves the Earth's orbit to explore the moon, other planets, or outer space. Its purpose is to make scientific observations, such as taking pictures, measuring atmospheric conditions, and collecting soil samples, and to bring or report the data back to Earth.

Over thirty space probes have been launched since the former **Soviet Union** first fired *Luna 1* toward the moon in 1959. **Probe**s have now visited every planet in the **solar system** except for Pluto. Two have even left the solar system and headed into the **interstellar medium.**

The earliest probes traveled to the closest extraterrestrial target, the moon. The former Soviet Union launched a series of Luna probes that provided us with our first pictures of the far side of the moon. In 1966, *Luna 9* made the first successful landing on the moon and sent back television footage from the moon's surface.

The National Aeronautics and Space Administration (NASA) initially made several unsuccessful attempts to send a probe to the moon. Not until 1964 did a Ranger probe reach its mark and send back thousands of pictures. Then, a few months after *Luna 9,* NASA landed *Surveyor* on the moon.

In the meantime, NASA was moving ahead with the first series of planetary probes, called Mariner. *Mariner 2* first reached Venus in 1962. Later Mariner spacecrafts flew by Mars in 1964 and 1969, providing detailed images of that planet. In 1971, *Mariner 9* became the first spacecraft to orbit Mars. During its year in orbit, *Mariner 9*'s two television cameras transmitted footage of an intense Martian dust storm, as well as images of 90 percent of the planet's surface and the two Martian moons.

The most recent, and most direct, encounters with Mars were made in 1976 by the U.S. probes *Viking 1* and *Viking 2*. Each Viking spacecraft consisted of both an orbiter and a lander. *Viking 1* made the first successful soft landing on Mars on July 20, 1976. Soon after, *Viking 2* landed on the opposite side of the planet. The Viking orbiters made reports on the Martian weather and photographed almost the entire surface of the planet.

The United States, however, was not the first country to send a probe to Mars. The Soviet Union was. The Soviets' *Mars 1* reached Mars in late 1962, but radio contact with the probe was lost after a few months. In 1971, Soviet engineers succeeded in putting *Mars 2* and *Mars 3* in orbit around Mars. Both of these spacecrafts carried landing vehicles which successfully dropped to the planet's surface, but in each case radio contact was lost after about twenty seconds.

From 1970 until 1983, the Soviets concentrated mostly on exploring Venus. They sent out a series of Venera and Vega probes that landed on Venus, analyzed its soil, took detailed photographs, studied the atmosphere, and mapped the planet using radar.

The next planet to be visited by a probe was Mercury. In 1974, *Mariner 10* came within 470 miles (756 kilometers) of the planet and photographed about 40 percent of its surface. The probe then went into orbit around the sun and flew past Mercury twice more in the next year before running out of fuel.

Space Probes to the Outer Planets

The U.S. space program next sent Pioneer probes to explore the outer planets. *Pioneer 10* reached Jupiter in 1973 and took the first close-up photos of the giant planet. It then kept traveling, crossed the orbit of Pluto, and left the solar system in 1983. *Pioneer 11* traveled to Saturn, where it collected valuable information about that planet's rings.

NASA next introduced the *Voyager 1* and *2* probes, more sophisticated versions of the Pioneers. Both were launched in 1977. Two years later they flew by Jupiter and took pictures of the planet's swirling colors and volcanic moons, and of its previously undiscovered ring.

The next destination for the Voyager space probes was Saturn. In 1980 and 1981, the world watched with wonder as they sent back detailed photos of Saturn, its spectacular rings, and its vast collection of moons. *Voyager 2* then traveled to Neptune, which it reached in 1989, while *Voyager 1* continued on a path to the edge of the solar system and beyond.

After many delays, the latest U.S. probe, *Galileo,* was launched from the **space shuttle** *Atlantis* in 1989. It reached Jupiter in December 1995, and dropped a barbeque-grill-sized mini-probe down to the planet's surface. That mini-probe spent fifty-eight minutes taking extremely detailed pictures of the gaseous planet before being incinerated near the surface.

Galileo will continue to orbit Jupiter and eight of its moons through late 1997, sending information back to Earth.

Currently, NASA has plans underway for at least two more space probes. October 6, 1997, is the planned launch date for *Cassini,* which will once again study Saturn and its moons. It is scheduled to reach its destination in 2004. *Cassini* will drop a mini-probe, called *Huygens,* onto the surface of Saturn's largest moon, Titan, for a detailed look, before going into orbit around Saturn.

Finally, NASA hopes to answer some questions about Pluto early in the next century when it will send off the *Pluto Express*. This probe will consist of two spacecraft, each taking about twelve years to reach Pluto.

See also **Galileo**; **Luna program**; *Magellan*; **Mariner program**; **Mars program**; **Pioneer program**; *Pluto Express*; **Vega program**; **Venera program**; **Viking program**; and **Voyager program**

The arrow is pointing to a Snap-19 radioisotope generator, which were used on NASA's Pioneer space probes when they traveled to Jupiter.

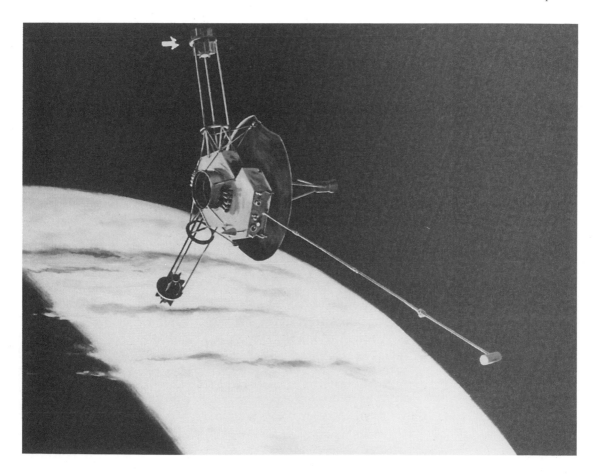

Space race

By the mid-1950s, space travel had moved from the realm of science fiction to the realm of possibility. The United States had publicly stated its intention of launching the world's first artificial satellite during the International Geophysical Year. This event was an eighteen-month period from July 1, 1957 to December 31, 1958, during which time a number of international projects to study the Earth and its atmosphere were scheduled. Then, much to the surprise of the world, the former **Soviet Union** beat the United States to the task with the launch of *Sputnik 1* on October 4, 1957. This event marked the beginning of the **space race,** a twenty-year-long contest for superiority in space travel that paralleled the **cold war** between the two world superpowers.

For several years the Soviet Union held an undisputed lead in the space race. Even as the United States launched its first satellite, *Explorer 1,* on January 31, 1958, the Soviets continued with ever more impressive accomplishments, particularly in the arena of lunar exploration.

In early 1959, the Soviets launched *Luna 1,* the first lunar fly-by (voyage past the moon). Over the next seven years, a series of twenty-four Luna **space probe**s thoroughly explored the moon and the space around it. These **probe**s accomplished a number of "firsts" in unpiloted space exploration, including orbiting, photographing, and landing on the moon. Two Luna craft even deposited robotic moon cars that crossed the lunar surface, analyzing soil composition.

On April 12, 1961, the Soviets scored another major victory in the space race by sending the first person, Yuri Gagarin, into space. In response, the U.S. space program went into high gear. Then-President John F. Kennedy vowed that not only would the United States match the Soviet accomplishment, but also that the United States would put a man on the moon by the end of the decade.

The Apollo program was begun for that purpose and became the focus of the National Aeronautics and Space Administration's efforts during the years 1967–1972. After a number of previous piloted and unpiloted Apollo flights, *Apollo 11* was launched on July 16, 1969, with astronauts Neil Armstrong, Buzz Aldrin, and Michael Collins on board. Four days later Armstrong and Aldrin climbed into the **lunar module** and, true to Kennedy's promise, landed on the moon. As Armstrong set foot on lunar soil, he stated his now-famous words: "That's one small step for [a] man, one giant leap for mankind." The *Apollo 11* mission was considered by many people to be the greatest achievement of the modern world. It finally gave the United States the upper hand in the space race.

Over the next three years five more Apollo missions landed twelve more Americans on the moon. The Soviets became progressively more pessimistic about their chances of getting one of their own **consmonaut**s to the moon. At the end of the 1960s, the Soviets quietly gave up this quest and shifted their focus to a series of **space station**s.

During the 1970s, the space race slowed considerably for a number of reasons. First, both countries needed to slow down after the completion of the exhausting and resource-intensive lunar landing segment. And toward the end of the Apollo series, the U.S. space program was faced with a decline in funding and waning interest. Meanwhile the Soviet space program was beset by the death of its founder and chief engineer, Sergei Korolëv. Also around this time, the field was widened to include the emerging space powers of Japan, China, India, and the European Space Agency (ESA).

Diverging Paths in the Space Race

The space programs of the United States and the Soviet Union took divergent paths in the 1970s, each accomplishing important goals. Following the *Apollo 17* flight in December 1972, NASA turned its attention to unpiloted flights to explore the rest of the **solar system** and to *Skylab,* a space station that operated from 1973 to 1979. Following that, in the 1980s, NASA focused on the development of re-usable **space shuttle**s.

The Soviets operated seven Salyut space stations from 1971 to 1991. Although the early stations met with mixed success, the later stations were quite impressive. Most importantly, the Salyut series laid the groundwork for the highly successful *Mir* space station, which continues to function today.

By many accounts, the space race ended in 1975, with the unprecedented U.S.-Soviet link-up in space: the *Apollo-Soyuz* Test Project. This joint venture, in which the U.S. *Apollo 18* and the Soviet *Soyuz 19* docked for a historic "handshake in space," came to symbolize a new era of peaceful relations in the space programs of the two nations.

The 1980s and 1990s have been dominated by a spirit of international cooperation. One example of this cooperation is the Russian *Mir* space station. Now in its eleventh year of operation, it has hosted numerous visitors from other nations, including the United States. Perhaps the greatest symbol of international cooperation, however, is the International Space Station, slated for completion early in the next century. The partners in this permanent international laboratory in space include the United States, Russia, Canada, Japan, and the fourteen member nations of the ESA. Once the space station is operational, six astronauts at a time will be able to spend periods of three to five months each there while conducting scientific research.

See also **Apollo program**; *Apollo-Soyuz* **Test Project**; *Explorer 1*; **International Space Station**; **Korolëv, Sergei**; **Luna program**; *Mir* **space station**; **Salyut program**; *Skylab* **space station**; **Space probe**; **Space shuttle**; **Space station**; **Spacecraft, piloted**; *Sputnik 1*; and **Vanguard program**

Space shuttle

The U.S. **space shuttle** is a winged space plane designed to transport humans into space and back. This 184-foot-long (56-meter-long) vessel acts like a spacecraft, but looks like an airplane. It contains engines, **rocket** boosters, living and work quarters (for up to eight passengers), and a cargo bay large enough to hold a bus. Plans for the first space shuttle began in 1969 at a time when the National Aeronautics and Space Administration (NASA) was designing a permanent station in space. It was clear that the construction and use of a **space station** would require a reusable transportation vessel.

The space shuttle (officially called the Space Transportation System) is launched vertically using its own engines, aided by two attached rocket boosters. The boosters fall away from the shuttle about two minutes after launch and parachute into the ocean, where they are captured and brought back for re-use. Once in orbit, the shuttle can use its own rocket motors to change direction. When it is ready to come back to Earth, the shuttle brakes with its engines. Its delta-shaped wings facilitate its re-entry into the Earth's atmosphere, and it glides in for a landing on a specially designed 3-mile-long (5-kilometer-long) runway.

In 1981, the first space shuttle to be launched was *Columbia*. Since that time, four other shuttles have been built and flown. Of the five, four are still in use today. Although the United States only had a space station (*Skylab*) in operation from 1973 to 1979, shuttles have been used for a variety of purposes, such as taking astronauts to the Russian space station

*The space shuttle
Challenger lifts off
on mission
51-F/Spacelab 2,
July 1985.*

Mir; delivering new satellites or **probe**s into space; and repairing equipment already in space.

The first shuttle, constructed for testing purposes only, was named *Enterprise,* in honor of the ship on the television series *Star Trek.* Although not intended to go into orbit, *Enterprise* proved capable of lifting off and gliding down to a safe landing. In 1981 its successor, *Columbia,* became the first shuttle to orbit Earth. It took a fifty-four-hour journey, after which it safely returned.

Three new shuttles were later added to the fleet: *Challenger, Discovery,* and *Atlantis.* From April 1981 to January 1986, the shuttles flew twenty-four consecutive successful missions. During these flights they put twenty-eight satellites into orbit, carried the *Galileo* and *Ulysses* **space probe**s and the European-built Spacelab into space, and retrieved four damaged satellites. Two of these satellites were repaired on-site and two others were brought back to Earth for repair and re-launch.

The shuttle program ran quite smoothly until the *Challenger* tragedy of January 28, 1986. That shuttle exploded seventy-three seconds after launch because of a faulty seal in a rocket booster, killing all seven people on board. As a result, all shuttle flights were put on hold for thirty-two months while hundreds of improvements were made in their construction.

In recent years, the only new shuttle built has been *Endeavour,* which replaced *Challenger.* While the space shuttles are still regularly used, there are no plans at present to expand the fleet.

See also **Atlantis**; **Challenger**; **Columbia**; **Discovery**; and **Endeavour**

Space station

The year 1971 saw the launch of the first **space station**, an orbiting spacecraft in which humans can be housed for long periods of time. The first space station was a diversion of sorts from the **space race,** the contest to achieve superiority in space flight between the United States and the former **Soviet Union.** At the end of the 1960s, the Soviets quietly gave up their quest to land a human on the moon and shifted their focus instead to the first space station.

Over the last two and one-half decades, a number of space stations have been placed into orbit, mostly by the Russians. Although originally envisioned as way-stations for piloted missions to the moon and beyond, these vessels have far surpassed that goal. They have been, for the most part, orbiting laboratories in which groups of men and women carry out important scientific experiments and act as subjects themselves in tests of the long-term effects of space on the human body.

On April 19, 1971, the Soviets launched *Salyut 1,* which was designed for both civilian and military purposes. This spacecraft was shaped like a tube that was skinnier in some parts than others. It was 47 feet (14 meters) long and 13 feet (4 meters) across at its widest point and weighed over 25 tons (27.6 metric tons). Four solar panels extended from its body like propellers, providing the station's power. It housed a work compartment and control center, a propulsion system, sanitation facilities, and a room for experiments. It contained a dock at one end through which **cosmonaut**s could leave and enter. *Salyut 1* remained in operation for six months, after which it burned up upon reentering the Earth's atmosphere.

Over the next twenty years, the Soviets operated six more Salyut stations, which met with mixed success. The last two—*Salyut 6* and *7*—were equipped with two docking ports, which made it easier to bring supplies into the station. This change meant that cosmonauts could remain on board for longer periods of time. The longest stay was 237 days. The crews of those stations, including astronauts from many other countries, performed astronomical research, plant growth experiments, and Earth observations.

Skylab and Mir

The only U.S. space station to date has been *Skylab.* Launched on May 14, 1973, this two-story craft was 118 feet (36 meters) long and 21 feet (6.4 meters) in diameter and weighed nearly 100 tons (110 metric tons). It contained a workshop, living quarters for three people, a module with multiple docks, and a solar observatory called the Apollo Telescope Mount.

Almost immediately after launch, *Skylab* encountered problems. Its **meteoroid** shield, heat shield, and one solar panel were lost, while the second solar panel became jammed. In addition, the station's power system was damaged. The temperature rose inside *Skylab,* endangering the sensitive scientific equipment. Eleven days after *Skylab*'s launch, a crew arrived and repaired most of the damage.

In its six years of operation, *Skylab* housed three different crews for a total of 171 days. They studied the effects of weightlessness; set a new record of seven hours for working outside the spacecraft; photographed

*A mock-up of the
Soviet space station
Mir, with the older
generation* Salyut *in
the background, at
the cosmonaut
training complex
near Moscow in
1986.*

the Earth; conducted biomedical experiments; studied the Comet Ko-houtek and a giant solar **flare**; and greatly increased our knowledge of the sun and its effect on the Earth's environment. In 1979, *Skylab* fell back to Earth.

Currently, the only space station in operation is the Russian vessel *Mir. Mir* is 43 feet (73 meters) long and 14 feet (4 meters) wide, with 98-foot-long (30-kilometer-long) solar panels. Launched in February 1986, it can accommodate six crew members. It was designed to afford greater comfort and privacy to its inhabitants, in the hopes that they will be able to remain on board for longer periods. The longest stay so far has been fifteen months.

Now in its eleventh year, *Mir,* which means "peace" or "community living in harmony," has hosted a series of Russian cosmonauts and international space travelers. The current joint Russian/American crew of *Mir,*

including astronaut Shannon Lucid, is conducting research into how humans, animals, and plants function in space.

After *Skylab,* the National Aeronautics and Space Administration (NASA) began planning an elaborate new U.S. space station called *Freedom.* Budget cuts, however, have prevented those plans from becoming a reality. Instead, the United States has joined with Russia, Canada, Italy, Japan, and the European Space Agency (consisting of fourteen member countries) to plan the construction of the International Space Station. It is due to be completed early in the twenty-first century.

See also **International Space Station**; *Mir* **space station**; **Salyut program**; and *Skylab* **space station**

Space telescope

The Earth's atmosphere provides an effective filter for many types of cosmic radiation. This fact is crucial to the survival of humans and other life forms because exposure to that radiation would be deadly. However, given that our atmosphere only allows visible light and **radio wave**s to pass through, it prevents us from observing many objects in space that emit other types of radiation. For instance, from the ground we cannot study celestial bodies that radiate only in wavelengths of infrared, ultraviolet, **X-ray**s, or **gamma ray**s. Many observatories have been constructed at high altitudes, where the atmosphere is thinner, but this solution improves the situation only slightly.

In the 1970s, scientists devised a better solution. They designed a telescope that could be placed into space beyond the Earth's atmosphere. Many people think only of the Hubble Space Telescope when they hear the term "**space telescope.**" However, dozens of other space telescopes have been put into orbit over the last two and one-half decades, each able to detect radiation in a particular range of wavelengths.

The first of these instruments, carried along on Apollo missions and on the *Skylab* **space station,** were small telescopes that could detect X-rays, gamma rays, or **ultraviolet radiation.** They made possible the discovery of hundreds of previously unknown entities, including one likely **black hole.**

In 1977, the first of three High Energy Astrophysical Observatories (HEAO) was launched by the National Aeronautics and Space Administration (NASA). During its year and a half in operation, it provided constant monitoring of X-ray sources, such as individual stars, entire **galaxies,** and **pulsar**s. The second HEAO, also known as the Einstein Observatory, operated from November 1978 to April 1981. It contained an extremely high resolution X-ray telescope which found that X-rays were coming from nearly every star. The third HEAO, launched in September 1979, spent two years monitoring gamma rays. It found that the greatest source of gamma rays is **cosmic ray**s.

International Programs

The late 1970s also saw the launch of the International Ultraviolet Explorer (IUE). This joint project of the United States, Great Britain, and the European Space Agency, was intended to function for only three to five years. Now in its eighteenth year of continuous operation, it holds the title of longest-lived astronomical satellite. The IUE, which recognizes ultraviolet radiation, has studied planets, stars, galaxies, and **comet**s. It has recorded especially valuable information from **nova**e and **supernova**e.

Another international effort—involving the United States, Great Britain, and the Netherlands—resulted in the 1983 launch of the Infrared Astronomical Satellite (IRAS). Since it was measuring **infrared radiation,** which is essentially heat, the satellite had to be cooled with liquid helium. And given that IRAS contained only a three hundred-day supply of helium, its life-span was fairly short. During that time, however, it managed to survey almost the entire sky. It discovered nearly two hundred-fifty thousand objects, including many new "infrared" galaxies, and learned about the formation of planets and stars.

A follow-up to IRAS, called the Infrared Space Observatory (ISO), was sent into space in November 1995 by the ESA. A highlight of its early operation was the observation of a collision between two galaxies and the resulting dust clouds, visible only at infrared wavelengths. ISO has also witnessed the birth and death of stars. Like its predecessor, ISO is cooled by liquid helium. Its supply is due to run out in November 1997.

Current U.S. Programs

In this decade, NASA has also been busily expanding its space telescope program. In April 1990, the Hubble Space Telescope (HST) was launched by the **space shuttle** *Discovery*. Scientists soon discovered that this much-touted piece of equipment had a serious flaw in its mirror. A few years later the crew of the space shuttle *Endeavour* visited the HST and made the necessary repairs. This space telescope now provides us with spectacular views of galaxies, **nebula**e, and other forms of matter, at much greater distances than we have ever been seen before.

One year after the HST launch, the Compton Gamma Ray Observatory was transported into space by the space shuttle *Atlantis*. It has detected gamma ray emissions from supernovae, star clusters, pulsars, **quasar**s, and possible black holes.

By the year 2000, NASA plans to launch at least one more space telescope—the Advanced X-Ray Astrophysics Facility (AXAF)—and, in the year 2001, the Space Infrared Telescope Facility.

See also **Advanced X-Ray Astrophysics Facility**; **Compton Gamma Ray Observatory**; **High Energy Astrophysical Observatories**; **Hubble Space Telescope**; **Infrared Astronomical Satellite**; **Infrared Space Observatory**; and **International Ultraviolet Explorer**

Space trash

Humankind's four decades of space exploration has left an unfortunate legacy: space trash. There are now thousands of human-made fragments larger than an inch and somewhere between ten billion and thousands of trillions of microscopic pieces of debris floating through our region of the **solar system.** There are even a few chunks ranging in size from a truck to a modest apartment building. Much of this debris gets pulled down by the Earth's gravitational field into progressively lower orbits until it enters the atmosphere and burns up. Some, however, is affected by **gravity** only slightly and will orbit the Earth for centuries.

Given the fact that over three thousand **rocket**s have launched about four thousand satellites into orbit since 1957, the presence of debris in space seems inevitable. When a satellite stops functioning (as happens inevitably), it can meet one of two fates. Most commonly, the satellite burns up in the Earth's atmosphere. In some cases, however, the satellite remains in orbit, either whole or in pieces.

Besides satellites and satellite parts, some examples of space trash include burned-out rocket components, tools that got away from space travelers, and pieces that have unexpectedly come loose from space vessels. For a period, the former **Soviet Union** was purposefully destroying their military satellites on completion of their missions for fear of them falling into enemy hands.

Some of the most famous objects orbiting Earth are the glove that floated away from the *Gemini 4* crew during the first U.S. **space walk**; the camera that astronaut Michael Collins lost during the *Gemini 10* mission; and the bags of trash that have been tossed from Soviet **space station**s. The least publicized items are small objects, such as showers of tiny pieces produced by explosions of used and discarded rocket parts and the intentional and unintentional destruction of satellites. Most people, however, are also unaware of the big objects floating around, such as rocket boosters and the **lunar module** from *Apollo 10*.

Potential Damage From Space Trash

The main problem with space trash is the danger it poses to currently operational satellites and piloted spacecraft. The larger pieces of debris are being tracked by ground stations to avoid collisions, but even tiny objects smaller than an inch across can do significant damage.

For instance, during a 1983 flight, one of the **space shuttle** *Challenger*'s windows was slightly damaged by a speck of paint less than a quarter of an inch wide. And panels from the *Solar Maximum Mission* satellite, retrieved by a space shuttle crew in 1984, were marked by 186 tiny craters, 20 caused by **meteoroid**s and the rest by paint chips from satellites. It has also been shown that a particle even a few inches across can have the destructive power of a hand grenade. The reason for this destructive potential is the very high speed at which particles in space are traveling (17,500 miles, or 28,158 kilometers, per hour). Such fast moving particles may have been the cause of the unexplained destruction of a Soviet *Cosmos* satellite in 1981. Scientists estimate there is a 1 percent chance that the Hubble Space Telescope could be similarly destroyed.

Not all trash from Earthly space missions is floating in space. Some is parked on the moon, Venus, and Mars. Between Soviet and American missions, 20 tons (18 metric tons) of human-made stuff has been left on the lunar surface. This trash includes big objects such as moon buggies, satellite parts, and equipment from science experiments, as well as smaller objects such as golf balls, cameras, and a flag. In addition, crashed **space probe**s litter the Martian and Venusian surfaces.

The United States and other nations with space programs are now attempting to reverse the tendency to clutter up the space around our planet. The first order of business has been to reduce the amount of debris produced by objects launched into space. Also, several damaged satellites have been picked up by space shuttle crews. And finally, research is underway into sophisticated methods of cleaning up the **cosmos.**

Spacecraft, piloted

In the early part of this century, scientists began to consider seriously what it would take to send humans into space. Only after the technology had been developed to launch an unpiloted ship into space, however, could they tackle the new challenge of developing an environment in which humans could survive.

Space is a hostile place for living beings. There is no air to breathe, no water to drink, no atmosphere to filter out radiation, and not enough **gravity** to walk around as we do on Earth. Therefore, astronauts must bring with them all the oxygen, food, and water they need on the journey. The cabin must be able to filter the sunlight and to compensate for weightlessness and extreme heat and cold. In addition, special exercise equipment must be provided to maintain the astronauts' muscle tone and blood circulation, both of which are affected by weightlessness.

Since 1961, dozens of men and women from just a few countries, mostly the United States and the former **Soviet Union,** have traveled in space. The Soviets were the first to launch an unpiloted satellite, *Sputnik 1,* in 1957. This event marked the beginning of the **space race** between the United States and the Soviet Union, a campaign for superiority in space exploration. For the next decade, scientists and engineers from the two countries worked at a frenzied pace to achieve "firsts" in a variety of categories: from launching a human into space; to keeping one in space for longer and longer periods of time; to the ultimate accomplishment of sending a human to the moon.

The first living being to travel in space was not a person, but a dog named Laika. She was sent into space on the Soviets' *Sputnik 2* in 1957. Laika survived the launch and the first leg of the journey. A week after launch, however, the air supply ran out and Laika suffocated. When the spacecraft re-entered the Earth's atmosphere in April 1958, it burned up (it had no heat shields) and Laika's body was incinerated. Then on April 12, 1961, Soviet astronaut Yuri Gagarin rode aboard the *Vostok 1,* becoming the first human in space. In 108 minutes, he made a single orbit around the Earth before re-entering its atmosphere. At about 2 miles (more than 3 kilometers) above the ground, he parachuted to safety. Only recently did scientists from outside of Russia learn that this seemingly flawless mission almost ended in disaster. During its final descent, the spacecraft had spun wildly out of control.

The American-Crewed Space Program

Gagarin's flight pressured officials at the National Aeronautics and Space Administration (NASA) to match the Soviet accomplishment. In a bold move, then-President John F. Kennedy announced that the United States would put a man on the moon by the end of the decade.

The first phase of that effort was the Mercury program. The Mercury spacecraft featured a heat-resistant, bell-shaped capsule designed to survive the intense heat and friction of re-entry into the Earth's atmosphere. It also contained numerous back-up systems in case of equipment malfunction on the spacecraft. On May 5, 1961, the first piloted Mercury flight, *Freedom 7,* was launched. It took astronaut Alan Shepard on a fifteen-minute flight that went 116 miles (187 kilometers) up and 303 miles (488 kilometers) across the Atlantic Ocean, at speeds of up to 5,146 miles (8,280 kilometers) per hour. The capsule then parachuted safely into the Atlantic Ocean with Shepard inside.

Two months later, another suborbital flight was launched, this one carrying the second U.S. man in space, Virgil "Gus" Grissom. Grissom's flight was similar to Shepard's, except at splashdown his capsule took in water and sank. Grissom was unharmed, but his capsule, the *Liberty Bell 7,* was not recovered. It was the only loss of its kind in the history of the U.S. space program.

Then, on February 20, 1962, just over nine months after Gagarin's flight, astronaut John Glenn became the first American to orbit the Earth. His spacecraft, *Friendship 7,* completed three orbits in less than five hours. Glenn's mission made him a national hero and gave the U.S. space program a tremendous boost.

Throughout the early and mid-1960s, both U.S. and Soviet space programs continued to deploy more sophisticated spacecraft, capable of hold-

*Opposite page:
Buzz Aldrin steps
down from* Apollo 11
*on the lunar
surface.*

Countdown (1968)

A drama about a fictional, first piloted mission to the moon. Directed by Robert Altman and starring James Caan and Robert Duvall, it focuses on the stresses placed upon the astronauts and their families. This film was released at the same time that NASA was making preparations to send the real first astronauts to the moon.

ing two, and then three men, and spending longer periods of time in space. U.S. astronauts, however, were the only ones to make it to the moon.

The Apollo program was created for the purpose of landing American astronauts on the moon. Engineers designed a craft consisting of three parts: a **command module** in which the astronauts would travel; a **service module,** which contained supplies and equipment; and a **lunar module,** which would detach to land on the moon.

The Apollo program was not without its snags. During a ground test in 1967, a fire engulfed the cabin of the *Apollo 1* spacecraft, killing Gus Grissom, Ed White, and Roger Chaffee. This tragedy prompted a two-year delay in the launch of the first Apollo spacecraft. During this delay, over fifteen hundred modifications were made to the command module.

On July 16, 1969, the *Apollo 11* spacecraft was ready to go, with astronauts Neil Armstrong, Buzz Aldrin, and Michael Collins on board. Four days later Armstrong and Aldrin climbed into the lunar module and, true to President Kennedy's promise, landed on the moon. As Armstrong set foot on lunar soil, he stated his now-famous words: "That's one small step for [a] man, one giant leap for mankind." The *Apollo 11* flight to the moon is considered by many to be the greatest technological achievement of the modern world.

Over the next three years, five more Apollo missions landed twelve more Americans on the moon. NASA then turned its attention to the development of re-usable **space shuttle**s and unpiloted flights to explore the rest of the **solar system.** The Soviet Union, meanwhile, was busy with the construction and launch of **space station**s. Today, the space race between the United States and Russia is over. That fact, combined with budget cuts, has greatly slowed the pace of piloted space flight.

See also **Apollo program**; **Gagarin, Yuri**; **Gemini program**; **Mercury program**; **Moon**; **Soyuz program**; **Space race**; **Space shuttle**; **Space station**; **Spacecraft equipment**; **Voskhod program**; and **Vostok program**

Spacecraft design

Spacecraft come in a wide variety of designs, with vast differences between those that carry human occupants and those that do not. Still, they all have a number of things in common. For instance, every spacecraft must have a launch system that will enable it to overcome the Earth's gravitational pull in order to reach space. The ship must be strong enough structurally to withstand the stresses of launch and, in some cases, reentry. The craft's design must also take into account the need for electricity to operate the instruments and control systems, including life support systems on piloted spacecraft.

Every flight into space begins with a **launch vehicle.** Launch vehicles generally consist of a series of successively smaller **rocket**s placed one on top of the other. A rocket is the only type of engine capable of producing the enormous, carefully controlled explosion needed to lift a spacecraft from the launch pad and send it, at tremendous speeds, hurtling past the edge of the Earth's atmosphere.

Unlike airplane engines, rockets cannot rely on oxygen from the air to burn their fuel. The reason is that within minutes they are beyond the Earth's atmosphere. Therefore, they must carry an "oxidizer" which, together with the fuel, is called the **propellant.** Before take-off, the fuel and oxidizer are kept in separate compartments of the rocket. To ignite the engines, the two are mixed and a combustion occurs. In this reaction, exhaust gases are produced that are allowed to escape through a hole in one end of the container. It is this forceful exit of exhaust gases that creates the thrust that pushes the rocket forward.

The most commonly used propellant is a liquid. Types of liquid fuel include alcohol, kerosene, liquid hydrogen, and hydrazine. The liquid oxidizer may be nitrogen tetroxide or liquid oxygen. One type of solid propellant, which is used in **space shuttle** boosters, is a mixture of ammonium perchlorate, powdered aluminum, and other additives.

Structural Design

Another important element in spacecraft design is the structure of the frame. The material of which the frame is made must be as light as possible. An aluminum alloy is often used. Heavier spacecraft are more difficult to launch than lighter ones. They require more thrust, which means burning more fuel.

The spacecraft frame also has to be durable and versatile enough to survive in three very different environments: Earth, the various layers of the Earth's atmosphere, and space. It must be able function in conditions of **gravity,** as on Earth, as well as in the near-zero gravity environment found in space. It also must be able to withstand the strong vibrations and intense heat of launch. And in space, a spacecraft must be prepared for extreme fluctuations in temperature, various types of dangerous radiation (such as **ultraviolet radiation, X-ray**s, and **gamma ray**s), and **magnetic field**s, in many cases for missions lasting several years.

The spacecraft's internal power source also has to be incorporated into the vessel's design. Power, in the form of electricity, is necessary to operate the instruments (including the communications system with Earth) and control systems. In order to generate electricity, a spacecraft must have solar cells, batteries, nuclear generators, or some combination of these.

Solar cells convert radiation from the sun into energy. Large spacecraft are commonly covered with solar cells or have solar panels extend like wings from its sides. Many spacecraft with solar cells also carry batteries (usually made of nickel and cadmium), to supplement the energy supply when the spacecraft is not in the sunlight (for example, when it is behind the moon). Batteries alone are sufficient to power most small satellites for at least ten years.

Nuclear power generators are used on spacecraft destined for very long journeys or on those venturing very far from the sun. For example, nuclear generators were used on *Voyager 1* and *2* which were launched in 1977 on a mission to the outer planets and beyond the **solar system.** The power is produced as heat, given off by the decay of uranium.

Many special factors must be incorporated into the design of piloted spacecraft, principally the need for a cabin with life support systems. Within the cabin, temperature and pressure must be kept constant and breathable air provided. In the Mercury flights—the first of the piloted space program—astronauts had to wear a spacesuit with circulating air the entire time. On later spacecraft, life support systems have been improved to the point that the ship's inhabitants have no need for spacesuits for most of a journey.

Another important consideration for a piloted spacecraft is the return trip. Any object entering the Earth's atmosphere encounters extreme heat and friction in the outer layers. Therefore, a spacecraft with human occupants must possess a heat shield or, in the case of the space shuttle, heat-resistant tiles made of silica.

A heat shield is built to withstand temperatures of up to 5,000 degrees Fahrenheit (2,760 degrees Celsius). It is made of a 2-inch-thick (5-centimeter-thick) reinforced plastic called phenolic epoxy resin. When the spacecraft enters the **thermosphere** the heat shield's resin chars and the peels off, carrying the heat away with it.

See also **Space probe**; **Spacecraft, piloted**; and **Spacecraft equipment**

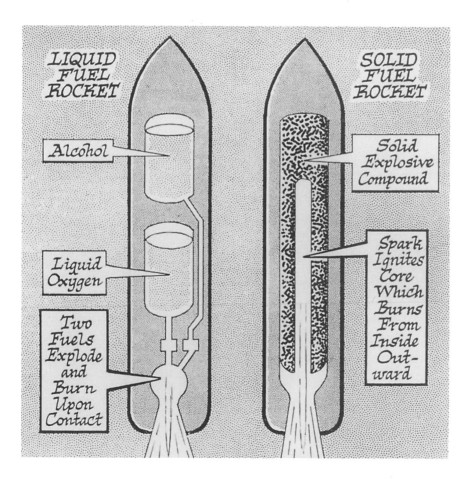

Launch vehicle design: the Jupiter-C rocket.

Spacecraft equipment

When human beings travel beyond the Earth's atmosphere, they encounter a hostile environment. Space is a vacuum, meaning that there is no air. Nor is there water or food or sufficient **gravity** to keep one's body from floating away. On the other hand, what does exist—harmful, direct sunlight and extreme changes in temperature—is just as inhospitable.

Spacecraft equipment is able to compensate for these conditions. To begin with, all the food, water, and oxygen required by the passengers is stored on board in tanks and other specialized storage units. The cabin of the craft screens out the sun's harmful rays and regulates temperature. Bathing facilities and a system for the elimination of human wastes are also present. Another consideration is the effect that weightlessness has on the human body. To prevent loss of muscle tone and poor blood circulation, the men and woman on board are provided with special exercise equipment.

Special attention is given to the packaging of food and drinks. Liquids must be contained in squeeze bottles or they will bubble up and float away. Even solid foods must be eaten from plastic pouches.

Both the cabin of the spacecraft and the spacesuit worn by an astronaut are equipped with life support systems. In the early Mercury missions, the cabin's system stabilized temperature and pressure while the spacesuit provided air for the astronauts to breathe. Air circulating throughout the spacesuit would exit through the helmet and be filtered and cooled before reentering the suit.

The first spacesuits were bulky and uncomfortable. They were made of many layers and restricted the astronauts' movement. And worse yet, they had to be worn continuously while in the spacecraft.

The Gemini spacecraft, in the series that followed the Mercury program, from 1958 to 1964, had a major improvement over their predecessors. The cabin's life support system was sufficient for astronauts to remove their spacesuits for periods of time. In addition, the new spacesuits were less bulky and allowed greater mobility. These suits also had an attachment for an oxygen hose, that allowed an astronaut to walk outside the spacecraft and perform tasks.

Space equipment was further improved Apollo missions, which took place in the late 1960s. Engineers had to design a whole new spacesuit, one that was suitable for walking on the moon. This suit was made of twenty-one layers of material, the outermost being made of fiberglass.

Tubes within the suit carried oxygen for breathing and maintained air pressure. Another set of tubes carried water to cool the person inside. This suit, which weighed 57 pounds (26 kilograms) on Earth, took an hour to put on. On the moon, because of weakened gravity, the suit weighed just 8 pounds (3.5 kilograms). The suit worn inside the spacecraft, in contrast, had just six layers of material and was much lighter.

Today's spacecraft equipment is both safer and easier to use. The spacesuit consists of liquid-cooled underclothes, pants and boots with flexible heat reflectors, and special locks that prevent the helmet and gloves from coming loose. The material is pleated in places where a person needs to bend.

The **space shuttle** contains a toilet similar to those on airliners, which is an improvement over the bags used on earlier spacecrafts. Since the shower tested on the *Skylab* **space station** was leaky and difficult to

Apollo 17 *astronauts (left to right) Harrison Schmitt, Ron Evans, and Gene Cernan pose in their missions' moon rover.*

use, astronauts on the space shuttle are back to taking sponge baths. And specialized sleeping bags on the shuttle mean that astronauts no longer have to strap themselves down to sleep. Food and exercise equipment have also been improved.

The recent emphasis on space stations means that humans will be spending longer and longer periods of time in space. Designers of space equipment are faced with the challenge of making sure that the astronauts' experience will be a safe and comfortable one.

See also **Space shuttle**; **Space station**; **Spacecraft, piloted**; and **Spacecraft design**

Spacecraft voyage

Spacecraft voyages have a common format. They begin with a launch; the spacecraft goes into orbit around the Earth; it breaks away to its final destination; and at the end (for piloted missions and some others) it returns to Earth. This sequence only begins to describe the missions of the more than four thousand vessels that have been sent into space since 1957, ranging from small communications and navigational satellites, to piloted ships, to interplanetary **probe**s. These spacecraft have ventured near and far. While some have merely orbited the Earth, others have traveled to the moon or approached the sun for a closer look. Spacecraft have visited every planet except Pluto and even some **asteroid**s and **comet**s. They have traveled throughout the **solar system** and beyond.

Every voyage is initiated with a launch, the main objective of which is to overcome Earth's **gravity** to the point where the craft ventures into space and, in most cases, goes into orbit around the Earth. To reach a height necessary to orbit Earth, a spacecraft must travel at about 17,500 miles (28,000 kilometers) per hour.

Most of the thrust needed to reach these speeds comes from a launch **rocket**. Engineers have also learned how to let the Earth's rotation contribute to the rocket's acceleration. To accomplish this goal, the rocket must be launched toward the east so that it travels in the same direction that the Earth rotates. It must also be launched from a position close to the equator, such as the Kennedy Space Center at Cape Canaveral, Florida, where the Earth turns fastest. By working with the motion of the Earth in this way, a spacecraft launched near the equator can gain an additional 900 miles (1,400 kilometers) per hour.

Another way to increase speed is through the use of multi-stage rockets. A multi-stage rocket is one that consists of three or four successively smaller rockets, called stages, set on top of one another. As each stage exhausts its fuel, it falls away and reduces the weight of the remaining spacecraft. Then the next stage fires and the rocket continues to accelerate. With its lighter load, a spacecraft can travel faster.

Another factor that contributes to the spacecraft's acceleration is the Earth's slowly diminishing gravitational field. The field extends farther than one might think. At 100 miles (161 kilometers) above the Earth, the gravitational force is still 95 percent of its strength at the planet's surface, and at an altitude of 1,600 miles (2,600 kilometers) it is at 50 percent strength. The greater distance a rocket travels, the less gravitational attraction it experiences. This fact, coupled with the reduced weight resulting from the consumption of fuel and the loss of rocket stages, means that the vehicle continues to accelerate as it ascends.

Attaining Earth Orbit

A spacecraft can go into orbit around the Earth when it reaches a state of equilibrium with Earth's gravitational field. Equilibrium is reached when gravitational attraction is not strong enough to pull the spacecraft back to Earth, yet it is sufficient to keep the spacecraft from traveling farther into space. The height at which the spacecraft goes into orbit determines how long it takes to complete a revolution. The closer to Earth, the shorter the path, and the less time it takes to circle the globe.

The orbital height selected depends on the type of spacecraft and the purpose of its mission. For communications and navigational satellites, for instance, it is desirable to remain over one spot on the Earth in order to maintain contact with ground stations. This type of orbit—one that takes twenty-four hours to complete and is 22,300 miles (35,700 kilometers) above the Earth—is called a **geosynchronous orbit.**

For spacecraft continuing on to other destinations, the next step is to break out of Earth's orbit. The vessel accomplishes this by firing rocket thrusters to reach the breakaway speed (or escape velocity) of 25,000 miles (40,000 kilometers) per hour (7 miles, or 11 kilometers, per second). Once free of the Earth's gravity, a spacecraft can travel great distances with relative ease.

Many spacecraft then approach and go into orbit around another body (for example, a planet or the moon) to make observations. To achieve this, a vessel sets out in the direction of that body at a particular speed (depending on the strength of the target body's gravitational field) on what is called a capture trajectory.

A spacecraft journeying on to distant planets, can use the gravitational field of one body to propel it toward another body, a technique known as **gravity assist.** This practice depends on the alignment of the planets. The ideal condition is one in which the planets are relatively close together on their orbits and line up in a continuous curve. An example of a journey on which gravity assist was used was the complex path of *Voyager 2*. This spacecraft visited Jupiter, Saturn, Uranus, and Neptune, in each case using the gravitational field of one planet to propel it toward the next without the need for additional rocket motors.

The Fate of Spacecraft

On completion of its mission, a spacecraft may face one of several fates. Some satellites, particularly those in low Earth orbits, re-enter the Earth's atmosphere and burn up. Some interplanetary probes are left to coast forever in orbit around the sun when they run out of fuel. Still others, such as *Pioneer 10* and *11* and *Voyager 1* and *2,* have continued beyond the edge of the solar system and into interstellar space.

Another class of spacecraft includes those carrying human occupants or valuable data or equipment. These spacecraft must come back to Earth intact. Returning to the Earth's surface from space is an especially difficult task. Any object entering the Earth's atmosphere encounters extreme heat and friction. Therefore, a spacecraft must possess a protective heat shield or, in the case of the **space shuttle,** heat-resistant tiles.

The angle at which a vessel re-enters the atmosphere is also of critical importance. It has to enter at an angle that is neither too steep nor too shallow. If it were to plunge straight down or at a steep angle, the effects of heat and friction would be intensified, rendering the heat shield ineffective and probably destroying the spacecraft. Then again, the angle of descent cannot be too shallow. In that case a spacecraft may actually bounce off the atmosphere and return to space, like a stone skipping off the surface of water. Some of the Apollo craft used this skipping effect to slow down in preparation for re-entry.

The final stage of a spacecraft voyage is touchdown, which can be accomplished in various ways. The early piloted spacecraft—those from the Mercury, Gemini, and Apollo missions—used parachutes to slow their descent before splashing down in the ocean. The spacecraft and occupants were then picked up by helicopters or ships. Another method of landing, used by the Russian Soyuz spacecraft, is to parachute to the ground. A final method is used by the space shuttle, which glides through the atmosphere in S-shaped curves and lands, like an airplane, on a runway.

See also **Space probe**; **Space shuttle**; **Spacecraft, piloted**; **Spacecraft design**; and **Voyager program**

Spacelab

Spacelab is a re-useable space laboratory that operates within the cargo bay of a **space shuttle.** From its initial run in 1983 to the present, Spacelab has been used on twenty-seven shuttle missions with one more scheduled for 1997. It has traveled on each of the five shuttles. A wide range of experiments have been carried out on Spacelab, most of them in the following areas: ultraviolet astronomy, **X-ray** astronomy, **infrared astronomy,** solar physics, material sciences, and the effects of weightlessness on humans and animals.

Spacelab is the product of an international effort initiated by the United States in the late 1960s. In the period of high hopes following *Apollo 11* (which landed the first man on the moon) the National Aeronautics and Space Administration (NASA) drew up plans for a **space station** and an ambitious program including piloted flights to Mars, and invited international participation. Over the next few years, NASA had to scale back its plans due to budgetary and technical restraints.

On August 14, 1973, NASA reached an agreement with the European Space Agency (ESA) stipulating that the ESA would build a space laboratory and the United States would provide a re-usable space shuttle. In recent years, the Japanese Space Agency has also participated in Spacelab missions.

The physical structure of Spacelab consists of a series of interchangeable modules. Some of these modules are pressurized, meaning that their environment is controlled, like the cabin of the space shuttle so that astronaut-scientists can work in ordinary clothing (they do not need spacesuits). These modules, which contain research instruments and control panels, are made of cylindrical aluminum segments coated with layers of thermal insulation. They receive their power supply from the space shuttle. Extending from the pressurized module is a tunnel, which leads first to the cargo-bay airlock, and then into the space shuttle cabin.

Other, non-pressurized Spacelab components include U-shaped platforms called "pallets" with attached Instrument Pointing System (IPS) platforms. The pallets hold equipment, such as telescopes and cameras, and particular experiments that require the vacuum of space. Each pallet is about 10 feet (3 meters) long by 13 feet (4 meters) across and weighs over 2.5 tons (2.3 metric tons). The IPS controls the instruments, aiming them at desired targets with great precision.

This equipment can be mixed and matched in various combinations, such as a pressurized module with two or three pallets or a train of five modules with no pressurized module. All components of the system are designed to be re-used.

Spacelab Missions

The first Spacelab mission, designated Spacelab 1, was launched on November 28, 1983, on the space shuttle *Columbia*. This mission was essentially a trial run, which in addition to carrying out a broad scientific survey tested the laboratory equipment. Dozens of experiments were conducted in the areas of astronomy, Earth observations, biology, and material sciences. Among the six-member crew was the first European astronaut, Ulf Merbold of Germany. The mission lasted ten days and proved that the Spacelab systems worked well.

Spacelab 2, an astronomy mission, was beset with technical difficulties and had to be delayed. Consequently, Spacelab 3 was launched before it, on April 29, 1985. Spacelab 3 flew on a seven-day journey aboard *Challenger*. Again, it was used for a variety of experiments, in particular examining the effects of launch and re-entry on animals and means of controlling space sickness.

Spacelab 2 finally made it into space on July 29, 1985, also on *Challenger*. This mission was devoted to a study of **plasma,** the sun, and stars. Because of the nature of the experiments, no pressurized module was necessary. The laboratory was comprised only of pallets.

The initial Spacelab runs have been followed by a series of missions that are too numerous to describe individually. In addition to experiments on astronomy, life sciences, and material sciences, Spacelab has been used to deliver scientific experiments to the *Mir* space station and to test hardware for use in the construction of the International Space Station (slated for completion early next century). Two Spacelab experiments were also designed to study tethered satellites, on board *Atlantis* in 1992 and *Columbia* in 1996. They returned no data, however because the miles-long tether jammed in each case, and the satellites were not successfully deployed.

In recent years, the number of planned Spacelab missions has been scaled back, in part due to their high cost, but also because experiments on board *Mir* have taken over in priority. Since 1994 at least seven planned scientific missions of Spacelab have been canceled or have been converted simply to supply runs to *Mir*. At this point, the only planned Spacelab journey is slated to launch on *Atlantis* on May 1, 1997, and is headed for *Mir*.

See also **Atlantis**; **Challenger**; **Columbia**; **Discovery**; **Endeavour**; **Mir space station**; and **Tethered Satellite System**

Spacetime

Every event in the universe can be described as occurring at a given point in space and time, or in a combination of the two called "**spacetime**." Spacetime is a four dimensional construct that unites the three dimensions of space (length, width, and height) and a fourth dimension, time. By observing an object's orientation in spacetime, you know not just where it is, but when it is.

The concept of spacetime becomes relevant when you observe a faraway object, such as the moon. In doing so, you're not just looking out into space, but back into time. This is because you must factor in the time it takes for light to travel between the object and yourself. (The **speed of light** is about 186,282 miles [299,728 kilometers] per second. A **light-year** is the distance light travels in one year, approximately 5.9 trillion miles [9.5 trillion kilometers]). Thus, you don't see distant objects as they are at that particular instant, but as they were in the past. This means that you perceive them as an event in spacetime.

When you look at the moon you see it as it was a second ago, since that's how long it took the light to reach you. And as for the sun, which is 93 million miles (150 kilometers) away, you see it as it was eight minutes ago. This phenomenon becomes more pronounced when looking at objects that are even more distant, such as stars. The closest star to our sun, Proxima Centauri, which is 24.8 trillion miles (39.9 trillion kilometers) away, appears to us on Earth as it was 4.2 years ago.

One way to visualize spacetime is with a spacetime diagram. This is a flat, two-dimensional map on which you label the vertical axis "time" and the horizontal axis "space." Of course this isn't quite accurate since space itself has three dimensions (length, width, and height). But for the purpose of this exercise, any one of these dimensions can represent "space."

You can make your own spacetime diagram for a series of events that occurred during your day. One example is to trace your bus ride home from school, using the number of blocks traveled as the measure for "space" and the minutes the ride took representing "time." Mark points on the diagram indicating how far you traveled after one minute, two minutes, and so on. When you connect the dots, you create what is called a "world-line," or a sequence of events. In this case your worldline represents the bus ride. You could also make a worldline to describe all the events of your day or even of your whole life.

It's also possible to create a worldline for a stationary object, like a mountain. In that case the worldline would be a straight vertical line—representing only the progression of time, with no movement in space.

The concept of spacetime originated with Albert Einstein's theory of relativity. According to this theory, the dimension of time is as necessary a component as the three dimensions of space in describing the location of an object or event.

The theory of relativity is divided into two parts—the **special theory of relativity** and the **general theory of relativity**—both of which explain the interdependence of time and space. Special relativity begins with the idea that space and time are not fixed, but change depending on how fast and in what direction the observer is moving. In other words, they depend on a observer's reference frame.

For example, imagine that you and a friend are on a train traveling at a constant 60 miles (97 kilometers) per hour and, to pass the time, you're playing catch. You are standing at the front end of the train and your friend is standing at the rear. When the ball is thrown, it appears to travel between the two of you at 30 miles (48 kilometers) per hour. Yet to an observer standing beside the railroad tracks watching the train go by, the ball appears to travel at 90 miles (145 kilometers) per hour (60 + 30) when you throw it and 30 miles per hour (60 - 30) when your friend throws it.

Thus, the ball appears to take different periods of time to travel between the two ball-players, depending on one's reference frame. The event cannot be described as "simultaneous" by the observer on the train and the one beside the tracks. It can only be adequately described by each observer by using the dimension of time as well as dimensions of space.

After the special theory of relativity came the general theory of relativity, in which Einstein connected the curvature of spacetime with **gravity.** Einstein argued that gravity is not a force (like magnetism), as was previously thought, but is the result of curved spacetime. He wrote that the reason large objects (such as the sun) draw smaller objects (such as the planets) toward them is that large objects curve spacetime and that smaller objects become trapped in those curves.

To illustrate this, imagine the sun curving spacetime into the shape of a shallow bowl. The planets are drawn into orbit around the sun like small balls rolling around the sides of the bowl. This describes how gravity is simply the changed motion of an object due to curved spacetime.

See also **Einstein, Albert** and **Speed of light**

Spectroscopy

Spectroscopy is the process of breaking down light into its component colors (its **spectrum**). The simplest example of spectroscopy is one that occurs in nature—a rainbow. A rainbow forms when sunlight passes through raindrops, each of which acts as a tiny prism. A prism is a transparent object with triangular ends and rectangular sides used to refract light or disperse it into a spectrum. You may have performed spectroscopy yourself, by shining light through a prism and casting a rainbow onto a surface.

Astronomers have been using spectroscopy to learn about celestial objects since the late 1800s. A spectrum is like a fingerprint, in that each one is unique. Spectral analysis provides information about an object's chemical composition, temperature, movement, pressure, and the presence of **magnetic field**s.

An instrument used to produce a spectrum is called a **spectroscope.** A spectroscope consists of a tube with a small opening at one end, through which light enters. The light passes first through one lens, which makes the light rays parallel, then through a prism. The prism produces a spectrum, which is then focused by a second lens. The final section of the instrument may be an eyepiece, through which **spectra** can be viewed directly. More commonly, however, a photographic plate is inserted in place of the eyepiece. In this case, the instrument is called a **spectrograph** and is capable of taking a picture of the object's spectrum.

Spectra generally appear as series of bright and dark lines. The bright lines, called **emission lines,** represent colors (or wavelengths) at which a particular object emits light. Dark lines, called **absorption lines,** indicate wavelengths at which an object absorbs light. The spectrum of a star, for example, can be compared to recorded spectra of elements (such as hydrogen and sodium). Whether or not they show similar patterns at particular wavelengths, indicates whether or not those elements are present in the star.

Simple Spectroscopy

When sunlight is refracted, or bent, it breaks down into the colors of the rainbow. Red, which has the longest wavelength, appears at one end of the visible light spectrum; and violet, which has the shortest wavelength, appears at the other. A handy way to remember the order of colors is by the mnemonic "ROY G. BIV" (an acronym for Red, Orange, Yellow, Green, Blue, Indigo, and Violet).

You can create your own visible light spectrum with this easy experiment. First, you need a bowl of clean water. Place it in direct sunlight. Then put a small mirror in the bowl and prop it against the edge of the bowl with a small rock. Arrange the position of the mirror so the sunlight strikes it and reflects onto a white wall (or white paper taped to a wall). Observe the spectrum on your wall and locate all the colors of ROY G. BIV.

Water bends the sunlight similar to the way a prism does. The same phenomenon occurs in nature when sunlight is refracted by raindrops and creates a rainbow.

Modern spectroscopy is not limited to the study of spectra of visible light. On the contrary, spectra can now be studied in radiation all across the **electromagnetic spectrum,** from **radio wave**s to **gamma ray**s.

See also **Kirchhoff, Gustav**

Speed of light

Light travels faster than anything else in the universe. Because of this, the **speed of light** is a standard measurement in astronomy, one against which the speeds of other entities can be compared.

Using modern methods, the speed of light in a vacuum (where it is not slowed down by air friction or any other forces) is 186,282.397 miles (299,728.377 kilometers) per second. At that speed, a particle of light can travel around the Earth's equator about seven times in just one second.

A **light-year** is the distance light travels in one year (approximately 5.9 trillion miles, or 9.5 trillion kilometers). If you look through a telescope at a star that is four and one-half light-years away, you are observing light that left that star four and one-half years ago. Therefore, you are actually looking four and one-half years into the past. As another example, it takes light from the sun eight minutes to reach Earth. So when we look at the sun, we see it as it was eight minutes ago. Very powerful telescopes that can see objects millions of light-years away (like looking back in time millions of years) provide us with clues about the evolution of the universe.

The speed of light was a figure that eluded scientists for centuries. One of the first attempts to calculate this number was made by Galileo Galilei, who in the late 1500s stood on a hilltop a set distance from his assistant. Galileo and his assistant flashed lanterns at one another to determine how long it took the light to get back and forth between them. However, the distance between the two was much too short to obtain accurate measurements, as light covered the distance in a fraction of a second.

In 1675, Danish astronomer Olaus Roemer tried to measure the speed of light over a much greater distance, millions of miles in fact, and had much better results. While watching Jupiter cross in front of its moons, he found that his observations did not agree with predicted times for the eclipses. The eclipses came a bit sooner than expected when the Earth's orbit brought it closer to Jupiter, and later than expected when the Earth and Jupiter were farther apart. He assumed, correctly, that the differences were due to the time it took light to travel from Jupiter to Earth.

Roemer measured these variations and concluded that light travels at a speed of 141,000 miles (226,870 kilometers) per second, 76 percent of the currently accepted value. More importantly than the accuracy of his estimation, Roemer showed that light travels at a finite speed. Previously, astronomers had assumed that the speed of light was infinite.

In the mid-1700s, English astronomer James Bradley devised a more precise method for measuring the speed of light. With his telescope pointed straight up, he observed an apparent movement of the stars and decided it was due to the Earth's motion forward into the starlight. That motion is called the **aberration of light.** Bradley realized that to observe stars from a moving Earth, he would have to angle his telescope slightly.

He used the degree at which his telescope was angled to determine the ratio between the speed of light and the speed at which the Earth

*Albert Michelson
was in charge of the
experiment in which
a beam of light was
flashed through this
mile-long vacuum
tube for the purpose
of making a final
check on the exact
speed of light.*

moves. He calculated first that light moves ten thousand times faster than the Earth, then that the Earth travels at 18.5 miles (29.8 kilometers) per second. This put the speed of light at 185,000 miles (297,665 kilometers) per second.

In the mid-1800s, French physicist Jean Bernard Léon Foucault was the first person to measure the speed of light in a laboratory accurately. His results were within 1 percent of the currently accepted value. Foucault's method involved the use of two mirrors, one rotating and one stationary. The moving mirror reflected light a distance of 65 feet (20 meters) to the still mirror, which bounced the light back. The light again struck the moving mirror, then reflected off to another point. Using geometry, Foucault calculated the angle of rotation of the moving mirror, the distance the light had traveled, and the time it took to get there.

In the late-1800s, American physicist Albert Michelson repeated Foucault's experiment, but on a much larger scale. Michelson reflected light from a rotating eight-sided mirror on Mount Wilson (near Pasadena, California) to a stationary mirror on Mount San Antonio, 22 miles (35 kilometers) away. Using his results, Michelson calculated the speed of light to be 186,243 miles (299,665 kilometers) per second, very close to the value now accepted by scientists.

See also **Bradley, James**; **Foucault, Jean Bernard Léon**; **Galilei, Galileo**; **Michelson, Albert**; and **Roemer, Olaus**

Spiral galaxy

The **Milky Way** and nearby Andromeda **galaxy** are both **spiral galaxies.** That term means that the galaxies have a group of stars at their center, surrounded by a **halo** and an invisible cloud of **dark matter,** with arms spiraling outward like a pinwheel. Spiral galaxies are flattened systems with a central disc, or nucleus, and arms of bright young stars, gas, and dust. Most of these galaxies have just one arm wrapped around the nucleus, although some have two or even three arms.

Galaxies are huge regions of space that contain hundreds of billions of stars, planets, glowing **nebula**e, gas, dust, empty space, and perhaps a **black hole.** They come in three main shapes. Besides spiral, they may be elliptical or irregular.

Two subsets of spiral galaxies can be found in approximately equal numbers: barred and unbarred. In barred spirals, a thick band of bright stars lies across the center of the galaxy. An arm emerges from each end of the bar and arches back toward the other end, forming a semi-circle above and below the nucleus. In unbarred spirals the arms emerge directly from the circular nucleus.

Both barred and unbarred spirals exist in numerous forms. In some cases the arms are just thin strands, tightly coiled around a large nucleus. In other cases they have large arms loosely surrounding a small nucleus.

Spiral galaxies include stars of a wide range of ages. The older stars tend to be clustered in the nucleus whereas the younger stars, including stars in formation, inhabit the arms. The **interstellar medium** (space between stars) of spiral galaxies is densely packed with clouds of gas and dust.

Image of a large spiral galaxy.

Spiral galaxies constitute the majority of bright galaxies (about 75 percent). However, if a count were made of all galaxies, including **dwarf galaxies,** then the majority would fall in the elliptical category.

Scientists have long theorized that an evolutionary relationship exists between spiral and elliptical galaxies, either that spiral galaxies lose their arms over time and become elliptical, or that elliptical galaxies eventually form arms and become spirals. However, it is now considered more likely that the different shapes represent entirely different species of galaxies, meaning that once a spiral galaxy, always a spiral galaxy, and once an elliptical galaxy, always an elliptical galaxy.

See also **Elliptical galaxy** and **Galaxy**

Sputnik 1

On October 4, 1957, the former **Soviet Union** launched the first artificial satellite into orbit around the Earth. It was called "Sputnik," the Russian word for "satellite." During its three months in space, *Sputnik 1* orbited the planet once every ninety-six minutes, at a speed of about 17,360 miles (27,932 kilometers) per hour. The Soviets' success caught U.S. engineers, who were expecting their country to be the first in space, by surprise. The launch of *Sputnik 1* thus ushered in a **space race,** paralleling the **cold war** between the two rival world superpowers.

Sputnik 1 was the brainchild of Russian engineer Sergei Korolëv. This leader of the Soviet space program was also largely responsible for his country's being the first nation to send a man into space and the first to land a spacecraft on the moon.

Sputnik 1 was a steel ball, 23 inches (58 centimeters) in diameter and weighing 184 pounds (83.5 kilograms). Attached to its surface were four flexible antennae ranging from 2.2 to 2.6 yards (201 to 238 centimeters) long. In addition to transmitting radio signals at two frequencies, *Sputnik 1* gathered valuable information about the **ionosphere** and space temperatures.

Over the next few years, in an attempt to test the viability of human space flight, the Soviets launched Sputnik satellites carrying animal passengers. In March 1961, they returned a Sputnik to Earth with the animals safely inside. Just a few months later, Russian **cosmonaut** Yuri Gagarin became the first man to travel in space.

See also **Space race**

Star cluster

Some of the over one hundred billion stars of our home **galaxy,** the **Milky Way,** are grouped together in either tight or loose star clusters. Over one hundred tight groupings, called **globular cluster**s, are located on the edges of the galaxy. The far more numerous loose groupings, called **open clus- ter**s, can be found more towards the center of the galaxy.

Globular clusters radiate with a continuous glow. These nearly spher- ical star systems contain anywhere from tens of thousands to a million stars, which appear to be tightly packed together. They are most heavily concentrated at the center of the cluster. While in reality there is a great distance between stars, an observer on Earth may find it impossible to pick out individual ones.

Russian Sputnik 1
Earth satellite,
October 9, 1957.

In contrast to globular clusters, which are thirteen to fifteen billion years old, open clusters are mere youngsters. These groups, formed just a few million to a few billion years ago, contain hot young stars and some stars still in formation. Open clusters have far fewer members than globular clusters (usually just a few hundred) and have no particular shape.

Over one thousand open clusters have been identified in our galaxy. However, many more may be hidden from view by dust and clouds. They reside within the galaxy's disk and for this reason are also called galactic clusters. In contrast, globular clusters occur in the galaxy's spiral arms.

In 1920, American astronomer Harlow Shapley identified numerous globular clusters dotting the edges of the galaxy. He measured the distance to **cepheid variable**s within those clusters and arrived at a new, much larger estimate of the size of the Milky Way than had previously been accepted.

Detail of a star cluster.

A few years later, his colleague Edwin Hubble measured the distance to other globular clusters and learned that they were well beyond our galaxy. In the process he discovered that the universe holds galaxies other than our own.

See also **Milky Way galaxy**

Steady-state theory

The **steady-state theory** claims that the universe has always been essentially the same as it is today, and that it will continue that way forever. The theory was first proposed in 1948 by Austrian-born American astronomer Thomas Gold, a believer in the cosmological principle. The cosmological principle states that the universe is the same everywhere. It states, in other words, that the same objects and gasses fill the universe from end to end and that the view from one **galaxy** is not much different than the view from any other galaxy.

Gold applied this concept of sameness to time as well as space to come up with the steady-state theory. He claimed that the universe should look the same, not only in all places, but at all times—past, present, and future.

The steady-state theory was offered in response to the other major theory of how the universe began, the **big bang theory.** In the late 1920s, Belgian astronomer Georges-Henri Lemaître suggested that the universe had originated as a great "cosmic egg," which billions of years ago exploded (with a "big bang") and then expanded outward. Out of this explosion came the building blocks of stars, planets, and other celestial bodies.

Gold and other steady-state theorists, such as English astronomer Fred Hoyle, found it impossible to accept the idea that the universe was created instantly, out of nothing, by a mysterious bang. They thought it more realistic that matter would be created continuously over time.

The strength of the big bang theory, at that time, rested mainly upon the 1929 discovery by Edwin Hubble that all matter in space is moving away from all other matter, implying that the universe is expanding. Gold and Hoyle incorporated this discovery into the steady-state theory by proposing that as matter in space moves apart, new matter is created to fill in the gaps. Furthermore, as older galaxies die, new galaxies take their place and everything remains basically the same.

Hoyle calculated that only one new atom per century would have to be added to a structure the size of a skyscraper to keep pace with the expansion of the universe. The new atoms were theorized to be hydrogen, which would be drawn together by their mutual gravitational force into huge clouds, and eventually for stars and galaxies. Critics protested this would be impossible to prove, because a single new atom a year would be undetectable among the trillions of atoms that exist in a region of space that size.

Evidence for the Big Bang Theory

Nevertheless, for two decades, the steady-state and big bang theories were considered to be equally likely explanations for how the universe began. But then three new pieces of evidence shifted the balance toward the big bang theory.

First came the discovery of **quasar**s in 1963. These extremely bright objects occur only at the farthest reaches from Earth. If, as the steady-state theory suggests, the universe looks the same, everywhere, in all directions, quasars should be distributed evenly throughout space. Since they are only old and distant though, they are not compatible with this theory.

The next year, radio engineers Arno Penzias and Robert Wilson found proof of the "big bang" itself. While looking for sources of satellite message interference, they detected radiation in space at the same temperature that astronomer George Gamow had predicted it should remain, even for billions of years, as a result of the initial explosion.

The most important piece of evidence was found in 1992, when the National Aeronautics and Space Administration's *Cosmic Background Explorer* (*COBE*) looked fifteen billion **light-year**s into space (the same as looking fifteen billion years into the past). It detected tiny temperature changes in the cosmic background radiation, which may be evidence of gravitational disturbances in the early universe. These ripples or fluctuations of temperature, which are as long as ten billion light-years, could have eventually come together to form the stars, galaxies, and other pieces of the universe, indicating that the universe has changed over time.

This last piece of evidence has pushed the steady-state theory out of the running for the explanation of how the universe began, at least for now.

See also **Big bang theory**; **Gold, Thomas**; and **Hoyle, Fred**

Stellar evolution

If one were to look up at the same stars night after night for years, one would probably never see them change. In reality, however, stars are constantly changing. The reason these changes are not apparent to the observer is that a star's life lasts for billions of years. Thus its changes occur very, very slowly.

Since astronomers cannot observe the entire life cycle of a single star, they learn about stellar evolution by observing many different stars at various stages of life.

A star is born when a hot cloud of gas and dust in space condenses. Depending on the size of the cloud, it may become a single star, a **binary star** (a system of two stars that orbit around a common center of **gravity**), or a **star cluster.** When the cloud gets hot and dense enough, fusion of hy-

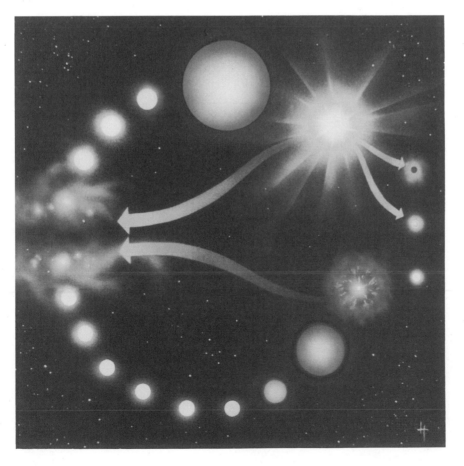

The main stages of the life of a star. The lower track shows the evolution of stars like our sun. After the hydrogen is burnt the star becomes a red giant. Eventually the outer layers are shed exposing the helium-rich core which becomes a white dwarf. The upper track shows more massive stars undergoing a supergiant phase and then a supernova explosion which leaves behind either a black hole or a neutron star.

drogen into helium begins to occur, producing starlight. The fusion process is taken as evidence that a star has been created.

As long as a star has plenty of hydrogen fuel, fusion will continue and the star will keep shining. When a star's hydrogen supply runs low, it enters the final stages of its life, and changes begin to occur. What happens next is determined by the size of the star, in one of the following two ways.

An average-sized star, like our sun, will spend the final 10 percent of its life as a **red giant.** In this phase of stellar evolution, a star's surface temperature drops to between 3,140 and 6,741 degrees Fahrenheit (1,727 and 3,727 degrees Celsius) and its diameter expands to ten to one thousand times that of the sun. The star takes on a reddish color, which is how the star gets its name.

Buried deep inside the star's atmosphere is a hot, dense core, about the size of the Earth. Helium left burning at the core eventually casts off the atmosphere, which floats off as a planetary **nebula.** The glowing core, called a **white dwarf,** is left to cool for eternity.

The second option, which applies to a star at least 1.4 times as massive as the sun, is that once it runs out of fuel it will go **supernova,** shedding much of its **mass.** In most cases the star will then end up as an extremely dense **neutron star.** For the most massive stars (at least two or three times the mass of our sun), the gravitational collapse of the supernova is so complete, that only a **black hole** remains. A black hole is a single point in space where pressure and density are infinite. Anything that gets too close to a black hole gets pulled in, stretched to infinity, and remains forever trapped.

See also **Black hole; Neutron star; Nova and supernova; Red giant star;** and **White dwarf star**

Stellar masses

Stellar **mass** can be directly determined for **binary star**s only. A binary star is a system in which two stars orbit each other around a central point of **gravity.** The mass of each star of the pair can be calculated from the size of its orbit and the length of time it takes to revolve around the other star.

Binary stars come in several varieties. A **visual binary** is a pair in which each star can be seen distinctly, either through a telescope or with the naked eye. In an **astrometric binary,** only one star can be seen, but its wobble implies another star is present and in orbit around the visible star. An **eclipsing binary** results when the orbital plane of each member of the binary is nearly edgewise to our line of sight. Thus each star is eclipsed by the other as they revolve around each other. A fourth type is a **spectroscopic binary,** the stars of which can be distinguished by using a **spectroscope.** If one apparent star gives two different **spectra,** this means it is actually a spectroscopic binary.

Determining Masses in Binary Systems

To determine the masses of stars in a binary system, an astronomer must first calculate the length of each star's orbit. The astronomer can then deduce the strength of the gravitational fields necessary to produce those orbits. And since gravity is a function of mass (the more massive a body, the larger the gravitational field it creates), astronomers can approximate the masses necessary to create those gravitational fields.

Visual binaries are the easiest cases for which to calculate stellar masses. In particular, for binaries with relatively short orbits (those taking less than one hundred years to complete), scientists can accurately assess the masses of both stars. For other types of binaries this calculation is more difficult.

For instance, with spectroscopic binaries, the angle at which the orbits of each star intersect is often difficult to discern. In cases where astronomers have only limited information about a binary's orbits, they can calculate each star's minimum possible mass. In other words, one can say that a star must equal at least "X" solar masses (the mass of the sun, which is used as a measurement of stellar mass) in order to produce the orbit that is observed. If the angle of inclination of the orbits is greater than perceived, the actual masses of the stars would be greater than the minimum value.

Single stars present a much greater challenge. Since their masses can not be calculated directly, the best that can be done is to make estimates based on comparisons with binaries for which masses have been accurately determined. These estimates are based on the **mass-luminosity law:** the relationship between mass and luminosity (brightness) of stars. By making a graph, in which the known mass of the binaries is plotted on one axis and their luminosities on the other, the points form a narrow, nearly straight band. Thus, if the luminosity of a single star is known, its position along the band can be found and its approximate mass determined. This method does not work, however, for stars that are **red giant**s or in other evolutionary stages that occur toward the end of a star's lifetime.

The smallest known stars are only about 8 percent as massive as the sun (the sun's mass is measured as 332,946 times the mass of the Earth). In theory, an object of lower mass could not produce the tremendous pressure necessary to initiate **nuclear fusion,** the process that makes a star bright and hot. It would instead be a **brown dwarf,** a small, dark, cool ball of dust and gas that never quite becomes a star.

The largest stars known are fifty times more massive than the sun. Astronomers do not know whether there is an upper limit as to how massive a star can be. One theory suggests that at over one hundred solar masses a star would become unstable and produce vibrations that would rip it apart.

See also **Binary star** and **Brown dwarf**

Stonehenge

One of the world's most famous ancient astronomical sites is Stonehenge. This complex assembly of boulders and ditches is located in the southwest of England, about 8 miles (13 kilometers) from the town of Salisbury. Stonehenge was built and re-built over three periods, most likely between the years 3100 B.C. and 1100 B.C. The architects of this monument were probably ancient druids, an order of Welsh and British priests. While Stonehenge is widely believed to have had some astronomical function, exactly what that function was remains in question.

The effects of about five thousand years of rain and wind, plus the action of vandals, have significantly altered Stonehenge from its original form. Studies undertaken by archaeologists and anthropologists indicate that at one time it contained thirty blocks of gray sandstone, each standing about 13.5 feet (4.1 meters) high, arranged in a 97-foot-diameter (29-meter-diameter) circle. Lying horizontally on top of these stones and forming a continuous ring were thirty smaller stone slabs. A second, inner circle of stones enclosed a third, horseshoe-shaped group of stones. Today, all that remains is a partial outer ring and a handful of inner stones.

The most popular theory about the astronomical function of Stonehenge is that it was a **calendar** of sorts, marking the summer **solstice.** According to this theory, the solstice can be observed by standing at the center of the ring of stones and looking toward the northeast. There, beyond the stones, framed by three segments of the circle (four upright stones topped by three horizontal stones) is a pillar called the Heel Stone. The top of the Heel Stone, which appears to line up with the distant horizon, is very close to the spot where the sun's first rays strike on the summer solstice.

This design, however, is not precise. The sun rises slightly to the north of the Heel Stone, raising questions about the validity of the theory. Some historians argue that the degree of error is not significant and that the ancient builders just did not hold themselves to the exact standards we do today. Others believe that it is merely coincidental that on the solstice the sun rises at a point near the Heel Stone and that the Heel Stone either served some other function or none at all. The answer to this question and others may lay beneath the nearly one-half of Stonehenge that has not yet been excavated.

Construction of Stonehenge

In the 1920s and 1950s, partial excavations revealed some of the history of the construction of Stonehenge. It seems most likely that the first stage of Stonehenge, built around 3100 B.C., consisted only of a circular ditch surrounded by an embankment, plus an inner circle of fifty-six pits. Several tall stones marking the entrance and the Heel Stone were probably also erected at this time.

Sunset over Salisbury Plain, home to Stonehenge.

The next phase of construction came in about 2150 B.C., with the erection of two concentric circles of stones in the center of the monument. Then, around 1550 B.C., a third group of stones was arranged in a horseshoe shape within the inner circle. The final stage—the addition of a long avenue leading up to the monument—probably took place around 1100 B.C.

In addition to the solstice-marker idea, many theories have been proposed as to the astronomical significance of the alignment of particular groups of stones. For instance, there are over fifty sets of stones that are believed to have been lined up with the sun and moon at various times of year. Too many unknowns remain, however, to determine which of these theories is true. Perhaps if the rest of the site is excavated in the future, more answers will be forthcoming.

Today Stonehenge is a popular tourist attraction. As a result of vandalism, however, the inner circle of stones has been closed off to the public by a fence topped with barbed wire. The only group to gain access to the inner circle is a modern-day order of white-robed druids who perform the same rituals on the summer solstice they claim have been performed by druids over the millennia.

See also **Solstice**

Sun

Our sun is an average-sized, middle-aged star. When considered in the context of the **galaxy,** the sun can easily be overlooked as just one star among over one hundred billion stars. The sun becomes even more insignificant when one considers that the **Milky Way** is just one galaxy among over fifty billion galaxies in the universe. Yet, on the stage that is our **solar system,** the sun truly is the star of the show.

The sun is a gas ball made mostly of hydrogen and helium, with a small amount of carbon, nitrogen, oxygen, and a smattering of heavy metals. It is about 865,000 miles (1,391,785 kilometers) in diameter, about 109 times the diameter of Earth. And it is so large that over 1.3 million Earths could fit inside it. The sun, which alone accounts for about 98 percent of the total **mass** in the solar system, is 332,946 times more massive than the Earth.

The sun is a mere eight light-minutes, or nearly 93 million miles (150 million kilometers), from Earth. In comparison, the next closest star, Proxima Centauri, is 4.2 **light-year**s, or 24.8 trillion miles (40 trillion kilometers) away. If a bridge to the sun existed, it would take 177 years at a constant speed of 60 miles (97 kilometers) per hour (with no stops) to drive there. Even if you lived long enough to make the entire trip, your car would overheat once you got to within about 10 million (16 million kilometers) of the sun. There you would encounter the edge of the **corona,** the outermost part of the sun's atmosphere, where the temperature is about 3.6 million degrees Fahrenheit (2 million degrees Celsius).

The Sun's Atmosphere

The corona is the thinnest part of the atmosphere and can be viewed only during a total eclipse of the sun. The corona is the region where **prominence**s appear. At the corona's outer edges it fades out into a sea of charged particles that flow out into space as the **solar wind.**

Beyond that boundary lies the **chromosphere,** which is cooler yet. This atmospheric layer is punctuated with **flare**s (bright, hot jets of gas) and **facula**e (consisting of bright hydrogen clouds known as plages). At its greatest distance from the sun's surface, the temperature of the chromosphere is about 180,000 degrees Fahrenheit (100,000 degrees Celsius). At its inner limit, a couple thousand miles nearer to the sun, the temperature falls to 7,200 degrees Fahrenheit (4,000 degrees Celsius). This is the region at which the sun's "surface," the **photosphere**, begins.

The photosphere is the part of the sun we can see. It is a layer about a few-hundred-miles thick, through which the sun's intense heat is given off into space. The inner part of the photosphere is about 3,600 degrees Fahrenheit (2,000 degrees Celsius) hotter than the outer region, where it meets the chromosphere.

The photosphere is made up of Earth-sized cells called **granules.** These cells constantly change in size and shape as they carry hot gas from the center of the sun out to the surface, and cycle the cooler gas back down to be re-heated. It is within this layer of the sun that **sunspot**s, or dark areas, appear. Sunspots are caused by magnetic disturbances. Their dark appearance is due to their relatively low temperature (about 2,700 degrees Fahrenheit, or 1,500 degrees Celsius) compared to the rest of the surface.

Further nearing the center of the sun is the convection zone, the region of the sun in which heat is carried toward the corona by slow-moving gas currents. This region is followed by the radiative zone, the region of the sun in which heat is dispersed into the surrounding hot **plasma** (a substance made of ions and electrons). Finally, about 312,000 miles (502,000 kilometers) below the surface is the core. With a diameter of 240,000 miles (386,160 kilometers), the core accounts for only about 3 percent of the sun's volume. Yet it is so dense that it contains about 60 percent of the sun's mass.

The temperature in this dense area where energy is created is an astounding 27 million degrees Fahrenheit (15 million degrees Celsius). There, **nuclear fusion,** the sun's heat-producing process, takes two hydrogen nuclei and combines them into one helium nucleus, releasing a tremendous amount of energy in the process. The amount of helium found in the sun indicates that the fusion of hydrogen to helium must have been going on for about 4.5 billion years. And it is estimated that the sun has enough hydrogen to continue producing energy for about 5 billion more years.

Artist's impression of the sun as it will appear from Earth when it nears the end of its life and begins to evolve into a red giant. The sun will gradually engulf Mercury, Venus, and the Earth and may extend as far as the orbit of Mars.

The sun will spend the final 10 percent of its life as a **red giant.** During this phase, its surface temperature will drop to between 3,000 and 6,700 degrees Fahrenheit (1,700 and 3,000 degrees Celsius), and it will take on a reddish color. Its diameter will expand tenfold, swallowing up the Earth in the process. After a billion or so years, the sun's atmosphere will float away, leaving only a glowing core called a **white dwarf.** This shrunken body will take perhaps a trillion years to cool completely.

Much of what we know about the sun has been discovered by the thirteen **space probe**s that have been sent to explore it since 1965. The first five, launched between 1965 and 1968, were members of the U.S. Pi-

oneer series (*Pioneer 5* through *9*). Two of those—*Pioneer 6* and *8*—are still transmitting data. The Pioneer **probe**s contain instruments to measure the sun's **magnetic field,** solar wind, and **cosmic rays** (invisible, high-energy particles).

In 1973, the sun was examined by the U.S. *Skylab* **space station** and a probe placed into lunar orbit, *Explorer 49*. There were two joint U.S.-West German solar probes, *Helios 1* and *2,* launched in 1974 and 1976, respectively. Then from 1984 to 1989 the U.S. *Solar Maximum Mission* observed solar flares during a period of intense solar activity. And in 1991 a joint U.S.-England-Japan probe called *Yohkoh* was deployed to study high-energy radiation from solar flares.

The two most sophisticated solar probes currently in operation are *Ulysses,* launched in 1990, and the Solar and Heliospheric Observatory (SOHO), launched in 1995. Both are joint projects of the U.S. and the European Space Agency (ESA). *Ulysses* is studying activity at the sun's north and south poles and in the space above and below the poles. SOHO, in addition to studying the sun, is collecting information on the **heliosphere**—the vast region permeated by the solar wind that surrounds the sun and extends throughout the solar system.

See also **Bethe, Hans**; **Pioneer program**; **Red giant star**; *Skylab* **space station**; **Solar and Heliospheric Observatory**; **Solar atmosphere**; **Sunspot**; *Ulysses*; and **White dwarf star**

Sunspot

Sunspots appear, through specialized telescopes, as blemishes on the sun. They are caused by magnetic disturbances at the sun's surface. Their dark appearance is a result of their low temperature, about 2,240 degrees Fahrenheit (1,227 degrees Celsius) lower than the rest of the surface.

A sunspot has two components, a small, dark, featureless core (the **umbra**) and a large, lighter surrounding region (the **penumbra**). Within the penumbra are delicate filaments, extending outward like spokes. Sunspots vary in size and tend to be clustered in groups. The larger groups exist for several weeks while the smaller groups usually fade out within a couple weeks.

A sunspot is often referred to as a magnetic "storm." Like a storm on Earth, it is brought about by the interaction of various environmental factors. On the sun, the storm is caused by the transfer of heat from the outer layers into the **photosphere,** the sun's visible surface, stirring up the weak **magnetic field** lying beneath it.

As the storm grows stronger, a sunspot erupts in a solar **flare** and ejects streams of subatomic particles along with **plasma, cosmic ray**s, **X-ray**s, and **gamma ray**s into space.

These particles approach Earth and are attracted toward the north and south magnetic poles. As they spiral downward, they ionize (create an electric charge within) the oxygen and nitrogen gas in the atmosphere, causing it to glow. These beautiful displays of light in the night sky are called **aurora**e, also known as the Northern and Southern Lights.

A connection between sunspots and large-scale climatic shifts on Earth is also thought to exist. Scientists have determined that increased sunspot activity corresponds with warmer temperatures on Earth, and that

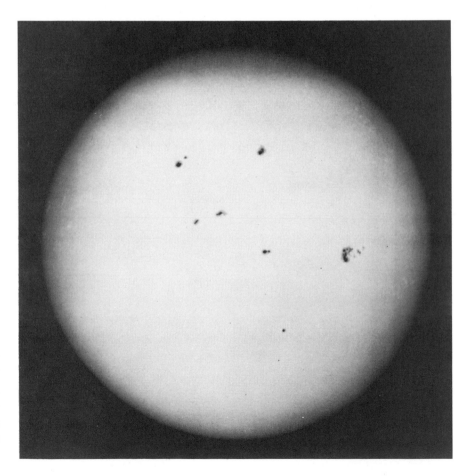

The sunspots at the upper center are about 21,000 miles (33,790 kilometers) in diameter, the large spot at the right is about 35,000 miles (56,315 kilometers) in diameter, and the small spot at the lower right is about the size of Earth.

decreased sunspot activity has the opposite effect. For instance, the spans of years from 1400–1510 and 1645–1715 were both cool periods on Earth and relatively inactive times for the sun.

See also **Sun**

Supergiant

The largest and brightest type of star is a **supergiant.** These stars possess over fifteen times the **mass** of the sun and shine over one million times more brightly than the sun. One of the best known supergiants, the star Betelgeuse in the Orion **constellation,** has a diameter the size of the orbit of Mars.

Supergiants represent the final stages of life of only the most massive stars and hence are quite rare. Astronomers believe that the fate awaiting a supergiant is to explode in a glorious burst called a **supernova,** during which its gravitational collapse is so complete that all that remains is a single point of infinite mass and **gravity** called a **black hole.**

Supergiants are similar in spectral type and temperature to their somewhat smaller counterparts, giants. Giants are the bloated stage that average-sized stars (like our sun) pass through toward the end of their lifetime. The only difference between the two classes of stars is that supergiants are larger and brighter.

Supergiants and giants are both located off the "main sequence" of the **Hertzsprung-Russell diagram** (H-R diagram). The H-R diagram is the graph showing the relationship between the brightness and temperature (or color) of stars. It places **absolute magnitude** (or brightness) on the vertical axis and color (or temperature) on the horizontal axis. When groups of stars are plotted, the majority appear on the main sequence, the diagonal line that runs from hot, bright, blue stars on the upper left to the cool, dim, red stars on the lower right. A star spends most of its lifetime at one position on the main sequence.

The significance of being off the main sequence is that a star has entered the final stages of life. It is no longer in the approximately 90 percent of its lifetime during which it has a supply of hydrogen to fuel the process of **nuclear fusion.** The stars that fall outside of the main sequence are either supergiants, giants, or **white dwarf**s (remnants of exploded stars). Supergiants and giants, being the brightest, coolest stars, are located on the upper right of the diagram. Since they are hot, dim, and small, white dwarfs are on the bottom left of the diagram.

Supergiants are so bright that they stand out in distant **galaxies,** which makes them useful as indicators of distance. The type of supergiants most famous in this regard are blinking yellow supergiants called **cepheid variable**s. Cepheids become brighter and dimmer (and larger and smaller) at regular intervals due to the expansion and contraction of their surface layers. The time it takes a cepheid to complete one pulsation is related to its brightness at a constant distance from Earth. For this reason, these stars have been given the name "astronomical yardsticks."

See also **Black hole**; **Cepheid variables**; **Nova and supernova**; and **Red giant star**

Tereshkova, Valentina (1937–)

Russian cosmonaut

Many Americans can tell you the name of the first American woman in space: Sally Ride. Far fewer, however, can tell you the name of the first woman in space from any nation: Valentina Tereshkova. The Russian Tereshkova accomplished this feat in 1963, two decades before her American counterpart.

Tereshkova rode into space on board *Vostok 6* on June 16, 1963. This spacecraft was the sixth in the historic Vostok series, which ushered in the era of human space flight. Just two years earlier, Yuri Gagarin, riding aboard *Vostok 1,* had become the first person in space.

Valentina Vladimirovna Tereshkova was born on March 6, 1937, in the Russian village of Maslennikovo, where her parents worked on a collective farm. Her father was killed during World War II, when Valentina was two, and her mother struggled to raise three children on her own. To assist with the family finances, Valentina went to work at a young age and did not begin school until she was ten years old.

When she was seventeen, Tereshkova went to work at a tire factory. The next year she transferred to the cotton mill where her mother and sister worked. Meanwhile, she completed correspondence courses and graduated from the Light Industry Technical School. She was also active in the Communist Party and in a parachuting club, eventually making over 150 jumps.

In 1961, at the age of twenty-four, Valentina applied to join the Soviet space program. As luck would have it, Soviet space officials were then seeking women to become **cosmonaut**s. Since there were very few female pilots, the most likely candidates were parachutists. Tereshkova was chosen to be one of the first four women cosmonauts, and in March 1962, she reported to Star City, just outside of Moscow, for training.

There are conflicting accounts as to how male cosmonauts reacted to the integration of women into their ranks. Official Soviet reports claim the men acted "like brothers" to the women. According to one American involved in the joint U.S.-Soviet *Apollo-Soyuz* Test Project, however, Tereshkova confided that she was shunned by male cosmonauts "because I have invaded their little playground and because I am a woman." However, Tereshkova was admired by at least one male colleague, Yuri Gagarin. He was quoted as saying, "It was hard for her [Tereshkova] to master **rocket** techniques, study spaceship designs and equipment, but she tackled the job stubbornly and devoted much of her own time to study, poring over books and notes in the evening."

*Valentina
Tereshkova, the
first woman in
space, rode aboard
the* Vostok *6 in 1963.*

Tereshkova and the other women underwent flight training in the Soviet Air Force. They were also subjected to rigorous exercises in preparation for the weightlessness they would experience in space. Tereshkova trained for fifteen months prior to her landmark journey into space.

Tereshkova's Flight in *Vostok 6*

There are rumors that Tereshkova, then a junior lieutenant in the air force, stepped in to pilot *Vostok 6* only at the last minute, when the scheduled cosmonaut failed her physical examination. Regardless of the circumstances that led to her flight, a smiling Tereshkova in space was shown on Soviet and European television, signaling that all was well. "I see the horizon," she said. "A light blue, a beautiful band. This is the Earth. How beautiful it is!"

Tereshkova spent nearly three days in space on *Vostok 6,* orbiting Earth forty-eight times. Her spacecraft came within three miles of *Vostok 5,* piloted by cosmonaut Valery Bykovsky. *Vostok 5* had been launched two days before *Vostok 6.* Tereshkova's flight proved that women, as well as men, are physically and psychologically capable enduring the stresses of space.

Tereshkova received a hero's welcome on her return. She became a symbol of the new Soviet feminism and of expanding opportunities for women everywhere. She embarked on a global tour, visiting the United Nations and Cuba, and attending the International Aeronautical Federation Conference in Mexico, where she expounded on the equality of the sexes in the **Soviet Union.**

In 1963, Tereshkova married cosmonaut Andrian Nikolayev, the pilot of the *Vostok 3* flight, one year after both had journeyed in space. It was a much-heralded, government-sponsored ceremony, in which then-Soviet leader Nikita Kruschev gave away the bride. They had one child, a daughter named Yelena, who was carefully examined for medical consequences that might have occurred as a result of being born to parents who had traveled in space. No negative effects were found. Their marriage ended in divorce in 1982.

Tereshkova continued her air force training at the Zhukovsky Air Force Engineering Academy. She graduated in 1969 and eventually attained the rank of colonel. Seven years later Tereshkova completed a technical sciences degree. In the meantime she served as an aerospace engineer in the Soviet space program and as a government official with the title Deputy to the Supreme Soviet.

Over the years, Tereshkova continued toward her way-up through the government ranks. In 1974, she became a member of the Supreme Soviet Presidium and in 1989 was elected as a People's Deputy. She also served on the Soviet Union's Women's Committee and International Cultural and Friendship Union. Since the breakup of the Soviet Union, she has chaired the Russian Association of International Cooperation.

Tereshkova has been the subject of at least one biography, entitled *It Is I, Sea Gull: Valentina Tereshkova, First Woman in Space,* by Mitchell Sharpe. She has also published an autobiography.

See also **Gagarin, Yuri** and **Vostok program**

Tethered Satellite System

The Tethered Satellite System (TSS) is a scientific experiment designed to fly on board a **space shuttle,** the purpose of which is to make measurements of electrical and **magnetic field**s in the Earth's upper atmosphere. The TSS consists of a small satellite designed to travel through space at the end of a nearly 14-mile-long (22.5-kilometer-long) cord, called a tether. The other end of the tether is attached to the cargo bay of a space shuttle. Two attempts have been made to deploy the TSS—first in 1992 and most recently in 1996—both times on the space shuttle *Atlantis.* In neither case was the deployment successful.

The TSS is a joint project of the National Aeronautics and Space Administration (NASA) and the Italian Space Agency. It consists of three parts: a re-usable satellite, a tether, and a satellite deployer system. The satellite is a 5.25-foot-diameter (1.6-meter-diameter) metal sphere. There are three windows carved out of its aluminum-alloy surface—one for each of the three sets of instruments making observations of the sun, Earth, and charged particles in the Earth's atmosphere. On the bottom of the satellite is a "bayonet pin" that secures the tether to the satellite.

The tether is a one-tenth-of-an-inch-thick copper and nylon cord. Its total length is nearly 14 miles, but it's only intended to be reeled out to 12.8 miles (20.5 kilometers). The copper wire running through the center of the tether conducts electricity, enabling the tether to measure electrical currents as it cuts across a wide portion of the Earth's atmosphere.

The TSS deployer system is the mechanism holding the tether in place in the space shuttle's cargo bay. This system also releases the satellite, which is a more complicated procedure than one might think. The satellite must first be lifted away from the shuttle, so that when the tether is released the satellite won't hit any part of the shuttle. This system also controls the tether reel mechanism, which in turn controls the length and tension of the tether. The final charge of the deployer system is to re-secure the satellite in the cargo bay at the end of the experiment.

The first TSS, launched on July 31, 1992, had to be aborted early on. Only 853 feet (260 meters) of tether had been unreeled when the tether reel mechanism jammed. Enough of the tether was extended, however, to prove that a tethered satellite could be deployed and controlled from a space shuttle.

On February 25, 1996, the second attempt at operating a TSS failed. This time the tether broke just before it reached full extension. Three weeks later, the satellite burned up as it entered the Earth's atmosphere.

Tethered Satellite System receiving finishing touches at the Kennedy Space Center, July 1995.

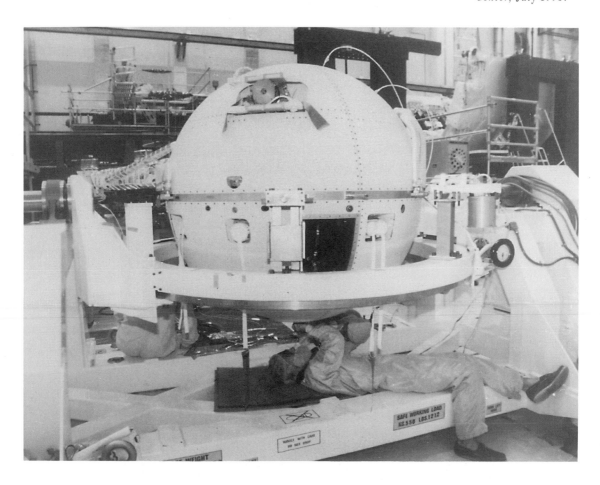

Although the future of the program is in question, it has been the hope of TSS operators that eventually a string of satellites could be deployed along the same tether. These satellites would take simultaneous readings of electrical and magnetic fields, as well as analyze **plasma** (a substance made of ions and electrons that flows out from the sun), at several locations in space. They could be used to take measurements in hard-to-reach layers of the Earth's atmosphere, places that are too high for aircraft and too low for spacecraft. The TSS is an economical way to conduct experiments, since it only requires one craft with propulsion systems while the satellites ride piggy-back.

Another possible use for tethered satellites is data retrieval. Scientists anticipate that shuttles could lower data-laden satellites toward Earth by long tethers to altitudes where the satellites could be picked up by aircraft. In this way, space shuttles could stay in space longer and conduct more experiments before returning to Earth.

The tether itself collects naturally occurring electricity—the type that produces **aurora**e (Northern and Southern Lights)—from ions in the Earth's upper atmosphere. Had the recent tethered satellite experiment been successful, the tether would have drawn 4,800 volts of electricity into the satellite. Scientists are considering the possibility that we may be able to use tethers as energy sources for future space missions, such as the International Space Station, slated for completion early in the next century.

Tethers also have the potential to be the world's longest antennae. They can detect radio signals from ships at sea and transmit these signals, as well as messages sent by astronauts, to ground stations on Earth. Tethers may even prove an efficient way to connect cellular telephone calls worldwide.

An investigative board at NASA concluded in June 1996 that the reason for the failure of the most recent TSS deployment was that the tether's insulation was punctured by small, sharp pieces of metal, either from braided wire or from the reel mechanism. This caused the tether to burn and float away, still attached to the satellite. The failure has been blamed on a flaw either in the manufacture or the handling of the tether.

Before the launch of the most recent TSS, plans had been underway for a third deployment using a 65-mile-long (105-kilometer-long) tether. Now, in light of the costly failures coupled with budget cuts faced by NASA, the future of the TSS program is in question.

See also **Aurorae** and **Earth's atmosphere**

Tides

If you have ever spent a day at the ocean, you have experienced tides, the rising and falling of water to different levels on the shore. Stand at the water's edge at low tide in ankle-deep water and you will find that at the same spot at high tide the water is knee-deep to over-your-head-deep. While many people know that the moon causes tides, few are aware of the complex way in which tidal forces operate.

Tides are caused not simply by water being pulled in the direction of the moon. If the relationship were this direct, only one high tide each day would take place, corresponding to the Earth's rotation. Water would be pulled toward the moon only when it had rotated to a position facing the moon. Yet two cycles of high and low tides occur each day, roughly thirteen hours apart. High tides occur both where water is closest to the moon and on the opposite side of the Earth, where it is farthest from the moon. At points in between, where the water has rushed away from the shores, there are low tides.

The reason for this effect is that tides are caused by the differential forces, different effects that the moon's **gravity** has on different locations on Earth. To illustrate this concept, draw two circles: a big one for the Earth and a small one for the moon. Now draw a dot at the center of the Earth and label it "B." Draw a second dot at the edge of the Earth closest to the moon and label it "A." And draw at third dot at the other side of the Earth, in line with the first two, and label it "C." "A" represents the water closest to the moon, "B" represents the solid Earth (beneath the oceans), and "C" represents the water farthest from the moon. (This example assumes that the Earth is entirely covered with water.)

The moon's gravitational pull is felt at all three points, but most strongly on the water that is closest to the moon ("A") and less so at points successively farther away ("B" and "C"). Thus, as water faces the moon, gravity pulls it and causes a high tide. The moon's gravity also pulls at the solid Earth beneath the ocean, but not as strongly. It is strong enough, however, to pull the solid Earth slightly away from the ocean on the opposite side, which creates a high tide there too.

During a twenty-six-hour period, each point on the Earth's surface moves through a series of tides: high, low, high, and low again. The twenty-six-hour figure is the sum of the Earth's twenty-four-hour rotation period and the moon's eastward movement around the Earth.

The sun's gravitational field also influences the tides, but only about half as much as does the moon's. The reason for this difference is that the sun is so far away that its gravitational pull, although very strong, is felt more-or-less evenly across the planet. And remember, it is the differential gravitational pull that causes tides.

The main way the sun influences tides is in conjunction with the moon. During a full moon or a new moon (when the moon, Earth, and sun are in line), the gravitational fields of the sun and moon work together, exerting a stronger pull on the tides. This alignment occurs twice a month and causes the highest tides of all, called spring tides. This term comes from the German word "springen," which means "to rise up" and has nothing to do with the season by the same name.

When the sun, moon, and Earth are at right angles to one another, during the first quarter and last quarter moons, the gravitational fields of the sun and moon are at odds, partially canceling each other out. This results in the year's smallest high tides (when there is the least difference between high and low tides), known as neap tides.

See also **Earth's rotation** and **Lunar phases**

Time

Time is a system for describing the continuous passage of events from past to present to future. Time can refer to the duration of a particular event

This page and opposite: High tide and low tide at Big Pine Key, Florida.

(how long it lasted), as well as the moment at which it took place. Measurements of time are divided into large increments such as years, months, and days; and smaller increments such as hours and seconds.

Every aspect of our lives in the busy, modern world is regulated by time. Think of how often you check the time. There are probably several clocks in your home and school and you may even wear a watch. Clocks and watches tell you when to wake up, when to catch a bus, when to eat supper, and when to watch your favorite television program. They also help you coordinate activities with other people, such as scheduling a ball game for a certain time, for example.

Time and the Natural World

This seemingly artificial concept of time has its roots in the natural world. In ancient times, before people had clocks, they relied on the sun, moon, and seasons to keep track of time. When the sun rose it signaled the time to get up and work and when the sun set they knew it was time to go to sleep. One complete cycle of the moon around the Earth marked a month and the changing seasons marked the progression of a year.

The passage of time during a single day—which is the focus of this essay—can be determined by following the sun's changing position in the sky. The sun appears each morning in the east. During daylight hours, due to the Earth's rotation about its axis from west to east, the sun appears to sweep westward across the sky. Finally it disappears below the western horizon. Hours later rises in the east again.

Sundials

The most basic form of timekeeping, based on the sun's position in the sky and the shadows it creates on the ground, is called apparent solar time. Beginning about four thousand years ago, people in Egypt, Greece, Rome, and China used an instrument called a sundial to measure apparent solar time. A **sundial** consists of a flat surface with hours marked at graduated intervals and a needle that points straight up, perpendicular to the surface. The sun's light falls on the needle, which casts a shadow on the appropriate hour. When the sun is directly overhead and casts little or no shadow, it's noon.

Sundials are best suited for measuring durations of time. For instance, if you're baking a cake that needs to stay in the oven for one hour, you could monitor the shadow cast by the needle on your sundial to know when the hour had elapsed.

The overall timekeeping capability of sundials, however, is limited. First, sundials only function during daylight hours and on sunny days. Even then, they give the time only for a particular **longitude.** As you travel eastward or westward (to different longitudes), the sun rises earlier or later each day. Thus, for example, if a sundial in one village reads "noon," a sundial in the next village to the west would read "11:30 A.M."

A Series of "Clocks"

Over the centuries, people came up with a range of timekeeping devices that did not rely on the sun to function. For instance, the Chinese used a wet rope with knots placed at regular distances apart. They set fire to the rope and as it slowly burned its way from knot to knot, it marked the lapse of a given time period.

The Greeks and Romans developed a "water clock." This consisted of a water-filled container with markings on the side representing increments of time. Water would leak from a small hole in the bottom of the container, causing the level to fall steadily. The revelation of new markings indicated the passage of time. Another example of a timekeeping device is the hourglass. In this case, sand travels through a narrow opening connecting two bulbous regions of glass. It takes one hour for all the sand to travel from the top half to the bottom.

Mechanical clocks were first developed around the year 1300. The earliest ones used a falling weight that turned a drum to run an hour hand

Making a Sundial

Before there were clocks and watches, people relied on the motion of the sun, and an instrument called a sundial, to keep track of time. You can construct your own sundial using simple materials that you'll find around the house.

First you need to locate a place outdoors or on a window sill that receives direct sunlight during all or most of the day. Then take a piece of cardboard and set it on that spot. Secure its corners with rocks or tape. Now take a compass to determine which way is north, and mark an "N" and an arrow in that direction on the edge of the cardboard.

Next find a pencil, ruler, or other long, straight object to act as a pointer and place it, pointing straight up, in the middle of the cardboard. If you're outdoors on the grass, you can drive the pointer straight through the cardboard and into the ground. Otherwise, you can affix it to the cardboard with a lump of clay. Be sure the pointer is straight up and down and that the cardboard is laying flat.

Now you're ready to mark the time. Start in the morning on a sunny day. Each hour throughout the day, mark an "X" at the end of the shadow cast by the pointer and write the time.

On the next sunny day, bring out your sundial and line it up facing north again. Repeat the experiment to make sure your markings are accurate. Observe how the sundial's time differs, as the months progress, from the time on a real clock. This is due to the changing position of the sun in the sky, as the Earth revolves around it.

(they didn't have minute hands). These big, heavy clocks were replaced by lighter, spring-driven clocks around 1550.

Standard Time

Even though mechanical clocks allowed people to keep track of time continuously, there still was still a problem—each town set its own time and there was no way of coordinating between them. The consequences of this became more pronounced when railroads were built and people began to travel more. A system of time was needed on which a train schedule could be based and which would allow travelers to make appointments in other towns.

This quest for uniformity led to an international agreement in October of 1884 that divided the world into twenty-four standard time zones. The zones are roughly based on areas 15 degrees of longitude across (their boundaries sometimes follow the borders of countries they pass through, and thus are irregular). The time within each zone is constant and the time changes by one hour whenever you enter a new zone.

In the United States there are four time zones. The time from one zone to the next, as you move westward, is set an hour earlier. Thus, if it's noon on the East Coast (Eastern Standard Time), it's 11 A.M. in the Midwest (Central Standard Time), 10 A.M. in Colorado (Mountain Standard Time), and 9 A.M. on the West Coast (Pacific Standard Time).

A handy adjustment to standard time, used by most states in the U.S. and many foreign countries, is daylight savings time. This means setting the time one hour later during the summer months, when days are longer.

See also **Calendar** and **Seasons**

Tombaugh, Clyde (1906–)

American astronomer

Clyde Tombaugh is best known for his 1930 discovery of the planet Pluto. He was then a self-described "farm boy amateur astronomer without a university education," hired to work at Lowell Observatory in Flagstaff, Arizona. The search for a suspected ninth planet, then referred to as Planet X, had been instigated twenty-five years earlier by observatory founder Percival Lowell. Tombaugh's job was to continue the tedious task of photographing the area of the sky where this planet was believed exist, a mission from which Lowell had emerged empty-handed, or so he believed.

Clyde William Tombaugh was born on February 4, 1906, to Muron Tombaugh and Adella Chritton Tombaugh. He grew up on a farm outside of Streator, Illinois, the eldest of six children. When he was sixteen, Tombaugh moved with his family to a farm in western Kansas.

The first telescope Tombaugh ever looked through was his uncle's 3-inch (7.5-centimeter) **refractor.** In 1925, with the help of his father who took a second job to finance the project materials, Tombaugh built his own 8-inch (20-centimeter) **reflector.** Although this telescope lacked precision

Astronomer Clyde
Tombaugh poses by
his homemade
telescope in his
backyard in Las
Cruces, New
Mexico, September
14, 1987.

and was of limited use, it set Tombaugh on a career of building telescopes. Throughout his lifetime, he built about thirty-six.

In 1928, Tombaugh completed construction of a very accurate instrument, a 9-inch (23-centimeter) reflector. That same year, as he was looking forward to beginning college and a probable career in astronomy, a hailstorm ruined his family's crops (and finances), and Tombaugh had to abandon his plans. Then he attempted to enter the field of astronomy through another route. Looking through his telescope, Tombaugh sketched Jupiter and Mars and sent his drawings to the Lowell Observatory. In return, he received a job offer.

Tombaugh Joins the Staff At Lowell

For the job they had in mind, the astronomers at Lowell had only enough funds to pay an amateur. Tombaugh's task, on which he worked for ten months, was to look for a ninth planet by photographing a selected region of the sky, one small piece at a time. Looking through Lowell's 13-inch (33-centimeter) refractor, he used a "blink comparator" to detect any object moving beyond the Earth's orbit. That device worked by alternately portraying two different photographs. Any moving object appeared as a pinpoint of light that would jump or "blink" between the images.

On February 18, 1930, Tombaugh's hard work paid off, when he discovered a small, moving body. He was able to rule out the possibility that the body was a **comet** or **asteroid** by comparing his results against a third photograph of the same area. He concluded that the object must be a planet. At the suggestion of an eleven-year-old English schoolgirl named Venetia Burney, the planet was called Pluto, for the Greek god of the underworld. Looking back at the photographs taken years earlier by Lowell, Tombaugh discovered that Lowell had indeed captured the image of Pluto. Because the planet was so small, however, Lowell's assistants had apparently overlooked it.

Having become something of a celebrity, Tombaugh was awarded a college scholarship. In 1932, he entered the University of Kansas, while still spending each summer at Lowell Observatory. By 1939, Tombaugh had earned both a bachelor's degree and a master's degree from the University of Kansas. In 1934 he married a fellow student named Patricia Edson, with whom he eventually had two children, Alden and Annette.

After his college years, Tombaugh held a variety of teaching posts while maintaining employment at the observatory. He first taught physics at Arizona State Teachers College, as well as navigation at Arizona State

University, both in Flagstaff. He subsequently taught astronomy and the history of astronomy at the University of California, Los Angeles.

At Lowell Observatory, Tombaugh participated in a project called the "planetary patrol," in which he recorded the positions of thousands of space objects, including **galaxies,** asteroids, and a **nova.** In the process he discovered several new celestial bodies, including two comets, hundreds of asteroids, a **globular cluster,** and a dense supercluster of eighteen hundred galaxies.

Tombaugh also made an extensive study of the surface of Mars. Although he could not view the markings (they were too fine), Tombaugh predicted that the Martian surface had been struck by asteroids and therefore was cratered. He made this assumption because of the planet's proximity to the asteroid belt. Observations made by the U.S. **space probe** *Mariner 4* in 1965 proved him correct.

In 1946, the year Tombaugh's employment ended at the observatory, he served in the U.S. Army, working at the White Sands Proving Grounds near Las Cruces, New Mexico, on missile development. His expertise with telescope optics was particularly useful in improving missile tracking systems.

Tombaugh's next post, in 1955, was at New Mexico State University in Las Cruces, where he helped found the astronomy department. In addition to teaching and research, Tombaugh helped maintain the university's collection of telescopes and participated in the construction of new ones. One of Tombaugh's research projects involved seeking small space objects near the Earth (such as asteroids) that could interfere with future spacecraft. He found none.

Since his retirement in 1973, Tombaugh has remained active in New Mexico State University's astronomy department giving seminars, attending programs, and participating in the local astronomy club. He continues to observe the skies through his decades-old, homemade 9-inch (23-centimeter) reflector telescope.

See also **Lowell, Percival**; **Lowell Observatory**; and **Pluto**

Tsiolkovsky, Konstantin (1857–1935)
Russian engineer

At the age of ten, Konstantin Tsiolkovsky contracted scarlet fever. The disease left him deaf and, as a result, he grew up a solitary child. At his father's encouragement, however, he studied and conducted experiments in mathematics, physics, and astronomy on his own.

At the age of twenty-two, Tsiolkovsky became a teacher. He also continued his experiments, which at that time were focused on air travel. To determine the air friction acting upon an airplane traveling at certain speeds, Tsiolkovsky built Russia's first wind tunnel.

Tsiolkovsky's experiments next led him to consider space travel. He first introduced his ideas on this topic in an article published in 1895. Three years later, he outlined many of the basic concepts of space travel that scientists still utilize today. His ideas were far more advanced than any other scientist in the field. For instance, he wrote that humans could survive in space only if supplied with oxygen inside a sealed cabin.

Tsiolkovsky also suggested that **rocket**s would be the vehicles necessary to power a craft in space, because rockets have self-contained propulsion systems and do not rely on oxygen. In 1903, he published an article entitled "The Exploration of Cosmic Space by Means of Reaction Devices," which detailed his theories about rocket propulsion and the use of liquid fuels.

*Konstantin
Tsiolkovsky.*

Tsiolkovsky is also credited with calculating the speed and amount of fuel a rocket would need in order to break free of the Earth's gravitational field and enter into orbit. He even wrote about aspects of rocketry as complex as methods of cooling the combustion (fuel-burning) chamber, navigation, and the design of multi-stage rockets.

At first, Tsiolkovsky was not taken seriously by the Russian government and scientific community. However, following the Bolshevik Revolution which overthrew the czar, the new Communist government took a closer look at his work. In 1921, it provided Tsiolkovsky with a salary so that he could continue to develop his theories. Within five years, his ideas became known to the international scientific community. He then gained fame among the general public with the publication of his futuristic novel, *Outside the Earth.*

Tsiolkovsky became a celebrated figure within the **Soviet Union.** On his seventy-fifth birthday, he was honored by his government for his achievements. The launch of the first satellite, *Sputnik 1,* was timed to coincide with the one hundredth anniversary of Tsiolkovsky's birth, but missed by twenty-nine days. Nonetheless, it brought to bear Tsiolkovsky's famous comment that "the Earth is the cradle of the mind, but one cannot live forever in the cradle."

See also **Rockets**

Uhuru

In 1970, the first National Aeronautics and Space Administration (NASA) **X-ray** detection satellite, *Uhuru,* was launched from a converted oil rig off the coast of Kenya in Africa. This satellite was number forty-two in the Explorer series of satellites. It was originally called the Small Astronomical Satellite 1. However, shortly before its launch on December 12, 1970, the satellite was renamed *Uhuru*—Swahili for "freedom." The name was chosen in honor of the seventh anniversary of Kenya's independence.

Uhuru was instrumental in advancing X-ray astronomy, the study of objects in space that emit X-rays. Examples of X-ray objects include stars, **galaxies, quasar**s, **pulsar**s, and **black hole**s. Since the Earth's atmosphere filters out most X-rays, the only way to view the X-ray sky adequately is through a space-based telescope.

As early as 1962, X-ray telescopes had been sent on short trips into space on board **rocket**s. *Uhuru,* however, was the first long-term space mission dedicated to X-ray astronomy. During *Uhuru*'s two-and-a-quarter years in space, it made the first detailed X-ray sky map. *Uhuru* discovered three hundred new X-ray objects, including **supernova** remnants, **globular cluster**s, and X-ray **binary star**s.

In July 1971, seven months after launch, *Uhuru*'s transmitter failed. Five months later, the transmitter made a partial recovery, and *Uhuru* continued to operate. Its mission came to a close in March 1973, when its battery died.

Uhuru was equipped only with simple X-ray counters. Thus, it was able to determine only approximate positions of X-ray sources. X-ray satellites launched since 1978 have had the advantage of more advanced technology, capable of producing high-quality pictures of X-ray objects and tracking their location with greater precision.

See also **Advanced X-Ray Astrophysics Facility**; **High Energy Astrophysical Observatories**; **Space telescope**; and **X-ray astronomy**

Ultraviolet astronomy

Until fairly recently, our knowledge of the universe was limited to that which can be seen with visible light. Most objects in space, however, emit radiation from all parts of the **electromagnetic spectrum.** In addition to light waves, the electromagnetic spectrum includes **ultraviolet radiation, radio wave**s, **infrared radiation, X-ray**s, and **gamma ray**s.

Ultraviolet astronomy is the study of matter in the sky that emits ultraviolet radiation. Ultraviolet waves are just shorter than the violet shortest wavelength end of visible light **spectrum.** This branch of space study has provided valuable additional information about stars (including our sun), **galaxies,** the **solar system,** the **interstellar medium,** and **quasar**s.

An ultraviolet telescope is similar to an optical telescope, with a special coating on the lens. However, due to the Earth's **ozone layer,** which filters out most ultraviolet rays, ultraviolet astronomy is almost impossible to conduct on the ground. In order to function, an ultraviolet telescope must be placed beyond the Earth's atmosphere, on board a satellite.

Beginning in the 1960s, a series of ultraviolet telescopes have been launched on spacecraft. The first such instruments were the eight Orbiting Solar Observatories, placed into orbit between 1962 and 1975. These satellites measured ultraviolet radiation from the sun. The data collected from these telescopes provided scientists with a much more complete picture of the solar **corona,** the outermost part of the sun's atmosphere.

The Orbiting Astronomical Observatories (OAO) were designed to provide information on a variety of objects, including thousands of stars, a **comet,** a **nova** in the **constellation** Serpus, and some galaxies beyond the **Milky Way.** Between 1972 and 1980, OAO Copernicus collected information on many stars, as well as the composition, temperature, and structure of interstellar gas.

The most successful ultraviolet satellite to date is the International Ultraviolet Explorer (IUE) launched in 1978. The IUE is a joint project of the United States, Great Britain, and the European Space Agency (ESA). It contains very sensitive equipment, with which it has studied planets, stars, galaxies, quasars, and comets. It has recorded especially valuable information from novae and **supernova**e.

The IUE allows astronomers to schedule time to conduct research at one of two ground stations associated with the project in the United States and Spain. The IUE was intended to function for only three to five years. Now in its eighteenth year of continuous operation, it holds the title of longest-lived astronomical satellite.

Ulysses

On October 6, 1990, after a series of delays, the *Ulysses* **space probe** was launched from the **space shuttle** *Discovery. Ulysses,* originally called the International Solar Polar Mission, was initiated in March 1979 as a joint project of the National Aeronautics and Space Administration (NASA) and the European Space Agency (ESA). Its goal is to study activity at the sun's north and south poles and in the space above and below the poles.

In order to study the sun's poles, a spacecraft must cross out of the ecliptic—the plane containing the orbits of all the major planets except Pluto. That is because the sun's poles can only be studied from above or below the sun, points outside of the two dimensions of the ecliptic. All spacecraft besides *Ulysses* have stayed within the ecliptic, since that is where their destinations, such as the moon or planets, have been located. *Ulysses* broke the mold by crossing out of the ecliptic and entering an orbit around the sun that is perpendicular to the orbits of most planets.

Ulysses was originally set for launch in the summer of 1986. It was delayed, however, by the explosion of the space shuttle *Challenger* the preceding January and the ensuing grounding of the entire shuttle fleet. *Ulysses* did not get another chance to launch until October 1990.

The **probe** initially headed away from the sun, toward Jupiter. It then looped around Jupiter in February 1992 and used the giant planet's gravitational field to propel itself southward, out of the ecliptic. In September 1994, *Ulysses* crossed beneath the sun's south pole and began heading north. A year later it passed over the sun's north pole. *Ulysses* then headed back toward Jupiter on the long leg of its six-year, oval-shaped path. It should pass over the sun's south pole again in the year 2000.

The main objectives of *Ulysses* are to study the sun's **corona,** the **solar wind,** the sun's **magnetic field,** bursts of solar **radio wave**s and **gamma ray**s, and **cosmic ray**s. Astronomers will compare data collected by *Ulysses* at different points to see how solar activity increases or decreases at different solar **latitude**s.

For almost four decades, scientists have launched probes to study the sun and its processes. Yet many more questions remain to be answered. For instance, why does the corona grow hotter, not cooler, at its outer reaches? Before *Ulysses,* only the equatorial regions have been examined, while the regions of presumed greatest activity, the poles, have been largely ignored. In exploring the sun's poles, there is a good chance that *Ulysses* will raise as many new questions as answers it provides.

See also **Solar atmosphere** and **Sun**

Uranus

Imagine a place where one day lasts forty-two years. Uranus is the seventh planet from the sun and the third in a line of four gas giants. Uranus rotates on its side, so that one of its poles faces towards the sun throughout half of its eighty-four year orbit, while the other pole faces away. Once it passes behind the sun and begins the return leg of its journey, the other pole faces the sun for forty-two years.

At some point in its history, Uranus was probably struck by a large object that knocked it sideways. As a result, its equator lies on a plane perpendicular to the plane of the other planets' orbits. In contrast, the Earth is positioned nearly upright. Our equatorial plane lies almost parallel to the plane of our orbit around the sun, so our entire planet experiences both night and day in every twenty-four hour period.

Uranus was discovered in 1781 by German astronomer William Herschel during a survey of the stars and planets. At first, Herschel thought he had spotted a **comet,** but the object's orbit was not as elongated as a comet's. It was more circular, like that of a planet. Six months later. he became convinced that this body was indeed a planet. The new planet was given two tentative names before astronomers decided to call it Uranus, the mythological father of Saturn.

Uranus is about 1.78 billion miles (2.86 billion miles) from the sun, more than twice as far from the sun as its closest neighbor Saturn. Thus, the discovery of Uranus doubled the known size of the **solar system.**

Uranus is 31,800 miles (51,166 kilometers) in diameter at its equator, making it the third largest planet in the solar system (after Jupiter and Saturn). It is four times the size of the Earth, yet less than half the size of Saturn. Similar to Jupiter, Saturn, and Neptune, Uranus consists mostly of gas. Its pale blue-green, cloudy atmosphere is made of 83 percent hydrogen, 15 percent helium, and small amounts of methane and hydrocarbons. Uranus gets its color because the atmospheric methane absorbs light at the red end of the visible **spectrum** and reflects light at the blue end. Deep down into the planet, a slushy mixture of ice, ammonia, and methane surrounds a rocky core.

The *Voyager 2* Mission to Uranus

Most of what we know about Uranus was discovered during the 1986 *Voyager 2* mission to the planet. The *Voyager 2* **space probe** left Earth in August 1977. It first visited Jupiter in July 1979, then Saturn in August 1981, before heading to Uranus.

Voyager 2 collected information on Uranus in January and February, 1986. At its closest approach, on January 24, it came within 50,600 miles

Artist's conception of Uranus and her thin rings.

(81,415 kilometers) of the planet. Among its most important findings were ten previously undiscovered moons (bringing the total to fifteen) and two new rings (bringing that total to eleven). *Voyager* also made the first accurate determination of Uranus' rate of rotation and found a large and unusual **magnetic field.** Finally, it discovered that despite greatly varying exposure to sunlight, the planet is about the same temperature all over, a chilly -350 degrees Fahrenheit (-212 degrees Celsius).

The Moons of Uranus

The two largest moons of Uranus, named Titania and Oberon, were discovered by William Herschel in 1787. The next two, Umbriel and Ariel, were found by William Lassell in 1851. It was not until 1948 that Gerard Kuiper detected the fifth moon, Miranda.

Before *Voyager 2*'s visit, Uranus appeared as a hazy disc, far out in space, surrounded by five tiny points of light. We now know that Uranus is the hub of a complex system of fifteen satellites, each with distinctive features. The previously discovered moons of Uranus range in size from about 1,000 miles (1,600 kilometers) in diameter (one-half the size of the Earth's moon) to 300 miles (482 kilometers) across (one-seventh the size of the Earth's moon). The largest moon discovered by *Voyager 2* is 90 miles (145 kilometers) in diameter, just larger than an **asteroid.** The smallest is a mere 16 miles (26 kilometers) across.

Voyager 2 determined that the five large moons are made mostly of ice and rock. Some are heavily cratered, others have steep cliffs and canyons, and yet others are much flatter. This discovery suggests varying amounts of geologic activity on each moon, such as lava flows and the shifting of regions of lunar crust. For instance, the largest moon, Oberon, has an ancient, heavily cratered surface, which indicates there has been little geologic activity. The craters remain as they were originally formed, no lava having filled them in. In contrast, Titania, the second largest moon, is punctuated by huge canyons and fault lines, indications of shifts in that moon's crust.

The original nine rings of Uranus were discovered only nine years before *Voyager 2*'s visit. We now know that Uranus has eleven rings plus ring fragments, consisting of dust, rocky particles, and ice. The eleven rings occupy the region between 23,560 and 31,700 miles (38,000 and 51,000 kilometers) from the planet's center. Each ring is anywhere from less than a mile to 1,550 miles (0.5 to 2,500 kilometers) wide. The outermost ring, called the epsilon ring, is several feet across and is made up of ice boulders.

Two of Uranus' small moons, Cordelia and Ophelia, act as shepherd satellites to the epsilon ring. This means that they orbit the planet within that ring and are possibly responsible for creating the gravitational field that confines the debris to the pattern of rings, keeping it from escaping into space. The presence of ring fragments indicate that the rings may be younger than the planet they encircle. One theory suggests that the rings are made of fragments of a moon that was smashed to pieces.

There is still much to be learned about Uranus. More secrets are likely to be revealed by the Hubble Space Telescope, which in recent years has made detailed observations of the planet.

See also **Herschel, William** and **Voyager program**

U.S. Naval Observatory

The U.S. Naval Observatory is located in northwestern Washington, D.C., near Georgetown University. In view of the fact that most observatories are located away from populated areas, usually on top of mountains, the Massachusetts Avenue site is one of the most accessible observatories in the country. It is also the country's oldest large observatory. Its original purpose was to provide navigational star charts for sailors. Today it is still noted for its work in tracking the position of celestial objects and time-keeping.

The observatory was initially part of the Depot of Charts and Instruments, a department established by the U.S. Navy in 1830 to care for navigational equipment. The Depot was located near the edge of the Potomac River, north of the Lincoln Memorial. In 1866, the U.S. Naval Observatory was established as a separate entity.

The riverside location turned out to be a poor spot for astronomical observations. Conditions were often foggy due to the river and nearby swampland. There was also smoke and light pollution from adjacent buildings to contend with. Even so, during that period the observatory made important advances in the fields of astronomy, navigation, and oceanography. These advances were largely due to the efforts of talented staff members, such as Simon Newcomb (who revolutionized methods of measuring and recording the motions of celestial objects) and Asaph Hall (who discovered Deimos and Phobos, the two moon of Mars, in 1877).

In 1887, the decision was made to move the observatory and construction was begun on the present site, at the highest elevation in the Washington, D.C., area. At the time the site was still a rural location. By 1893, the new facility—known as Observatory Hill—was up and running.

Observatory Hill today is also the site of the U.S. vice-president's residence. This location was first established during the tenure of vice president Walter Mondale, who served with president Jimmy Carter from 1977 to 1981. Before that time, vice presidents had no official residence.

Activities At the Observatory

*The U.S. Naval
Observatory in
Washington, D.C.*

The U.S. Naval Observatory is one of the few observatories in the world that specializes in the field of astrometry, also known as "positional astronomy." Astrometry is defined as the study of the positions of celestial objects. The observatory's precision instruments are continually trained on the sun, moon, planets, and stars, measuring and recording their

movements. This data is used to keep track of time, as well as for the navigation of vessels in the sea, air, and space.

The data collected at the observatory is passed on to the Nautical Almanac Office, which together with the British government publishes the *Astronomical Almanac,* the annual compendium of the motions of the sun, moon, and planets. This information is then used as a daily reference by navigators, surveyors, and astronomers.

The U.S. Naval Observatory is also the country's official keeper of time. And its navigational information is used by the Navy and the Department of Defense in designing missile guidance systems and other forms of warfare technology.

Among the Naval Observatory's instruments are two **refractor telescope**s. The largest has a lens 26 inches (66 centimeters) in diameter and it dates back to 1873. It is used primarily for observing multiple star systems and moons of various planets, as well as planets, **comet**s, and **asteroid**s. It is equipped with a motor that turns it at the rate of the Earth's rotation, so that it can follow celestial objects across the sky.

The smaller of the two refractors has a 12-inch (30-centimeter) lens. It became operational in 1895 and was originally used to observe the positions of stars. It was put aside to make room for other instruments in 1957 and has been in and out of storage several times since then. In 1980 it was restored and upgraded and is now used during public tours and for personal observing by staff members.

The third noteworthy instrument at the observatory is a 6-inch (15-centimeter) "transit" telescope. This small ninety-year-old telescope is specially designed to record very small motions of stars with great precision. It is stabilized by the massive concrete piers on which it is mounted. Its movement is restricted to a programmed arc that follows the motion of a star across the night sky.

The Naval Observatory also has a station in Flagstaff, Arizona, where skies are clearer than they are over the nation's capital. This facility has two **reflector telescope**s, a 61-inch (155-centimeter) and a 40-inch (101-centimeter). The primary function of the reflectors is to measure distances to faint objects and to record the brightness and colors of stars. It was on the larger of these two reflectors that astronomer James Christy discovered Pluto's moon Charon in 1978. The telescopes at Flagstaff have also been used to observe **brown dwarf**s—small, dark, cool balls of dust and gas that never quite become stars.

U.S. Naval Observatory

The Naval Observatory is home to one of the world's leading astronomical libraries, containing over seventy-five thousand volumes. Among these are some very old, rare publications including works by Isaac Newton, Galileo Galilei, Johannes Kepler, and Nicholas Copernicus.

See also **Newcomb, Simon**

Van Allen, James (1914–)
American physicist

James Van Allen was born in Iowa, the state he still calls home. He was educated at Iowa Wesleyan College and the University of Iowa, earning his Ph.D. in physics from the latter in 1939. He then spent three years as a research fellow at the Carnegie Institution in Washington, D.C., before enlisting in the Navy as an ordinance and gunnery officer during World War II.

After the war, Van Allen moved to Baltimore where he served as supervisor to the High Altitude Research Group at Johns Hopkins University. There he studied the conditions that **rocket**s encounter high in the Earth's atmosphere. This project led to Van Allen's later research in the areas for which he is best known, the Earth's **magnetic field**; **cosmic ray**s; and the extraterrestrial region that bears his name, the **Van Allen belts.**

In 1951, Van Allen received an appointment to teach physics at the University of Iowa. Over the next few years, he participated in Project Matterhorn, a study of controlled thermonuclear reactions. He also helped plan events for the International Geophysical Year, a period during July 1, 1957, and December 31, 1958, aimed at studying the upper atmosphere and other physical characteristics of the Earth.

In the 1950s, Van Allen's primary research concerned cosmic rays, the high-energy particles that constantly flow out of from the sun in all directions, bombarding the Earth in the process. Most cosmic rays are high-speed protons, although they also include the nuclei of all known elements. Van Allen conducted his research at the White Sands Proving

Grounds in Nevada, using German V-2 rockets that were captured after World War II. He equipped the rockets with Geiger counters that would measure the radiation encountered by a rocket on its flight.

During these tests, Van Allen invented the rockoon technique. A rockoon consists of a balloon that lifts a small rocket into the **stratosphere,** where the rocket ignites. Since the rocket does not have to overcome air friction encountered by a rocket launched from the ground, it is able to travel farther into the atmosphere.

When the V-2 test phase was complete, Van Allen and his crew turned to a new line of rockets, called Aerobees. Using these rockets, they studied solar radiation, sky brightness, the composition of the atmosphere, and **auror**ae. Van Allen was the first scientist to show the relationship of aurorae with high levels of cosmic radiation.

James Van Allen examines a partially completed stratosphere spectrograph which he used in rocket tests at White Sands, New Mexico.

Discovery of the Van Allen Belts

In 1957, Van Allen was put in charge of designing a set of miniature scientific instruments for the United States' first satellite, *Explorer 1*. With the radiation detector invented by Van Allen, *Explorer 1* discovered bands of charged particles encircling the Earth, bands that were later named the Van Allen belts.

The Van Allen belts contain cosmic rays that have been trapped by the Earth's **magnetosphere.** Once trapped within the Van Allen belts, the cosmic rays spiral around the lines of the Earth's magnetic field. They are led away from the Earth's equator and shuffled back and forth between the two magnetic poles. Subsequent satellites showed that there are actually two distinct bands of cosmic radiation, one encircling the Earth at about 2,000 feet (610 meters) and the other at about 10,000 feet (3,048 meters).

In order to protect crew members, the position of the Van Allen belts is now taken into consideration when planning space flights. National Aeronautics and Space Administration (NASA) engineers and their Russian counterparts plot courses that take a spacecraft through the weakest part of these radiation zones.

See also **Cosmic rays** and **Van Allen belts**

Van Allen belts

In 1958, the United States launched its first satellite, *Explorer 1,* into orbit, just months after the **Soviet Union** launched its *Sputnik 1* satellite. James Van Allen, a professor of physics at the University of Iowa and an expert on **cosmic ray**s, had equipped *Explorer 1* with a radiation detector, among other instruments. The detector found two rings of charged particles encircling the Earth, rings that were later named the **Van Allen belts.**

Van Allen belts contain trapped cosmic rays, high-energy particles that constantly flow out from the sun in all directions, bombarding the Earth in the process. Most cosmic rays are high-speed protons although they also include the nuclei of all known elements. As cosmic rays approach the Earth's **magnetosphere,** they become trapped and spiral around the lines of the Earth's **magnetic field.** They are led away from the

Van Allen belts

Earth's equator and shuffled back and forth between the two magnetic poles.

Explorer 1 mapped out the shape of the radiation-filled region and found that it was like a fat doughnut, widest above the Earth's equator and curving downwards toward the Earth's surface near the polar regions. The doughnut's "hole" was at the Earth's axis.

A later satellite, *Pioneer 3,* found that the Van Allen belts are actually two distinct bands, one closer to Earth and one farther away. The peak radiation within the first belt is located at a distance of 2,000 miles (3,218 kilometers) from Earth. The second belt, which contains fewer and less-energetic particles than the first, has its peak radiation at an altitude of 10,000 miles (16,090 kilometers).

See also **Cosmic rays**; **Earth's magnetic field**; and **Van Allen, James**

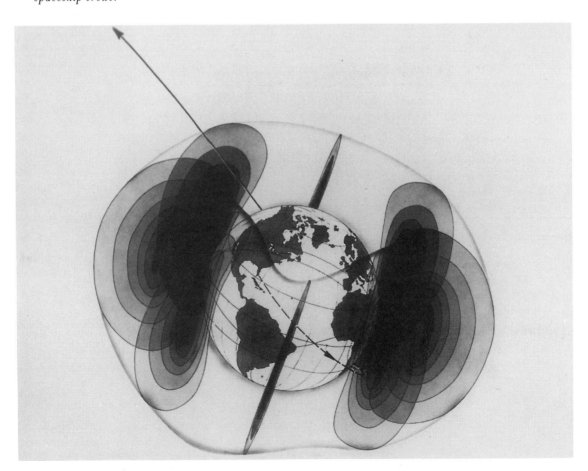

Vanguard program

The name "Vanguard" has come to represent the first, fumbling stages of the U.S. space program, similar to the clumsy attempts of a young bird learning to fly. The embarrassing failures of the early Vanguard program, especially in light of the **Soviet Union**'s success in launching the first artificial satellite (*Sputnik 1*), led to nicknames such as "Flopnik" and "Kaputnik" being bestowed on the U.S. program.

In late 1957, the pressure was on the United States to get a satellite into orbit around the Earth. With their launch of *Sputnik,* the Soviets were winning the **space race,** the contest for superiority in space exploration. The United States adopted as its goal the launch of a scientific satellite between July 1, 1957, and December 31, 1958, a period that had been designated the International Geophysical Year. The aim of this eighteen-month period was to study the physical characteristics and upper atmosphere of the Earth.

The Department of Defense (DOD), which was in charge of the U.S. satellite program, accepted two satellite-launch proposals. The first, the Vanguard project, called for launching a 20-pound (9-kilogram) satellite from a newly designed three-stage **rocket.** The second, called Project Orbiter, suggested using the army's powerful Jupiter-C rocket to propel a 5-to-15 pound (2-to-7 kilogram) satellite. The DOD chose the Vanguard option, primarily because of the military associations of Jupiter-C. President Dwight D. Eisenhower wanted to present the satellite launching as a civilian undertaking, one that would demonstrate the peaceful applications of rockets.

The first attempted Vanguard launch was on December 6, 1957, two months after the launch of *Sputnik.* Just a few feet off the ground, the rocket burst into flames. This failure prompted the DOD to give the go-ahead to Project Orbiter, headed by former German rocket scientist Wernher von Braun. On January 31, 1958, von Braun succeeded in placing the first U.S. satellite, *Explorer 1,* into orbit, a little less than four months after *Sputnik.*

The second Vanguard launch was attempted in early February, just a few days after *Explorer.* This one also failed. Fifty-seven seconds after lift-off, the rocket veered off course and broke apart.

The next U.S. satellite to be launched was *Explorer 2* on March 5, 1958, which failed to reach orbit. This was followed by the Vanguard program's first success. On March 17, 1958, Vanguard placed into orbit a 3-pound (1.4 kilogram) satellite that was only 6 inches (15 centimeters) in diameter—so small that the Soviets jokingly called it "the grapefruit." It turned out to be a hearty fruit, however, remaining in orbit and transmitting information about the Earth's shape and gravitational field until the middle of 1964.

Eight more launch attempts were made in the Vanguard series between the first successful Vanguard satellite and September 1959. Only two of those launches succeeded in placing satellites in orbit.

See also **Braun, Wernher von**; **Rockets**; **Space race**; and *Sputnik 1*

Variable stars

Variable stars are stars that vary in brightness over time. In most cases, these changes occur very slowly, over a period of months or even a couple of years. In some cases, however, the changes take place in a matter of hours.

The category "variable stars" encompasses several different types of stars that vary in brightness for entirely different reasons. Some types of variable stars are **red giant**s, **eclipsing binaries,** RR Lyrae, and **cepheid variable**s.

The most common variables, with the longest bright-dim cycles, are red giants. Red giants are stars of average size, similar to our sun, in the final stages of life. For the last several million years of its multi-billion-year lifetime, one of these stars will puff up and shrink many times. It becomes alternately brighter and dimmer, generally spending about one year in each phase until it completely runs out of fuel.

The apparent variable behavior of a second group of stars, eclipsing binaries, is caused by a very different process. A **binary star** is a double star system in which two stars orbit each other around a central point of **gravity.** An eclipsing binary occurs when the plane of a binary's orbit is nearly edgewise to our line of sight. Each star is then eclipsed by the other as they complete their orbits.

A special class of variables, discovered by American astronomer Henrietta Swan Leavitt, consist of blinking yellow **supergiant**s called cepheid variables. The pulsation of these stars seems to be caused by the expansion and contraction of their surface layers. They become brighter and dimmer on a regular cycle (lasting three to fifty days), the period of which is related to their true brightness. For this reason, astronomers use these stars as a way of measuring distances in space.

Another type, similar to cepheids but older, is the group known as RR Lyrae stars. These stars are usually found in densely packed groups called **globular cluster**s. Because of their age, RR Lyrae stars are relatively dim. They also have very short cycles, lasting less than a day.

Two American women astronomers have been instrumental in tracking variable stars. Leavitt, in a search of the southern skies in the early 1900s, discovered about 2,400 variable stars. And Helen Sawyer Hogg, in 1939, created the first complete listing of the known 1,116 variable stars in our **galaxy.** In 1955, she updated this catalogue, adding 329 new variables, one-third of which she discovered herself.

See also **Cepheid variables** and **Red giant star**

Vega program

The destinations of the two Soviet Vega **space probe**s is evident from their name—if you speak Russian, that is. "Vega" is a contraction of the Russian words for "Venus" (Venera) and "Halley" (Gallei). Launched six days apart in December 1984, the Vega **probe**s were the first Soviet spacecraft to visit more than one celestial body: Venus and Halley's **comet.** These missions were also noteworthy in that they represented a considerable international cooperative effort.

Each Vega spacecraft was about 36 feet (11 meters) long and consisted of a cylindrical mid-section with a landing capsule at one end and an experiment platform at the other. The platform held cameras and other scientific instruments provided by several nations including the **Soviet Union,** France, Germany, and the United States. Protruding from the craft's central portion were a dish-shaped antenna and electricity-generating solar panels.

Vega 1 reached Venus on June 9, 1985, and dropped its capsule to the surface. Two days later the capsule landed safely and for two hours relayed pictures and information about soil composition. At the same time, the spacecraft released a French-designed, helium-filled balloon which hovered for two days about 30 miles (48 kilometers) above the planet's surface. During that time, the balloon was blown by the Venusian winds to a point about 6,200 miles (9,976 kilometers) from its original position. Hanging about 36 feet (11 meters) below the balloon was a set of instruments that measured atmospheric temperature and pressure, as well as wind speeds. Astronomers in the Soviet Union, Europe, Brazil, the United States, and Australia tracked the balloon's flight using **radio telescope**s. The entire capsule-and-balloon sequence was repeated a few days later by *Vega 2*.

The two spacecraft then used a technique called **gravity assist,** in which they circled Venus and used its gravitational force to propel them on an intercept course with Halley's comet. In 1986, the comet was at its closest point to Earth on its seventy-six-year-long orbit around the sun. Along with probes sent by Japan and the European Space Agency (ESA), the *Vega*s were part of the International Halley Watch, coordinated by over one thousand astronomers from forty countries.

Vega 1 was the first probe to reach Halley's comet, coming within 5,600 miles (9,010 kilometers) of its nucleus on March 6, 1986. For three hours, *Vega 1* took hundreds of photographs of the comet. *Vega 2,* which approached the comet on March 9, also took photographs and collected information on the composition of the comet. Both *Vega*s relayed information on the comet's location, which was used by the ESA to reposition its probe *Giotto*. On March 13, *Giotto* flew right into the center of the comet and took very detailed pictures.

After passing the comet, the *Vega*s remained in orbit around the sun until they were programmed to shut down in early 1987.

See also **Giotto**; **Halley's comet**; **and Venus**

Venera program

The Venera program was an intensive, two-decade-long effort by the former **Soviet Union** to explore the atmosphere and surface of Venus. "Venera," Russian for "Venus," was the name given to the sixteen spacecraft sent to that planet between 1961 to 1983. During those years, the exploration of Venus was almost exclusively the domain of the Soviets, who shared some of their information with the international community.

*Soviet Venera 3
spacecraft. It
succeeded in
reaching Venus, but
communications
failed as it entered
the planet's
atmosphere and it
crash-landed on the
surface.*

While the Venera program got off to a shaky start, over the years it went on to record an impressive list of "firsts" about our mysterious, cloud-covered neighboring planet. Venera spacecraft were the first to probe Venus' atmosphere, the first to both land on and return pictures of the surface, the first to analyze the soil, and the first to map the surface.

The original *Venera* spacecraft somewhat resembled the character "R2D2" in the movie *Star Wars*. This **space probe** weighed 1,420 pounds (644 kilograms). It had a cylindrical body with a domed top and solar panels on its sides. Attached to one side of the body was a radio antenna in the shape of an umbrella top, with the concave side and handle pointed outward.

The vessels used in successive missions were larger and more complex. Those later than *Venera 3* consisted of two parts: a carrier vessel and a lander. The lander dropped from the spacecraft onto Venus' surface while the carrier remained in orbit around the planet, receiving signals from the lander. The last two *Venera* craft, numbers *15* and *16,* each weighed 8,840 pounds (4,010 kilograms) and were equipped with large radio antennae.

The first three Venera missions, launched between 1961 and 1965, were unsuccessful. Radio contact with *Venera 1* and *Venera 2* was lost about two weeks into each vessel's journey. These spacecraft eventually flew past Venus and went into orbit around the sun. *Venera 3* looked more promising as it reached Venus, but communications failed as it entered the planet's atmosphere and it crash-landed on the surface.

The First Venera Successes

Venera 4, the first to carry a landing capsule (**probe**), finally met with a measure of success. Launched in June 1967, it reached Venus four months later. The capsule was released into the atmosphere and for ninety-four minutes transmitted data on the temperature, pressure, and chemical composition of the planets atmosphere. About 15 miles (24 kilometers) above the surface the capsule was crushed by the intense pressure of the atmosphere.

Designing a probe that could land intact on the Venusian surface was no easy feat. The probe would encounter an atmospheric pressure ninety times that on Earth and temperatures of about 850 degrees Fahrenheit (454 degrees Celsius). Following *Venera 4,* landing probes were built stronger and with smaller parachutes so they would reach the surface more quickly.

Despite these changes, *Venera 5* and *6* met with fates similar to that of *Venera 4*. It was not until *Venera 7,* launched in August 1970, that the first successful landing of a spacecraft on another planet was achieved. This capsule was equipped with a cooling device, which helped it withstand the extreme temperature conditions. It sent back data for thirty-five minutes during its descent and for another twenty-three minutes after reaching the surface.

Two years later, *Venera 8* built on the success of its predecessor. It measured variations in wind speed as it floated down through the atmosphere. Then for fifty minutes after landing, it transmitted data on the amount of sunlight reaching the surface, as well as basic information on soil composition.

First Pictures of Venus' Surface

Venera 9 and *10* were launched six days apart in June 1975 and both went into orbit around Venus. They spent a month photographing cloud layers in the upper atmosphere before releasing their landing probes. Equipped with cameras, the probes returned the first pictures of the rock-strewn Venusian surface. The carrier spacecrafts remained in orbit and acted as radio relay stations for the landers.

The next four *Venera* crafts, numbers *11, 12, 13,* and *14,* which reached Venus between December 1978 and March 1982, each dropped landing probes to the surface. Between them, they measured the chemical composition of the atmosphere and surface rocks, confirmed the presence of lightning, and took the first color pictures of the surface.

The final two probes in the series—*Venera 15* and *16*—arrived at Venus in October 1983. Rather than to drop probes to the surface, their mission was to remain in orbit and to construct detailed maps of the planet's surface using radar. They accomplished this task by bouncing **radio wave**s off the surface and recording the echoes that were returned. Over the next year, they mapped a large part of Venus' northern hemisphere, including areas that were probably volcanoes in the distant past.

The Venera program was the most thorough exploration ever undertaken of another world. Following on its success, from 1990 to 1994 the U.S. *Magellan* space probe surveyed 99 percent of Venus' surface using sophisticated radar equipment.

*See also **Magellan** and **Venus***

Venus

Venus is the planet closest to Earth. It is visible in the sky either just after dark or just before sunrise, depending on the season. This pattern prompted ancient astronomers to refer to the planet as the "evening star" or "morning star." Venus, named for the Roman goddess of love and beauty, has been thought of throughout history as one of the most beautiful objects in the sky. It is often referred to as a brightly glittering jewel.

Venus and Earth have long been considered sister planets. The reason for this comparison is that they are similar in size, **mass,** and age. And while astronomers could not see beneath Venus' thick cloud cover until recently, they assumed that Venus would have seas and plant life like that on Earth. We now know, however, that this is not the case. The two planets are so different that one would be hard pressed to still call them "sisters."

Venus, Earth's "sister" planet.

Beginning in 1961, the United States and former **Soviet Union** have deployed a long string of **space probe**s that have examined the Venusian atmosphere and peered beneath its dense cloud cover. The **probe**s have revealed that Venus is an extremely hot, dry planet, with no signs of life. Its atmosphere is made primarily of carbon dioxide with some nitrogen and trace amounts of water vapor, acids, and heavy metals. Its clouds are laced with sulfur dioxide.

Venus provides a perfect example of the **greenhouse effect.** Heat from the sun penetrates the planet's atmosphere and reaches the surface. The heat is then prevented from escaping back into space by atmospheric carbon dioxide. The result is that Venus has a balmy surface temperature of 900 degrees Fahrenheit (482 degrees Celsius), even hotter than that of Mercury, its neighbor closer to the sun.

Venus is also unusual in that it is the only planet besides Uranus to rotate from east to west. Thus, if you lived on Venus, the sun would rise in the west and set in the east. In addition, it rotates very, very slowly. In fact, it takes Venus 243 Earth days to complete one rotation. A day on Venus lasts even longer than its year, which is 225 Earth days.

The U.S. and Soviet space probes uncovered a rocky surface covered with volcanoes (some still active), volcanic features (such as lava plains), channels (like dry riverbeds), mountains, and medium- and large-sized craters. No small craters exist apparently because small **meteorite**s cannot get through the planet's atmosphere. Another set of features found on the surface are arachnoids. These features are circular formations ranging anywhere from 30 to 137 miles (48 to 220 kilometers) in diameter, filled with concentric circles with spokes extending outward.

The most recent probe, *Magellan,* mapped the entire Venusian surface from 1990–1994. It discovered that, from a geological viewpoint, the planet's surface is relatively young. Astronomers analyzing *Magellan*'s data have concluded that about three hundred to five hundred years ago, lava surfaced and covered the entire planet, giving it a fresh, new face. One indication of this event is the presence of craters and other formations on the surface that lack the same weathered appearance of that of older formations. Also, relatively few craters occur on Venus. In fact, more craters in a slice of the moon can be seen through a small telescope than occur on the entire surface of Venus.

Magellan collected enough information to keep scientists busy with analysis for years to come. Even so, discussions are now taking place about the possibility of sending a joint U.S.-Russian space-probe laboratory back to Venus to learn more as early as 1997.

See also **Magellan**; **Mariner program**; **Vega program**; and **Venera program**

Very Large Array

There is a stretch of New Mexico, known as the Plains of San Augustine, that looks for all the world like the setting of a science fiction novel. The flat, stark landscape is dotted with an assemblage of immense **radio telescope** dishes, all looking up at the same point in the sky. Awesome, yes; but fictional, no. Those dishes are components of the world's most famous **radio interferometer,** the Very Large Array (VLA).

The VLA is located just west of Socorro, New Mexico, at an elevation of nearly 7,000 feet (2,134 meters) above sea level. Completed in 1980, it consists of twenty-seven radio telescopes, each about 82 feet (25 meters) in diameter. A radio telescope is an instrument made of a concave dish with a small antenna at the center that observes **radio wave**s emitted by celestial objects. The series of telescopes moves about on railroad tracks arranged in a "Y" shape. At their farthest distance apart, the telescopes stretch over 22 miles (35 kilometers), an area about one-and-a-half times the area of Washington, D.C.

The telescopes are all trained on the same part of the sky and are linked electronically. The information collected by each one is transmitted to a central computer, which combines the data from all telescopes.

A radio interferometer works on a simple but ingenious principle: two telescopes are better than one. And, by extension, a group of telescopes is best of all. The telescopes of an interferometer act as a single telescope with a diameter equal to the distance separating them. The result is a radio "picture" with much finer detail than could be produced by any one telescope.

The 230-ton (209-metric ton) radio dishes can be placed in four different arrangements. In the tightest configuration, all twenty-seven dishes are squeezed into an area six-tenths of a mile (about 1 kilometer) wide. In other arrays the instruments are positioned farther apart, covering either 2.2 miles (3.5 kilometers), 6.2 miles (10 kilometers), or the full 22 miles.

Paradoxically, in the tightest configuration, the interferometer can survey the largest area of the sky, but with the lowest resolution (meaning it has the least ability to distinguish fine detail).

Research With VLA

The VLA is a branch of the National Radio Astronomy Observatory (which also includes the Arecibo Observatory in Puerto Rico, the Green Bank Telescope in West Virginia, and telescopes at various other field stations) and is funded by the National Science Foundation. It is used by astronomers from around the world for projects such as general sky surveys, studies of specific celestial objects, satellite tracking, and atmospheric or weather studies. Observing time on the VLA is awarded on a competitive basis. Astronomers must submit proposals several months in advance. Those fortunate enough to have their proposals accepted are granted anywhere from one to twenty hours on the interferometer.

The Very Large Array in the southern New Mexico desert is composed of twenty-seven radio telescopes, each about 82 feet (25 meters) in diameter.

One recent project at the VLA has been the study of the **supernova** explosion in a **galaxy** known as M81, roughly twelve million **light-year**s from Earth. The star exploded in 1993 and since that time radio astronomers have been studying the cloud of debris spreading outward from the star's core.

Another highlight of VLA studies in 1996 has been the aftermath of the 1994 collision of fragments from Comet Shoemaker-Levy with Jupiter. The radio emissions produced by the impacts have yielded a wealth of information about the composition of Jupiter's atmosphere.

The VLA has also been the site of a study of possible **black hole**s within our galaxy. Astronomers have trained the interferometer on **binary star**s, looking for energy variations and other signs that may indicate that one member of the pair is a black hole.

The longest currently running project is a large-scale sky survey. Begun in 1993, the goal of this survey is to produce detailed radio maps of the entire portion of the sky visible from the VLA. The maps produced thus far have already been extensively used by radio astronomers worldwide.

The best way to experience this impressive set-up is to see for yourself. The VLA is about a one hour drive south of Albuquerque, New Mexico. The installation includes a welcome center, and visitors are free to tour the grounds.

See also **Interferometry**; **Radio astronomy**; **Radio interferometer**; and **Radio telescope**

Viking program

In the mid-1970s, the U.S. Viking **space probe**s established without a doubt that life does not exist on Mars. Earlier **probe**s, including the Soviet Mars series and U.S. Mariner series, had shown that conditions do not presently exist on the planet to support life. Data collected by *Mariner 9,* however, indicated that cold, dry periods (like the present) may alternate with warm, moist ones, with each cycle lasting about fifty thousand years. This raised the possibility that life forms may have evolved to lay dormant during cold, dry spells and then re-activate when the climate was more hospitable. It was the job of the Viking probes to examine Mars thoroughly for any signs of life, dormant or otherwise.

There were two Viking spacecraft, designated *Viking 1* and *Viking 2.* Like the Soviet *Mars 2* and *Mars 3,* each consisted of an orbiter and a lander. The *Vikings,* however, differed from their Soviet predecessors in that the entire Viking vessel was designed initially to go into orbit around the planet. In comparison, the Mars spacecraft dropped their landers immediately to the surface while only the orbiters remained in orbit. The *Vikings* had the advantage of scouting out an acceptable landing site before releasing the landers.

Each Viking orbiter was an eight-sided structure, nearly 8 feet (2.4 meters) wide. Contained in this body were most of the ship's control systems. The **rocket** motor and fuel tanks (used to guide the ship into orbit around Mars) were attached to the rear face of the structure. Solar panels extended from another face. These panels were folded up at launch. Once in space, they were extended to a cross-shaped structure over 30 feet (9 meters) wide. The orbiter also contained a movable platform, on which sat

The Viking 1 *spacecraft. It went into orbit around Mars in June 1976 after almost a year-long journey.*

two television cameras and instruments for measuring the planet's temperature and detecting water.

The landers, enclosed in protective casing for the journey through space, were bound to the orbiters. A lander and orbiter together stood 16 feet (5 meters) tall. The central portion of each lander was a six-sided compartment with alternating longer and shorter sides. Attached to each short side was a landing leg with a circular footpad. A remote control arm for the collection of soil samples, which resembled an extended fourth leg, protruded from one of the lander's long sides. Soil samples were transferred to the biological analyzer, which was perched on top of the body, for testing.

Other instruments affixed to the top of the lander included two cylindrical television cameras, a seismometer (for measuring quakes beneath the surface), atmospheric testing devices, and a radio antenna dish. Beneath the vessel were rockets that slowed the lander's descent. **Propellant** tanks were stored on opposite sides of the lander.

Viking Launches

Following two years of delays due to technical problems, the two *Viking*s were launched two weeks apart in August and September 1975. *Viking 1* went into orbit around Mars in June 1976. It immediately began transmitting photos of the surface back to Earth, where mission controllers studied them for possible landing sites. The site that had been pre-selected for the lander to hit on July 4, 1976 (the American bicentennial), was discovered to be too rough. A different landing site was chosen, and on July 20, 1976, the *Viking 1* lander made the world's first soft-landing on Mars.

The lander's cameras began operating minutes later. They showed rust-colored rocks and boulders (due to the presence of iron oxide) with a reddish sky above.

Viking 2 arrived at Mars that August and went into orbit. Its lander was released on the opposite side of the planet from the *Viking 1* lander, making a successful touchdown on September 3, 1976. Over the next few years, the landers collected and analyzed soil samples from many parts of the planet, none of which showed signs of past or present life on the planet.

By the summer of 1980, the two Viking orbiters had sent back numerous weather reports and pictures of almost the entire surface of the planet. They found that although the Martian atmosphere contains low levels of nitrogen, oxygen, carbon, and argon, it is principally made of carbon dioxide and thus is not capable of supporting human life. In addition, they detected **ultraviolet radiation** at levels lethal to any life form with which we are familiar. The high temperature on Mars was measured at -20 degrees Fahrenheit (-28 degrees Celsius) in the afternoon, and the low was -120 degrees Fahrenheit (-84 degrees Celsius) at night.

More than fifty-six thousand pictures taken by both landers and orbiters confirmed that Mars is a barren, desolate, crater-covered world prone to frequent, violent dust storms. Wind gusts during those storms reached 62 miles (100 kilometers) per hour.

The orbiters and landers of both *Viking*s operated far longer than anticipated. The first to lose contact was the *Viking 2* orbiter in July 1978; the last, in November 1982, was the *Viking 1* lander.

See also **Mariner program**; **Mars**; and **Mars program**

Voskhod program

"Voskhod," Russian for "sunrise," was the **Soviet Union**'s second series of piloted spacecraft. It was very similar in design to its predecessor—the world's first piloted vessels—the Vostok series. The main difference between the two was that the Voskhod cabins were enlarged to carry up to three **cosmonaut**s at a time. In contrast, Vostok could hold only one.

Voskhod was a stopgap spacecraft in the Soviet space program. A stopgap spacecraft is an improvised substitute craft—one that is quickly developed to fill the gap between two planned series of spacecraft. The more sophisticated Soyuz spaceship was supposed to succeed Vostok, but was taking longer than anticipated to complete. In the meantime, the United States was developing the Gemini two-seat spacecraft, and the Soviets could wait no longer. Being the first to put a man in space had given the Soviets the lead in the **space race**—the competition between the two superpowers for superiority in space exploration—and they did not want to jeopardize their standing. Hence, they modified Vostok to a three-seater.

Both Voskhod and Vostok vehicles were small and relatively simple in design, each consisting of a cabin and an instrument module. In Vostok crafts, one cosmonaut sat in an ejection seat, which could be used for a quick escape in the event of an emergency during launch or landing. In Voskhod vessels the cosmonauts sat on small couches. Safety was given second consideration as there was not enough room in the cabin for ejection seats and hence, no emergency escapes. The fit was too tight even for the cosmonauts to wear spacesuits. The Voskhod program was fraught with risk, and it was lucky that no mishaps occurred.

Voskhod 1 and Voskhod 2

Following one unmanned test flight, Voskhod 1 was launched on October 12, 1964. It was occupied by pilot Vladimir Komarov, medical expert Boris Yegorov, and spacecraft designer Konstantin Feoktistov. The crew reportedly carried out medical experiments during the vessel's one day in space, although details of the tests were never disclosed.

Voskhod 2, launched on March 18, 1965, was a much more memorable mission. It was on this flight that cosmonaut Alexei Leonov took the first "**space walk**" in which he floated in space outside of his vehicle. On Voskhod 2's second orbit around the Earth, Leonov donned a white spacesuit and an oxygen-tank backpack and exited the spacecraft. He floated 17.5 feet (5.3 meters) away from the spacecraft—the total length of his safety tether—and took photographs of the spaceship and the Earth. At the end of his planned twelve-minute space walk, Leonov found that his space-suit had ballooned out in places, making it impossible for him to fit back inside the hatch. He solved the problem by releasing air from the suit. Eight minutes later, he made it back inside the spacecraft.

Later in the flight, as Leonov and his crewmate Pavel Belyayev were preparing to return to Earth, they noticed their ship was pointed in the wrong direction. It took them another orbit to turn the spacecraft around, causing them to alter their landing site. The two cosmonauts parachuted to Earth in a remote region of the Ural mountains and spent two cold days in the woods before rescue teams reached them.

A third Voskhod mission was rumored to have been planned, in which two cosmonauts were to remain in space for up to two weeks. This flight never took place, perhaps because by that time the Soviets had decided to focus their energies on the Soyuz flight program.

See also **Leonov, Alexei**; **Soyuz program**; and **Vostok program**

Vostok program

On April 12, 1961, Vostok 1 was launched with **cosmonaut** Yuri Gagarin on board. The world was awestruck at the realization that human space flight—which had been merely a dream for decades—had finally been accomplished. The journey lasted only 108 minutes, during which time the spacecraft orbited Earth once and then returned. When his capsule was about 2 miles (3 kilometers) above ground, Gagarin parachuted to safety.

The Soviet *Vostok 1* flight was an important milestone in the **space race,** the contest between the United States and the former **Soviet Union** for superiority in space exploration. It put pressure on the U.S. National Aeronautics and Space Administration (NASA) to begin its own piloted space program and led to President John F. Kennedy's promise of landing an astronaut on the moon by the end of the decade.

"Vostok," Russian for "East," was a small, relatively simple spacecraft, consisting of a cabin and an instrument module. The spherical, 7.5-foot-diameter (2.3-meter-diameter) cabin was large enough to accommodate only one cosmonaut. That person sat in an ejection seat, which could

The finishing touches are put on the Soviet Vostok 6 *spacecraft in June 1963.*

be used for a quick escape in the event of an emergency during launch or landing. The outside of the cabin was coated with a protective heat shield. Communication antennae extended from the top of the cabin, and nitrogen and oxygen tanks for life support were stored beneath it. (Since the *Apollo 1* ground test fire, in which the pure oxygen environment ignited, spacecraft cabin environments have been a mixture of gases that will not ignite.) The instrument module, containing a small **rocket** and thrusters, was strapped to the cabin with steel bands.

The Vostok Series of Flights

A series of unpiloted test flights, named *Sputnik 4* through *10,* led up to the launch of *Vostok 1.* Only recently did American scientists learn that this seemingly flawless, human venture into space almost ended in disaster when the spacecraft, on descent, spun wildly out of control. Gagarin's craft regained stability only when his capsule separated from the lurching rocket.

Vostok 2, flown by cosmonaut German Titov, went into space on August 6, 1961. *Vostok 2* stayed in orbit for twenty-five hours and eighteen minutes, far longer than *Vostok 1.* The reason it stayed up so long was that its landing had to be made at a time when the spacecraft was over Soviet territory. As the Earth rotated, the Soviet Union moved away from its position along *Vostok*'s orbit. Only within five hours of the spacecraft's launch, or after twenty-four hours (after a complete rotation of the Earth), would Soviet territory once again be under the path of the spacecraft.

Titov was the first person to eat a meal in space and, as a result, the first to experience space sickness. He soon recovered, however, and after a good night's sleep, brought his craft in for a perfect landing.

Vostok 3 and *4* were launched one day apart in August 1962. These two vessels came within 4 miles (6.4 kilometers) of each other and remained close for three hours, after which their orbits began to drift apart. On August 15, the two spacecraft simultaneously re-entered the Earth's atmosphere. Their landing times differed by just a few minutes.

In June 1963, the Soviets repeated this maneuver with the last two vehicles in the Vostok series, numbers *5* and *6.* The only difference this time was that one of the spacecraft was flown by Valentina Tereshkova, the first woman in space. At one point, these two spacecraft were only 3 miles (5 kilometers) apart. *Vostok 5* remained in space for five days, setting a new endurance record. Tereshkova's *Vostok 6* spent nearly three days in space.

See also **Gagarin, Yuri**; **Space race**; **Tereshkova, Valentina**; and **Voskhod program**

Voyager program

In 1977, the National Aeronautics and Space Administration (NASA) launched *Voyager 1* and *2,* the second set of **space probe**s to explore the outer planets (those past Mars) and space beyond our **solar system.** The *Voyagers,* which are still in operation, are much more sophisticated than their predecessors, *Pioneer 10* and *11,* which took flight in 1972 and 1973, respectively. The more recent **probe**s are equipped with nuclear power generators, capable of producing a far greater power supply than the *Pioneers'* solar panels, which is especially important as the spacecraft get farther and farther from the sun. And with their high-powered cameras, the *Voyagers* have captured much more highly detailed images than those taken by the *Pioneers.* The *Voyagers* have vastly increased our knowledge of the outer planets and are widely considered the most successful interplanetary missions ever launched.

The core component of each 1,820-pound (826-kilogram) *Voyager* spacecraft is an octagonal equipment module. This module contains the ship's electronic systems, fuel, and sixteen small **rocket** motors that are used to make minor adjustments to the vessel's flight path. Three containers of uranium (the radioactive isotope that decays to provide nuclear power) are attached to one side of the module. Sitting atop this section is a 12-foot-diameter (3.7-meter-diameter) radio dish antenna that sends a concentrated beam of radio signals back to Earth. The scientific instruments—including television cameras, an infrared telescope, and an ultraviolet telescope, as well as devices to measure **plasma**—are located on a boom extending from the equipment module.

Voyager 1 headed first for Jupiter and then for Saturn, after which it exited the solar system. *Voyager 2,* however, took what is called the "Grand Tour," visiting four planets before traveling to deep space. *Voyager 2's* complex path was only possible because of the particular way the outer planets were lined up in the late 1970s. They were situated along a continuous curve so that a spacecraft could rely on the **gravity assist** technique to travel from planet to planet without the need for additional rocket motors. Gravity assist uses the gravitational field of one planet to propel it toward the next planet.

Accomplishments of *Voyager 1* and *2*

Voyager 2 was launched first, on August 20, 1977, toward Jupiter. *Voyager 1* followed just sixteen days later, but was placed on a more direct route to the giant planet than was its sister ship. Consequently, *Voyager 1* was the first to arrive at Jupiter, in March 1979; *Voyager 2* reached the planet four months later. *Voyager 1* spent several weeks photographing the planet. It revealed in great detail the turbulence in Jupiter's atmosphere, discovered a thin ring surrounding the planet, and took the first close-up pictures of Jupiter's moons. *Voyager 2* then went in for closer looks at Jupiter's ring and the volcanoes on Io, the innermost of Jupiter's moons.

Voyager 1 headed first for Jupiter and then for Saturn after which it exited the solar system.

Curious about the *Voyager* record?

It's available on CD-ROM, along with a book called *Murmurs of Earth* which tells the story behind the record, from the Planetary Society (the astronomy organization formerly headed by the late Carl Sagan). They can be reached by calling (818) 793-1675.

The next destination of both vessels was Saturn. *Voyager 1* arrived at the planet in November 1980. It transmitted dazzling pictures of the planet's spectacular rings, showing them to be comprised of thousands of ringlets. *Voyager 1* also discovered many members of Saturn's vast collection of moons. The final step in its mission was to survey Titan, Saturn's largest moon. It analyzed the composition of Titan's atmosphere, as well as revealing that Titan has seas of liquid nitrogen, bordered with a substance that may be organic. *Voyager 1* then swung around Titan and headed out of the solar system.

Voyager 2 reached Saturn in August 1981 and added to the series of images of the planet taken by *Voyager 1*. It did not fly by Titan, but instead headed for Uranus and Neptune. In January 1986, *Voyager 2* approached Uranus. Unfortunately, the probe arrived at the planet at about the same time as the **space shuttle** *Challenger* explosion. With that tragedy dominating the headlines, little attention was paid to *Voyager 2*'s exploration of Uranus, its five largest moons, and its obscure rings.

In 1989, *Voyager 2* arrived at the final planet on its journey, Neptune. The probe's photos were the first to reveal Neptune's five very faint rings, as well as six of the planet's eight moons. *Voyager 2* then followed *Voyager 1* into deep space, where both are expected to continue transmitting information on the **interstellar medium** until early in the next century.

Like *Pioneer 10* and *11* before them, both *Voyager*s carry information about Earth, should they encounter an alien civilization. The *Voyager*s' message, however, is far more detailed than the *Pioneer*s'. Affixed to each *Voyager* is a gold-plated phonograph record filled with sounds from Earth, a needle, and instructions (in a language of symbols) on how to play the record. The record contents were selected by a NASA committee headed by astronomy writer Carl Sagan. They include a sampling of sounds heard in nature (such as bird songs and the surf crashing on the seashore), greetings spoken in fifty-five languages, and music from around the world. It also contains salutations from then-U.S. President Jimmy Carter and then-United Nations Secretary General Kurt Waldheim.

To protect it during its long journey, the record is housed in a protective aluminum jacket. It has to last at least forty-thousand years—the estimated time to the nearest planetary system.

See also **Jupiter**; **Neptune**; **Pioneer program**; **Saturn**; **Space probe**; and **Uranus**

Whipple Observatory

The Whipple Observatory is the largest of the three field stations operated by the Cambridge, Massachusetts-based Harvard-Smithsonian Center for Astrophysics (CfA). It is located on a 4,744-acre (1,920-hectare) tract atop Mount Hopkins, Arizona, 35 miles (56 kilometers) south of Tucson. At 7,600 feet (2,315 meters) above sea level, Mount Hopkins is the second highest peak in the Santa Rita Range of the Coronado National Forest. The exceptionally dark skies, dry climate, and high elevation at this site make for excellent observing conditions.

The observatory was established as the Mount Hopkins Observatory in 1968 by the Smithsonian Astrophysical Observatory (SAO), which merged with the Harvard College Observatory in 1973 to form the CfA. Mount Hopkins Observatory was renamed in 1981 for its founder and former director of the Smithsonian Astrophysical Observatory, the late planetary expert Fred L. Whipple.

The most famous telescope at the Whipple Observatory is the Multiple Mirror Telescope (MMT), constructed in 1980. This instrument is made of six individual **reflector telescope**s, each one with a primary mirror 71 inches (180 centimeters) in diameter. The mirrors are arranged in a hexagonal array with an electronic guidance system that brings all six images into focus at the same time, giving the instruments a combined observing power of a 177-inch (450-centimeter) reflector. The telescope is used primarily by researchers from the CfA, as well as the University of Arizona, Arizona State University, and Northern Arizona University.

Construction is currently underway to replace the array with a single 265-inch (673-centimeter) mirror, that will have a much wider field of view. The 11 million dollar alteration is slated for completion in late 1996. The new mirror will enable the telescope to detect much fainter objects, meaning that it will be able to see four times as much of the universe as does the present instrument. In addition, the new mirror will produce a field of view several hundred times wider than the current telescope, allowing for the observation of up to three hundred **galaxies** at a time.

Future plans call for the improved MMT to be used in a survey of the distribution of galaxies in space—a process involving the measurement of distances of galaxies from Earth. Since the farther away an object is, the older it is, the survey will also demonstrate how the galaxies are distributed in time. By looking at the numbers of galaxies that existed at different points in time, we can learn about the evolution of the universe.

Telescopes At the Whipple Observatory

Whipple Observatory also has a 59-inch (150-centimeter) reflector telescope, used mainly for spectroscopic observations of galaxies, stars, and planets. In recent years, this telescope was used in an important survey of **red-shift**ed galaxies throughout a large portion of the Northern Hemisphere sky. A red-shifted object is one with a **spectrum** in which the pattern of wavelengths is shifted toward the red end, implying that the object is moving away from the observer.

The observatory also has a 328-inch (833-centimeter) wide optical reflector, a honeycomb-shaped array of 248 individually adjustable, spherical glass mirrors. This instrument is used to study **cosmic ray**s, invisible, high-energy **gamma ray**s that constantly bombard Earth from all directions. The goal of the study is to determine the source of these rays.

Cosmic rays do not penetrate the Earth's atmosphere, but when they strike the top layer of the atmosphere they produce a shower of secondary particles, which take the form of barely detectable bursts of light. The optical reflector, with its array of photomultiplier tubes (devices that increase the intensity of light), is specially designed to detect this light. It has traced the light bursts (and the cosmic rays that produced them) back to a **supernova** in the Crab Nebula, which was visible on Earth in A.D. 1054. All that remains of the supernova now is the dense, pulsating core of a star known as a **pulsar.**

When you next visit Tucson, stop in at the Whipple Observatory visitor's center and check out the exhibits on astronomy and natural history.

Then take a guided tour of the mountaintop facilities. If you time your visit properly, you can catch a "star party." These public viewing nights are held four times a year. The visitors center also offers a host of programs, conducted in both English and Spanish.

See also **Cosmic rays**; **Harvard-Smithsonian Center for Astrophysics**; and **Spectroscopy**

White, Edward (1930–1967)

American astronaut

Edward White had a short but spectacular career as an astronaut. His initial claim to fame was being the first American astronaut to walk in space. He accomplished this feat in June 1965 during the four-day-long *Gemini 4* mission. That mission also set an American endurance record in space. Throughout his twenty-one-minute **extravehicular activity (EVA),** White steered himself with a hand held maneuvering unit. He remained attached to the ship by a tether, while in orbit around the Earth at a speed of 18,000 miles (28,962 kilometers) per hour. White's **space walk** generated a huge amount of public interest. In fact, pictures of White floating outside of his spacecraft are among the most recognizable images of the U.S. space program.

Edward White.

White was selected next to fly the first piloted mission of the Apollo series, the program designed to land astronauts on the moon. On January 27, 1967, shortly before the scheduled liftoff, however, the celebrated mission ended in tragedy. White, along with crewmates Gus Grissom and Roger Chaffee, were sealed inside the **command module** of *Apollo 1* during a routine countdown test when a fire broke out in the cabin. All three astronauts were killed.

The fire was caused by faulty wiring. All it took was one spark to make contact with the pure-oxygen atmosphere to start the fire. Within seconds the crew had died of smoke inhalation.

As a result of this incident, the first Apollo launch was delayed by nearly two years while a number of improvements were made to the command module. The most important of these improvements was the addition of an escape hatch and a modification of the cabin atmosphere from pure oxygen to a mixture of gases.

Edward Higgins White II, born on November 14, 1930, in San Antonio, Texas, was destined to fly. His father was a pilot who became a general in the Air Force. The younger White followed his father's example and enrolled in West Point Military Academy. He graduated from West Point with a bachelor of science degree in 1952.

For the next year, White trained to be an Air Force pilot. He then spent nearly four years in Germany, flying fighter planes. On his return to the United States, White went to the University of Michigan where he completed a master of science degree in aeronautical engineering in 1959.

White's next move was to become a test pilot. He was stationed at the Wright-Patterson Air Force Base in Ohio when he was selected to be an astronaut by the National Aeronautics and Space Administration (NASA).

While *Gemini 4* was White's only mission in space, he logged over 4,200 hours flying aircraft. White was buried with full military honors at West Point and was survived by his wife, Beth, and their two children.

See also **Apollo program** and **Gemini program**

White dwarf star

A **white dwarf** is the fate awaiting our sun and other stars of a similar size. It is the core of a star, left to cool for eternity.

Nuclear fusion, the process by which two small particles join together to form one larger particle, occurs in the early stages of every star's life. It provides an outward pressure that acts as a balance to the star's tremendous **gravity.** In the absence of fusion, gravity takes over and causes the star to collapse upon itself. The larger the original star, the smaller white dwarf it becomes. The reason for this pattern is that larger stars have stronger gravitational fields, which produce a more complete collapse.

In the case of a star with greater than 1.4 times the **mass** of the sun, the collapse is so complete that it all matter in the star is concentrated either into an extremely densely packed **neutron star** or into a single point of infinite gravity, a **black hole.**

An average-sized star like our sun will spend the final 10 percent of its life as a **red giant.** In this phase of a star's evolution, its surface temperature drops to between 3,140 and 6,741 degrees Fahrenheit (1,727 and 3,727 degrees Celsius) and its diameter expands to ten to one thousand times that of the sun. The star takes on a reddish color, which is how the star gets its name.

Buried deep inside the star is a hot, dense core, about the size of the Earth. The core makes up about 1 percent of the star's diameter. The helium left burning at the core eventually ejects the atmosphere, which explodes off into space as a planetary **nebula.** The glowing core has become a white dwarf, all that remains of the star.

The term "white dwarf" is a bit misleading. The reason is that the core starts out white, but displays a range of colors as it cools—from yellow to red. When all heat within the core has escaped, the body ceases to glow and becomes a **black dwarf.** Billions of white dwarfs exist within our galaxy, many of them now in the form of black dwarfs. These cold, dark globes, however, are next to impossible to detect.

See also **Black hole; Red giant star;** and **Stellar evolution**

A close up (right) of white dwarfs (circled) in galaxy M4, August 28, 1995.

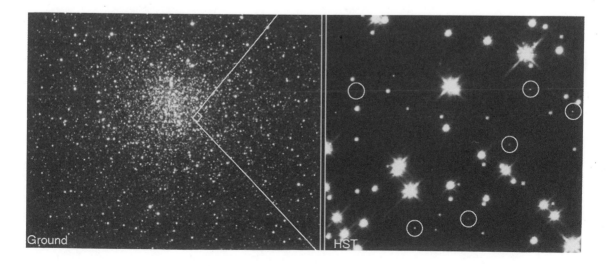

Wyoming Infrared Observatory

The top of Jelm Mountain in Wyoming is home to the Wyoming Infrared Observatory (WIRO), one of this country's most precise infrared telescopes. For the last two decades, observers at WIRO have been quietly conducting cutting-edge research on **nova** and **comet**s.

WIRO is a facility of the University of Wyoming. It is located far from any population center, 25 miles (40 kilometers) southwest of Laramie and 125 miles (200 kilometers) northwest of Denver, Colorado. The advantages of being in such a remote area include the low levels of air and light pollution which make for very clear observations. And on Jelm Mountain, at an altitude of 9,656 feet (2,935 meters), the air is dry and turbulence is relatively low. These conditions are important for **infrared astronomy** since moisture in the air absorbs **infrared radiation** and turbulence scatters the radiation, making images appear blurry. Two other reasons why that site was chosen are its closeness to the University of Wyoming and the existence of a road, electricity, and phone lines. The site of the observatory was once occupied by a U.S. Forest Service fire lookout station.

Among the disadvantages of the location is bad weather on Jelm Mountain, which gets exceedingly cold and windy in the winter. Temperatures dip to -40 degrees Fahrenheit (-40 degrees Celsius) and the wind gusts up to 100 miles (161 kilometers) per hour. The road leading up the mountain is covered with snow from October until May and can be traversed only by all-terrain vehicles. The summer brings a hazard of its own: lightning. One year a lightning bolt disabled nearly the entire electronic system. Since that time, lightning rods and other protective devices have been installed.

The WIRO telescope became operational in September 1977. It was the first large computer-controlled infrared telescope in the country. An infrared telescope detects **electromagnetic radiation** in infrared wavelengths, which are longer than visible light waves but shorter than **radio wave**s. This telescope is remarkable for its ability to track objects with great accuracy. It has a 92-inch-diameter (234-centimeter-diameter) thin primary mirror. The mirror's thinness gives it a great deal of flexibility and mobility, factors that enhance the telescope's positional accuracy.

The telescope also has an 8-inch-diameter (20-centimeter-diameter) secondary mirror, which is used to adjust for background infrared radiation present everywhere in the sky. It works like this: the secondary mirror "wobbles" to reflect, alternately (at five to ten times per second), the object under study (such as a star) and the "empty" sky. The infrared radiation from the sky is then subtracted from the radiation of the object (which includes background radiation from the sky), to get an accurate measure of the radiation coming solely from the object.

Research At WIRO

Through an infrared telescope, astronomers can observe a host of objects that would be invisible, barely visible, or blocked from view in an optical telescope. Examples of objects that emit infrared light include **stellar nurseries,** areas where new stars are in formation; **dwarf galaxies, galaxies** which contain relatively few stars and may be the precursors to visible galaxies; and parts of the **Milky Way** that are blocked by dust.

Wyoming Infrared Observatory.

Wyoming Infrared Observatory

The Wyoming Infrared Observatory is open for public tours only twice a year, in the spring and fall. Call (307) 766-6150 for more information.

Researchers at WIRO are presently involved in an ongoing study of novae in our region of the **galaxy.** A nova occurs when the smaller member of **binary star** system—typically a **white dwarf**—temporarily becomes brighter. This brightening is the result of matter being transferred from the larger to the smaller partner, initiating a nuclear chain reaction on the smaller star's surface. When the reaction ceases, the material blows away from the star, causing it to glow brightly. That material then "seeds" the galaxy, providing the material from which new stars are made. Days or weeks later the nova fades, and the process begins again.

The novae that WIRO researchers are looking at vary in brightness over relatively short periods, from ten to a few hundred days. Thus, within a couple of years it is possible to study a nova's complete bright-dim cycle. One example described by WIRO observer Charles Woodward as a typical nova in the study, is Cygnus 1992, located within the **constellation** Cygnus, about 9,780 **light-year**s away.

Another research area for which WIRO is noted is the observation of comets. In recent years, comets Hyakutake, Hale-Bopp, Halley, Shoemaker-Levy 9, and others have come under study at WIRO. Of great interest to WIRO astronomers is the period when a comet is nearest the sun. It is during this period that gas and dust boil away from the nucleus and sweep back to form the tail. Observers can then study the tail to determine its chemical composition.

See also **Comets**; **Infrared astronomy**; and **Nova and supernova**

X-ray astronomy

When we look out at the night sky, we see the moon and stars shining with visible light. Most objects in space, however, emit radiation from other parts of the **electromagnetic spectrum** as well, with wavelengths longer or shorter than those of visible light. For instance, some objects give off **radio wave**s or **infrared ray**s, which have longer wavelengths than those of visible light. And others emit **ultraviolet radiation, X-ray**s, or **gamma ray**s, with wavelengths shorter than those of visible light. Each of these types of radiation can be detected only with specialized instruments, and each gives a different view of the sky.

X-ray astronomy is a relatively new field that includes the study of objects in space that emit X-rays. Such objects include stars, **galaxies, quasar**s, **pulsar**s, and **black hole**s.

The Earth's atmosphere filters out most X-rays. This fact is fortunate for humans since a large dose of X-rays would be deadly. On the other hand, this fact makes it difficult for scientists to observe the X-ray sky. Radiation from the shortest-wavelength end of the X-ray range, called hard X-rays, can be detected at high altitudes. The only way to see longer X-rays, called soft X-rays, however, is by traveling outside the Earth's atmosphere, by means of special telescopes placed on artificial satellites.

In 1962, an X-ray telescope was launched into space aboard an Aerobee **rocket** by physicist Ricardo Giacconi and his colleagues. During its six-minute flight, the telescope detected the first X-rays from interstellar space, coming in particular from the **constellation** Scorpius. Later flights detected X-rays from the Crab Nebula (where a pulsar was later discovered) and from the constellation Cygnus. X-rays in the latter site are believed to be coming from a black hole. By the late 1960s, astronomers had become convinced that while some galaxies are strong X-ray sources, all galaxies, including our own **Milky Way,** emit weak X-rays.

The first satellite designed specifically for X-ray research, *Uhuru,* was launched by the National Aeronautics and Space Administration (NASA) in 1970. It produced a detailed map of the X-ray sky. Then in 1977, the first of three High Energy Astrophysical Observatories (HEAO) was launched. During its year and a half in operation, it provided constant monitoring of X-ray sources, such as individual stars, entire galaxies, and pulsars. The second HEAO, also known as the Einstein Observatory, operated from November 1978 to April 1981. It contained a high resolution X-ray telescope, which found that X-rays were coming from nearly every star.

Now in the planning stages is the Advanced X-Ray Astrophysics Facility (AXAF), which NASA intends to have in operation by the year 2000.

See also **Advanced X-Ray Astrophysics Facility**; **High Energy Astrophysical Observatories**; and **X-ray stars**

X-ray stars

X-rays are a form of high-energy radiation. On the **electromagnetic spectrum** they occupy a position between longer wavelength **ultraviolet radiation** and shorter wavelength **gamma ray**s. Further along on the electromagnetic spectrum, occupying a band of longer wavelength radiation, is visible light.

An X-ray star is one that gives off X-rays. A star produces X-rays when **plasma** ions in its core collide with one another. The resultant X-rays contain enough energy to leave the star's core and can be detected on its surface.

Many X-ray stars exist as part of a **binary star**—a double star system in which two stars orbit each other around a central point of **gravity.** In cases where the two are in close proximity, plasma may flow from one star on to the second, causing the second star to become an X-ray star.

The Earth's atmosphere filters out most of these X-rays, making it nearly impossible to observe X-ray stars and other X-ray objects from the ground. Radiation from the shortest-wavelength end of the X-ray range, called hard X-rays, can be detected at high altitudes, such as up in a hot air balloon. The only way to see longer X-rays, called soft X-rays, however, is from a position outside the Earth's atmosphere, through special telescopes placed on artificial satellites. Thus, it was not until the **space age** (beginning in the late 1950s) that scientists began to learn about the X-ray universe.

The first X-rays in space, coming from the **constellation** Scorpius, were detected by an X-ray telescope launched on board an Aerobee **rocket** in 1962. X-rays were then found in the Crab Nebula, where a **pulsar** was later discovered. The constellation Cygnus also proved a strong X-ray source, probably due to the presence of a **black hole.**

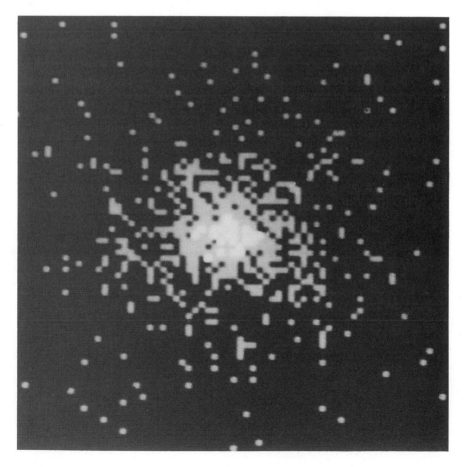

First picture taken of an X-ray star, transmitted by NASA's HEAO-2 to the control center at Goddard Space Flight Center, November 18, 1978.

By the late 1960s, astronomers had become convinced that while some **galaxies** are strong X-ray sources, all galaxies, including our own **Milky Way,** emit weak X-rays. Even our sun emits X-rays, but they are up to one thousand times weaker than the strongest X-ray sources in our galaxy. The most powerful sources of X-rays, however, come from galactic clusters and quasars, well beyond our galaxy.

See also **Advanced X-Ray Astrophysics Facility; High Energy Astrophysical Observatories;** and **X-ray astronomy**

Yerkes Observatory

In 1997, Yerkes Observatory will celebrate its centennial. This historic observatory, which is owned and operated by the University of Chicago, is the home of the world's largest **refractor telescope.** With a 40-inch-diameter (102-centimeter-diameter) lens, however, this telescope pales in comparison with such modern giants as the Keck Telescope at Mauna Kea Observatory in Hawaii. The primary mirror in this **reflector telescope** measures 394 inches (1,016 centimeters) across.

The Yerkes refractor was built during a pivotal period in the history of telescope-making. Astronomers at the turn of the century were just realizing that the best images of celestial objects could be obtained through the largest instruments, since they let in the most light. Reflectors are much better suited for large designs than refractors for a number of reasons. The principal one is that mirrors reflect light from only one surface and can, therefore, be supported from behind. Lenses, on the other hand, must allow light to pass through them. Thus, they can be supported only at the edges, their thinnest and most fragile part. Astronomers now believe that the Yerkes refractor marks the limit of the weight that could be supported in that way and is, therefore, the end of the line for the great refractors.

Yerkes Observatory is located in Williams Bay, Wisconsin, on the shore of Lake Geneva, about 80 miles (129 kilometers) northwest of Chicago, Illinois. The site was chosen for its proximity to Chicago and for its dark skies. At the time the observatory was erected, Williams Bay was one of the least populous areas in the region, meaning that there was min-

Yerkes Observatory, Williams Bay, Wisconsin. The dome on the left houses the 40-inch (102-centimeter) refractor telescope installed in 1897.

imal light pollution. Over the last century, however, Williams Bay has grown up around Yerkes to its present population of two thousand. Neighboring towns have also been established in recent years. Gone are the dark skies. Yerkes now holds the distinction of being the last great observatory to be situated in a poor location. Another factor contributing to the present poor viewing at Yerkes is that it sits only 1,095 feet (334 meters) above sea level, meaning it experiences the full impact of the Earth's atmosphere. (Given that atmospheric molecules scatter light and blur images, most major observatories are situated high above sea level where the atmosphere is thinner.) Also, the weather is average-to-poor. On more nights than not, overcast skies prevent any observations from being made.

Yerkes Observatory was founded in 1897 by pioneering astronomer George Hale, then a faculty member at the University of Chicago. Hale had been following the efforts of a group of Harvard astronomers to set up a research station atop Mount Wilson in southern California. The re-

searchers were planning to construct a 40-inch (102-centimeter) refractor and had already ordered the lens, when an extraordinarily harsh winter caused them to abandon the site.

Learning of this, Hale approached the president of the University of Chicago, William Rainey Harper, with the idea of raising funds to establish an observatory which would have as its centerpiece the orphaned 40-inch instrument. Hale located a wealthy donor, Chicagoan Charles Yerkes, and solicited a sum of money large enough for the construction of the telescope and a dome in which to house it.

Hale was the observatory's first director. Under his short-lived tutelage (he soon headed west for bigger astronomical adventures) the facility was set well on its way to becoming a world-class observatory.

Yerkes' Contributions to Astronomy

A number of famous astronomers followed Hale at Yerkes, leaving in their wake an impressive list of accomplishments. Yerkes is the site at which Edward E. Barnard crafted his classic photographic atlas of the **Milky Way** in 1916. Then in the 1930s, Subrahmanyan Chandrasekhar shocked the scientific world with the discovery that above a certain **mass** a star would not become a **white dwarf** at the end of its lifetime, but a **black hole.** And, in the late 1940s, Gerard Kuiper used the Yerkes refractor to discover the fifth moon of Uranus and the second moon of Neptune, as well as the presence of carbon dioxide in the atmosphere of Mars.

Today, Yerkes Observatory houses three reflector telescopes—a 41-inch (104-centimeter), a 24-inch (61-centimeter), and a 10-inch (25-centimeter)—in addition to the original refractor. Research at the site focuses primarily on a long-term study of the motion of stars within tightly packed clusters in **galaxies** beyond our own. Most of the work of the Yerkes staff, however, is conducted off-site. Examples of this research include conducting astrophysical studies at a field station in Antarctica; operating infrared telescopes on board the Kuiper Airborne Observatory; and making observations, in both infrared and visible light, at the Apache Point Observatory in New Mexico.

Every Saturday, Yerkes Observatory is open to the public. Tours include a visit to the original refractor and its 90-foot (27-meter) dome, as well as lectures and slide shows on the history of Yerkes and the astronomical research conducted there.

See also **Hale, George**

Zwicky, Fritz (1898–1974)

Swiss astronomer

Fritz Zwicky, one of this century's most brilliant astronomers, is as well known for his distinctive personality as he is for his scientific achievements. Zwicky's high energy and quick wit won him the affection of some and the disdain of others. No question exists, however, that his insightful and accurate theories—particularly pertaining to **supernova**s, **neutron star**s, and **dark matter**—led to a much greater understanding of our universe.

Zwicky was born to Swiss parents in Varna, Bulgaria. He went to college at Albert Einstein's alma mater, the Federal Institute of Technology in Zürich, Switzerland. There he conducted research on salt crystals and earned his Ph.D. in 1922. A few years, later Zwicky emigrated to the United States, where he joined the faculty of the California Institute of Technology (CalTech). He also worked at the Palomar and Mount Wilson observatories.

Zwicky spent almost his entire career at CalTech. During World War II, he served as director of research for the Aerojet Engineering Corporation, conducting research into jet propulsion. Following the war, he was sent to Japan by the U.S. government to measure the damage caused by the nuclear bombs dropped on Hiroshima and Nagasaki.

From the 1930s through the 1950s, Zwicky studied a number of astronomical concepts. He began with a careful study of **galaxies,** eventually cataloging close to thirty thousand of them in a part of the sky called the Coma Supercluster.

Studying the stars, Zwicky found something puzzling about brighter-than-usual **nova**s, stars that undergo a temporary brightening. He focused on a particular nova in the Andromeda galaxy, unable to understand how a star so far away could appear so bright. In collaboration with astronomer Walter Baade, Zwicky came up with a revolutionary concept. Zwicky and Baade claimed that this star, which they called a supernova, was exceptionally bright because it was experiencing an explosion marking the end of its lifetime. They also concluded that a supernova is a rare event, occurring only two or three times every one thousand years per galaxy. (Recent studies, however, have put that number at closer to one supernova every fifty years per galaxy. Many supernovas are never seen because of interference by interstellar clouds.)

Zwicky Hypothesizes the Neutron Star

Zwicky and Baade also predicted in 1934 that a neutron star would

Fritz Zwicky looks up from his chart of lunar exploration space vehicles at CalTech.

be left behind after a star went supernova. A neutron star is an object made of extremely densely packed neutrons. In 1967, they were proven correct when the first **pulsar,** a type of neutron star, was discovered.

Zwicky's studies then led him to suggest the existence of a "cosmic glue" called dark matter. He calculated that the **mass** of known matter in galaxies is not great enough to hold a cluster of galaxies together. Yet, even though each independent galaxy moves at too great a speed for them to remain in a cluster, they are not moving away from each other. Zwicky theorized that an as-of-yet undetected substance creates a gravitational field to counter-balance the galaxies' outward expansion.

Again, Zwicky's prediction appears to be correct. In early 1996, after decades of searching, astronomers announced that they had discovered one possible form of the mysterious dark matter—**white dwarf**s, the cooling, shrunken cores left when stars die. The remaining dark matter could be made of **black hole**s, **black dwarf**s, **brown dwarf**s, or any number of unusual subatomic particles.

Zwicky died in Pasadena, California, just six days before his seventy-sixth birthday, and was buried in Switzerland. The seemingly contradictory sides of Zwicky's nature were summed up in an obituary by Harvard astronomer Cecilia Payne-Gaposchkin, published in *Sky & Telescope* magazine: "Aggressively original, outspoken to the point of abrasion, he seemed to his contemporaries stubbornly opinionated." At the same time, Payne-Gaposchkin wrote that Zwicky was "one of the kindest men, with a deep concern for humanity."

See also **Dark matter** and **Neutron star**

Sources

Books

Abbott, David, ed. "Seyfert, Carl Keenan," *The Biographical Dictionary of Scientists: Astronomers,* New York: P. Bedrick Books, 1984.

Abell, George O. *Realm of the Universe,* 3rd edition, Philadelphia: Saunders College Publishing, 1984.

Anderson, Julie. "Edward Mills Purcell," *Notable Twentieth-Century Scientists,* Volume 3, Ed. Emily J. McMurray, Detroit: Gale Research, 1995.

Apfel, Necia H. *Astronomy Projects for Young Scientists,* New York: Prentice Hall Press, 1984.

Asimov, Isaac. *Isaac Asimov's Library of the Universe: Ancient Astronomy,* Milwaukee: Gareth Stevens Publishing, 1989.

Asimov, Isaac. *Isaac Asimov's Library of the Universe: Projects in Astronomy,* Milwaukee: Gareth Stevens Publishing, 1990.

Bali, Mrinal. *Contemporary World Issues: Space Exploration,* Santa Barbara, CA: ABC-CLIO, Inc., 1990.

Barone, Michael and Grant Ujifusa. *The Almanac of American Politics 1996,* Washington, D.C.: National Journal Inc., 1995, pp. 1032-36.

Beck, R. L. and Daryl Schrader. *America's Planetariums & Observatories,* St. Petersburg, FL: Sunwest Space Systems, Inc., 1991.

Bernstein, Joanne E. and Rose Blue. *Judith Resnik: Challenger Astronaut,* New York: Lodestar Books, 1990.

Blaauw, Adriaan. *ESO's Early History,* Garching bei München, Germany: European Southern Observatory, 1991.

Blaauw, Adriaan. "Sitter, Willem de," *Dictionary of Scientific Biography,* Volume XII, Ed. Charles Coulston Gillispie, New York: Charles Scribner's Sons, 1973.

Bonnet, Robert L. and G. Daniel Keen. *Space and Astronomy: 49 Science Fair Projects,* Blue Ridge Summit, PA: Tab Books, 1992.

Booth, Nicholas. *Encyclopedia of Space,* London: Brian Trodd Publishing House Limited, 1990.

Brecher, Kenneth and Michael Feirtag, eds. *Astronomy of the Ancients,* Cambridge, MA: The MIT Press, 1979.

Carroll, Peter N. *Famous in America: The Passion to Succeed,* New York: Dutton. 1985.

Cassut, Michael. *Who's Who in Space: The First 25 Years,* Boston: G. K. Hall & Co., 1987.

Cornell, James. *The First Stargazers: An Introduction to the Origins of Astronomy,* New York: Charles Scribner's Sons, 1981.

Couper, Heather and Nigel Henbest. *How the Universe Works,* Pleasantville, NY: Reader's Digest Association, Inc., 1994.

Davies, J. K. *Space Exploration,* Edinburgh: W & R Chambers Ltd., 1992.

Davies, Kay and Wendy Oldfield. *The Super Science Book of Time,* New York: Thomson Learning, 1992.

D'Occhieppo, Konradin Ferrari. "Oppolzer, Theodor Ritter Von," *Dictionary of Scientific Biography,* Volume X, Ed. Charles Coulston Gillispie, New York: Charles Scribner's Sons, 1973.

Drake, Frank D. *Is Anyone Out There?: The Scientific Search for Extraterrestrial Intelligence,* New York: Delacorte Press, 1992.

"Drake, Frank Donald," *American Men and Women of Science,* 18th edition, Vol. 2, New Providence, New Jersey: R. R. Bowker, 1972.

Eastwood, Bruce S. "Grimaldi, Francesco Maria," *Dictionary of Scientific Biography,* Volume V, Ed. Charles Coulston Gillispie, New York: Charles Scribner's Sons, 1973.

Friedman, Herbert. *The Astronomer's Universe,* New York: W.W. Norton & Company, 1990.

Gatland, Kenneth. *The Illustrated Encyclopedia of Space Technology,* New York: Crown Publishers, Inc., 1981.

Goldsmith, Donald. *The Astronomers,* New York: St. Martin's Press, 1991.

Graham, Judith, ed. "Jemison, Mae C.," *Current Biography Yearbook 1993,* New York: H.W. Wilson, 1993.

Gray, Chris Hables. "Carl Sagan," *Notable Twentieth-Century Scientists,* Volume 3, Ed. Emily J. McMurray, Detroit: Gale Research, 1995.

Gump, David P. *Space Enterprise: Beyond NASA,* New York: Praeger, 1990.

Hadingham, Evan. *Early Man and the Cosmos,* New York: Walker and Company, 1984.

Haskins, Jim and Kathleen Benson. *Space Challenger: The Story of Guion Bluford,* Minneapolis: Carolrhoda Books, Inc., 1984.

Hathaway, Nancy. *The Friendly Guide to the Universe,* New York: Penguin Books, 1994.

Hawking, Stephen W. *A Brief History of Time: From the Big Bang to Black Holes,* Toronto: Bantam Books, 1988.

Heidman, Jean. *Extraterrestrial Intelligence,* Cambridge, England: Cambridge University Press, 1995.

Hoffleit, Dorrit. "Mitchell, Maria," *Dictionary of Scientific Biography,* Volume IX, Ed. Charles Coulston Gillispie, New York: Charles Scribner's Sons, 1973.

Hunley, J. D. "Hermann Oberth," *Notable Twentieth-Century Scientists,* Volume 3, Ed. Emily J. McMurray, Detroit: Gale Research, 1995.

Ilingworth, Valerie, ed. *The Facts on File Dictionary of Astronomy,* 3rd edition, New York: Facts on File, Inc., 1994.

Itard, Jean. "Legendre, Adrien-Marie," *Dictionary of Scientific Biography,* Volume VIII, Ed. Charles Coulston Gillispie, New York: Charles Scribner's Sons, 1973.

Kaufmann, William J., III. *Discovering the Universe,* 3rd edition, New York: W. H. Freeman and Company, 1993.

Kippenhahn, Rudolf. *Bound to the Sun: The Story of Planets, Moons, and Comets,* New York: W. H. Freeman and Company, 1990.

Kirby-Smith, H.T. *U.S. Observatories: A Directory and Travel Guide,* New York: Van Nostrand Reinhold Company, 1976.

Kopal, Zdenek. "Römer, Ole Christensen (or Roemer, Olaus)," *Dictionary of Scientific Biography,* Volume XI, Ed. Charles Coulston Gillispie, New York: Charles Scribner's Sons, 1973.

Kragh, Helge. "Lemaitre, Georges," *Dictionary of Scientific Biography,* Volume 18-Supplement II, Ed. Charles Coulston Gillispie, New York: Charles Scribner's Sons, 1990.

Krauss, Lawrence M. *The Physics of Star Trek,* New York: BasicBooks, 1995.

Lerner, Eric. *The Big Bang Never Happened,* New York: Times Books, 1991.

Lévy, Jacques R. "Le Verrier, Urbain Jean Joseph," *Dictionary of Scientific Biography,* Volume VIII, Ed. Charles Coulston Gillispie, New York: Charles Scribner's Sons, 1973.

Lohne, J. A. "Harriot (or Hariot), Thomas," *Dictionary of Scientific Biography,* Volume VI, Ed. Charles Coulston Gillispie, New York: Charles Scribner's Sons, 1973.

MacDonald, D.K.C. *Faraday, Maxwell, and Kelvin,* Garden City, NY: Doubleday & Company, Inc., 1964.

Mallas, John H. and Evered Kreimer. *The Messier Album: An Observer's Handbook,* Cambridge, MA: Sky Publishing Corp, 1978.

Marsden, Brian G. "Newcomb, Simon," *Dictionary of Scientific Biography,* Volume X, Ed. Charles Coulston Gillispie, New York: Charles Scribner's Sons, 1973.

Marx, Siegfried and Werner Pfau. *Observatories of the World,* New York: Van Nostrand Reinhold Company, 1982.

McDonald, Avril. "Grote Reber," *Notable Twentieth-Century Scientists,* Volume 3, Ed. Emily J. McMurray, Detroit: Gale Research, 1995.

Moore, Patrick. *Fireside Astronomy: An Anecdotal Tour through the History and Lore of Astronomy,* Chichester, England: John Wiley & Sons, 1992.

Moore, Patrick. *The Guinness Book of Astronomy,* Middlesex, England: Guinness Publishing Ltd., 1988.

Moore, Patrick. *The International Encyclopedia of Astronomy,* New York: Orion Books, 1987.

Moore, Patrick. *Patrick Moore's History of Astronomy,* 6th edition, London: MacDonald & Co. Ltd., 1983.

Moyer, Don F. "Langley, Samuel Pierpont," *Dictionary of Scientific Biography,* Volume VIII, Ed. Charles Coulston Gillispie, New York: Charles Scribner's Sons, 1973.

Multhauf, Lettie S. "Olbers, Heinrich Wilhelm Matthias," *Dictionary of Scientific Biography,* Volume X, Ed. Charles Coulston Gillispie, New York: Charles Scribner's Sons, 1973.

Munitz, Milton K., ed. *Theories of the Universe,* Glencoe, IL: The Free Press, 1957.

Neal, Valerie, Cathleen S. Lewis and Frank H. Winter. *Spaceflight: A Smithsonian Guide,* New York: Macmillan • USA, 1995.

Newton, David E. "Martin Ryle," *Notable Twentieth-Century Scientists,* Volume 3, Ed. Emily J. McMurray, Detroit: Gale Research, 1995.

North, John. *The Norton History of Astronomy and Cosmology,* New York: W. W. Norton & Company, Inc., 1995.

O'Connor, Karen. *Sally Ride and the New Astronauts: Scientists in Space,* New York: Franklin Watts, 1983.

Office of Technology Assessment. *Civilian Space Policy and Applications,* Washington, D.C.: U.S. Government Printing Office, 1982.

O'Neil, W. M. *Early Astronomy from Babylonia to Copernicus,* Sydney, Australia: Sydney University Press, 1986.

Parker, Barry. *Stairway to the Stars: The Story of the World's Largest Observatory,* New York: Plenum Press, 1994.

Pasachoff, Jay M. *Contemporary Astronomy,* 4th edition, Philadelphia: Saunders College Publishing, 1989.

Pasachoff, Jay M. *Journey Through the Universe,* Fort Worth, TX: Saunders College Publishing, 1992.

Pendick, Daniel. "Clyde W. Tombaugh," *Notable Twentieth-Century Scientists,* Volume 4, Ed. Emily J. McMurray, Detroit: Gale Research, 1995.

Riabchikov, Evgeny. *Russians in Space,* Garden City, New York: Doubleday & Company, Inc., 1971.

"Rocket and Rocket Engine," *Science and Technology Illustrated: The World Around Us,* Volume 22, Chicago: Encyclopedia Britannica, Inc., 1984.

Ronan, Colin A. *The Natural History of the Universe,* New York: MacMillan Publishing Company, 1991.

Sagan, Carl. *Cosmos,* New York: Random House, 1980.

Schmittroth, Linda, Mary Reilly McCall, and Bridget Travers, eds. *Eureka!* 6 Volumes, Detroit: U•X•L, 1995.

Smith, Julian A. "Valentina Tereshkova," *Notable Twentieth-Century Scientists,* Volume 4, Ed. Emily J. McMurray, Detroit: Gale Research, 1995.

Smith, Julian A. "Vera Cooper Rubin," *Notable Twentieth-Century Scientists,* Volume 3, Ed. Emily J. McMurray, Detroit: Gale Research, 1995.

Smith, Robert W. *The Space Telescope: A Study of NASA, Science, Technology and Politics,* Cambridge, MA: Cambridge University Press, 1993.

Stuewer, Roger H. "Gamow, George," *Dictionary of Scientific Biography,* Volume V, Ed. Charles Coulston Gillispie, New York: Charles Scribner's Sons, 1973.

Swenson, Loyd S. Jr. "Michelson, Albert Abraham," *Dictionary of Scientific Biography,* Volume IX, Ed. Charles Coulston Gillispie, New York: Charles Scribner's Sons, 1973.

Swift, David W. *SETI Pioneers: Scientists Talk About Their Search for Extraterrestrial Intelligence,* Tucson, AZ: The University of Arizona Press, 1990.

Thurston, Hugh. *Early Astronomy,* New York: Springer-Verlag, 1994.

Travers, Bridget, ed. *The Gale Encyclopedia of Science,* 6 Volumes. Detroit: Gale Research, 1996.

Travers, Bridget, ed. *World of Invention,* Detroit: Gale Research, 1994.

Travers, Bridget, ed. *World of Scientific Discovery,* Detroit: Gale Research, 1994.

Tucker, Wallace H. *The Star Splitters: The High Energy Astronomy Observatories,* Washington, D.C.: National Aeronautics and Space Administration, 1984.

Walter, William J. *Space Age,* New York: Random House, 1992.

Wilson, Colin. *Starseekers,* New York: Doubleday & Company, Inc., 1980.

Wilson, Philip K. "Allan R. Sandage," *Notable Twentieth-Century Scientists,* Volume 4, Ed. Emily J. McMurray, Detroit: Gale Research, 1995.

Zeilik, Michael and John Gaustad. *Astronomy: The Cosmic Perspective,* 2nd edition, New York: John Wiley & Sons, Inc., 1990.

Articles

Acton, Scott. "Untwinkling Our Own Star," *Sky & Telescope,* June 1994: 26-27.

"Allan Sandage Receives 1991 Crafoord Prize," *Physics Today,* December 1991: 91.

Allen, Jane E. "Probe Finds Jupiter Surprisingly Windy, Drier Than Expected," *Detroit Free Press,* 23 January 1996: A1.

Allen, Jane E. and Russell Grantham. "By Jupiter! Probe's Findings Surprise Scientists," *The Ann Arbor News,* 23 January 1996: A3.

"Americans Get the Mir Experience," *Astronomy*, April 1995: 28.

"Astronaut at Home on Mir," *The Ann Arbor News*, 26 March 1996: A4.

"Astronomers Are Closer to Agreeing on the Age of the Universe," *Chronicle of Higher Education*, 17 May 1996: A10.

Banke, Jim. "The Story of Apollo 13: The Movie," *Ad Astra*, March/April 1995: 50.

Bartusiak, Marcia. "Head in the Stars," *The New York Times Book Review*, 10 December 1995: 22.

Bond, Bruce. "100 Years on Mars Hill," *Astronomy*, June 1994: 28-39.

Boyd, Robert S. "Astronomers See Potential for Life on Newly Found Planets," *Detroit Free Press*, 18 January 1996: A3+.

Boyd, Robert S. "Exploring the Big Bang and Beyond," *Detroit Free Press*, 7 January 1996: H1+.

Boyd, Robert S. "Origin of Life on Earth Eludes Scientists," *Detroit Free Press*, 7 January 1996: H4.

Boyd, Robert S. "Somewhere, Some Other Planet Must Sustain Life," *Detroit Free Press*, 7 January 1996: H4.

Broad, William J. "Could Life on Loose Bit of Mars Survive a Short Cut to Earth?" *The New York Times*, 12 March 1996: C1.

Broad, William J. "Russian Space Momentos Show Gagarin's Ride Was a Rough One," *The New York Times*, 5 March 1996: B12.

Browne, Malcolm W. "'Neutrino Bomb' Idea Expands Debate on Human Extinction," *The New York Times*, 23 January 1996: D4.

Brunier, Serge. "Temples in the Sky," *Sky and Telescope*, February 1993: 18-24.

Bruning, David. "Hubble: Better Than New," *Astronomy*, April 1994: 44-49.

Chang, Kenneth. "Two More Planets Found Near Stars Similar to the Sun," *The Los Angeles Times*, 18 January 1996: A3.

Chartrand, Mark. "A Measure of Space," *Ad Astra*, November/December 1993: 52.

Clary, Mike. "U.S. Woman Will Spend Months in Mir," *The Los Angeles Times*, 21 March 1996: A18.

"COBE Mission Launched," *Astronomy*, February 1990: 16+.

Cole, Richard. "NASA Mission May Unlock a Few Cosmic Secrets," *The Detroit News*, 3 December 1995: A2.

Cowley, Anne. "The Catherine Wolfe Bruce Medal to Maarten Schmidt," *Mercury*, November-December 1992: 197-98.

"Dr. Mae Jemison Becomes First Black Woman in Space," *Jet*, 14 September 1992: 34-38.

Drago, Mike. "Shuttle Retrieves NASA Probe," *The Ann Arbor News*, 16 January 1996.

Dunn, Marcia. "Female Astronaut Settles In on Mir," *USA Today*, 25 March 1996: A3.

Dunn, Marcia. "Shuttle, Mir Are Linked After Tricky Docking," *The Boston Globe*, 16 November 1995: A3.

Dyson, Freeman. "Hidden Worlds: Hunting for Distant Comets and Rogue Planets," *Sky & Telescope*, January 1994: 26-30.

Eicher, David J. "Descent Into Darkness," *Astronomy*, April 1995: 66-69.

Friedlander, Blaine P. Jr. "The Comet With Two Tails," *The Washington Post*, 6 March 1996: B5.

"Gamma-Ray Telescope Takes Shape," *Astronomy*, July 1995: 26.

Gauthier, Daniel James. "One Hundred Stars of Space," *Ad Astra*, July/August 1991: 8+.

Goldman, Stuart J. "Astronomy On the Internet," *Sky & Telescope*, August 1995: 21-27.

Grantham, Russell. "By Jupiter! Instruments From U-M to Explore It," *The Ann Arbor News*, 6 December 1995: B1+.

Grantham, Russell. "Expert Shares Jupiter Surprises," *The Ann Arbor News*, 8 February 1996: B3.

Grantham, Russell. "Hyakutake Brightest Comet in Sky Since 1976," *The Ann Arbor News*, 20 March 1996: B1+.

Grantham, Russell. "New Technology Has Accelerated Advances In Field of Astronomy," *The Ann Arbor News*, 11 April 1996: D1+.

Grantham, Russell. "Star Potential," *The Ann Arbor News*, 11 April 1996: D1+.

Gurshtein, Alexander. "When the Zodiac Climbed into the Sky," *Sky & Telescope*, October 1995: 28-33.

Hathaway, David H. "Journey to the Heart of the Sun," *Astronomy* January 1995: 38-43.

Horgan, John. "Beyond Neptune: Hubble Telescope Spots a Vast Ring of Ice Protoplanets," *Scientific American*, October 1995: 24+.

Hotz, Robert Lee. "Quest for Ice: Polar Prospecting." *The Los Angeles Times*, 14 January 1996: A1.

Hoversten, Paul. "Hubble's Time Travel Finds Galaxies," *USA Today*, 16 January 1996: A1.

"Hubble Observes the Violent Birth of Stars," *Astronomy* October 1995: 22.

Jaroff, Leon. "Listening for Aliens," *Time*, 5 February 1996: 55+.

"Jemison, Endeavour Crew Return To Earth After Successful Science Mission," *Jet*, 5 October 1992: 9.

Johnson, George. "Dark Matter Lights the Void," *The New York Times*, 21 January 1996: E1+.

Knight, Tony. "To Explore Strange New Worlds—Galileo Streaks Toward Jupiter," *Daily News of Los Angeles*, 27 November 1995.

Lemonick, Michael D. "Astronomers Have Detected Water-Bearing Planets Around Nearby Stars. Now They're Focused on a Deeper Mystery: Where Are the Friendly, Earthlike Worlds?" *Time*, 5 February 1996: 53+.

Lemonick, Michael D. "Beyond Pluto," *Time*, 28 September 1992: 59.

Luxner, Larry. "Southern Space: Down South Looks To The Stars," *Ad Astra*, November/December 1992: 46-47.

Mallon, Thomas. "Galileo, Phone Home," *The New York Times Magazine*, 3 December 1995: 57+.

Mann, Paul. "Spacelab's Demise?" *Aviation Week & Space Technology*, 1 August 1994: 23.

McDonald, Kim A. "A Great Comet," *The Chronicle of Higher Education*, 5 April 1996: A10.

Nash, Nathaniel C. "Starry-Eyed But Resolute: Astronomers in Race," *The New York Times*, 6 January 1994: A4.

"New Life for McMath Solar Telescope," *Sky & Telescope*, October 1990: 346.

Nicholson, Thomas D. "Observatory Hill," *Natural History*, April 1991: 78+.

"100-Inch Mount Wilson Telescope to Reopen," *Astronomy*, January 1988: 86-87.

O'Toole, Thomas. "The Man Who Didn't Walk On the Moon," *The New York Times Magazine*, 17 July 1994: 26+.

Owen, Tobias. "Ice in the Solar System: How the Earth Got its Atmosphere," *Ad Astra*, November/December 1995: 26-29.

Powell, Andrew. "Spaced Out," *Harper's Bazaar*, September 1994: 332-36.

Preston, Richard. "Beacons in Time: Maarten Schmidt and the Discovery of Quasars," *Mercury*, January-February 1988: 2-11.

Recer, Paul. "And It's Colder Than Michigan in March: Hubble Telescope Captures First Surface Images of Remote, Frozen Pluto," *The Ann Arbor News*, 8 March 1996: A6.

"Rendezvous in Space," *Astronomy*, October 1995: 23.

"Report: Insulation Puncture Caused Tether Failure," *The Ann Arbor News*, 5 June 1996: A4.

Ressmeyer, Roger H. "Tradition & Technology at Yerkes Observatory," *Sky & Telescope*, September 1995: 32-34.

Robinson, Cordula. "Magellan Reveals Venus," *Astronomy*, February 1995: 32-41.

Roylance, Frank D. "'Right Stuff' Old Stuff to Him; 'I Love Space': A 29-Year Astronaut, Dr. Storey Musgrave at 61 Will Be the Oldest Human to Fly in Space When Columbia Takes Off in November," *The Baltimore Sun*, 26 April 1996: 1A.

Rudich, Joe. "The Electronic Frontier," *Ad Astra*, September/October 1995: 32-36.

Sawyer, Kathy. "Space Fleet Stares Deep Into Sun," *The Washington Post*, 20 May 1996: A3.

Sawyer, Kathy. "'Tadpoles' In Nebula Suggest Presence of Rogue Planets," *The Washington Post*, 20 April 1996: A3.

Shibley, John. "Glow Bands & Curtains," *Astronomy*, April 1995: 76-81.

"Space Flight: Endeavor Is a Symbol of Dreams," *The Ann Arbor News*, 14 January 1996.

Stephens, Sally. "The End of Hubble's Troubles," *Ad Astra*, March/April 1994: 50-52.

Stephens, Sally. "Telescopes that Fly," *Astronomy*, November 1994: 46-53.

Stern, Alan. "Chiron: Interloper From the Kuiper Disk?" *Astronomy*, August 94: 26-33.

Stevens, William K. "One Hundred Nations Move To Save Ozone Shield," *The New York Times*, 10 December 1995: A6.

"Subrahmanyan Chandrasekhar (1910-1995)," *Astronomy*, December 1995: 32.

"Taking the Long View: Hubble Images Shed Light On the Unknown, the Unseen," *Detroit Free Press*, 18 January 1996: F8.

Tyson, Neil de Grasse. "Romancing the Mountaintop," *Natural History*, January 1995: 70-73.

Watson, Traci and William J. Cook. "A New Solar System?" *U.S. News & World Report*, 30 October 1995: 69-72.

Weissman, Paul R. "Comets At the Solar System's Edge," *Sky & Telescope*, January 1993: 26-29.

Wilford, John Noble. "Ear to Universe Is Plugged by

Budget Cutters," *The New York Times,* 7 October 1993: B12.

Wilford, John Noble. "Found: Most of Missing Matter Lost Around Edges of Universe," *The New York Times,* 17 January 1996: A1+.

Wilford, John Noble. "Gifts Keep Alive Search for Other Life In Universe," *The New York Times,* 25 January 1994: C5.

Wilford, John Noble. "Life in Space? Two New Planets Raise Thoughts," *The New York Times,* 18 January 1996: A1+.

Wohleber, Curt. "The Rocket Man," *Invention & Technology,* Summer 1996: 36-45.

Websites

About La Silla. [Online] Available http://lw10.ls.eso.org/lasilla/generalinfo/html/aboutls.html, April 7, 1996.

Allen, Jesse S. The Uhuru Satellite: December 1970-March 1973. [Online] Available http://heasarc.gsfc.nasa.gov/docs/heasarc/missions/uhuru.html, June 5, 1996.

Altschuler, Daniel. General Information on Arecibo Observatory. [Online] Available http://www.naic.edu/, April 4, 1996.

Arnett, Bill. Pluto. [Online} Available http://seds.lpl.arizona.edu/billa/tnp/pluto.html, March 14, 1996.

Astronaut Alan B. Shepard, Jr. News & Photo Archives, NASA Ames Public Affairs Home Page. [Online] Available http://ccf.arc.nasa.gov/dx/basket/storiesetc/Shepa.html, May 9, 1996.

Bartlett, Don. A Practical Guide to GPS. [Online] Available http://www.fys.uio.no/~kjetikj/fjellet/GPS1.html, June 25, 1996.

Beatty, J. Kelly. Life from Ancient Mars? *Sky & Telescope's Weekly News Bulletin: Special Edition.* [Online] Available http://www.skypub.com/news/marslife.html, August 8, 1996.

Behr, Bradford. Big Bear Solar Observatory. [Online] Available http://astro.caltech.edu.observatories/bbso/bluebook.html, July 26, 1996.

Behr, Bradford. Palomar Observatory. [Online] Available http://astro.caltech.edu.observatories/palomar/, May 27, 1996.

Bell, Edwin V. Cassini. [Online] Available http://nssdc.gsfc.nasa.gov/planetary/cassini.html, March 18, 1996.

Bell, Edwin V. Pluto Express. *NSSDC Master Catalog Display Spacecraft.* [Online] Available http://nssdc.gsfc.nasa.gov/cgi-bin/database/www-nmc?PFF, July 22, 1996.

Biography of Dr. Buzz Aldrin. [Online] Available http://www.nss.org/askastro/biography.html, April 3, 1996.

Capt. Charles 'Pete' Conrad, Jr. (Ret.). [Online] Available http://www.nauts.com/astro/conrad/conrad.html, May 8, 1996.

Columbia Lands in Florida. [Online] Available http://shuttle.nasa.gov/sts-75, May 8, 1996.

Dettling, J. Ray. Beyond Hubble. [Online] Available http://ori.careerexpo.com/pub/docs/hubble.html, July 22, 1996.

Donahue, Bob. Mount Wilson Observatory. [Online] Available http://www.mtwilson.edu/, April 7, 1996.

Double Nucleus of the Andromeda Galaxy M31. [Online] Available http://galaxy.einet.net/images/galaxy/m31c.html, May 1, 1996.

Dr. Buzz Aldrin. *The National Space Society and the Space, Planetary, and Astronomical Cyber-Experience Present...Ask An Astronaut.* [Online] Available http://www.nss.org/askastro/#question, April 3, 1996.

Duarte, Luis Sánchez. SOHO-Solar and Heliospheric Observatory Home Page. [Online] Available http://sohowww.nascom.nasa.gov/, July 17, 1996.

Dumoulin, Jim. Space Shuttle Orbiter Atlantis. [Online] Available http://www.ksc.nasa.gov/shuttle/resources/orbiters/atlantis.html, April 6, 1996.

Dumoulin, Jim. Space Shuttle Orbiter Challenger. [Online] Available http://www.ksc.nasa.gov/shuttle/resources/orbiters/challenger.html, April 6, 1996.

Dumoulin, Jim. Space Shuttle Orbiter Columbia. [Online] Available http://www.ksc.nasa.gov/shuttle/resources/orbiters/columbia.html, April 6, 1996.

Dumoulin, Jim. Space Shuttle Orbiter Discovery. [Online] Available http://www.ksc.nasa.gov/shuttle/resources/orbiters/discovery.html, April 6, 1996.

Dumoulin, Jim. Space Shuttle Orbiter Endeavour. [Online] Available http://www.ksc.nasa.gov/shuttle/resources/orbiters/endeavour.html, April 6, 1996.

Educator's Guide to Convection. [Online] Available http://bang.lanl.gov/solarsys/edu/convect.html, April 22, 1996.

Educator's Guide to Eclipses. [Online] Available http://bang.lanl.gov/solarsys/edu/eclipses.html, April 22, 1996.

Frommert, Hartmut. M31: The Andromeda Galaxy. [Online] Available http://ftp.seds.org/messier/m/m031.html, April 30, 1996.

George Ellery Hale. *The Bruce Medalists-Brief Biographies*. [Online] Available http://yorty.sonoma.edu/people/faculty/tenn/BM2H-L.html#13, June 5, 1996.

Goldstein, Bruce E. Welcome to the Ulysses Mission Home Page! [Online] Available http://ulysses.jpl.nasa.gov/ULSHOME.html, May 30, 1996.

Grote Reber. *The Bruce Medalists-Brief Biographies*. [Online] Available http://yorty.sonoma.edu/people/faculty/tenn/BM2Q-R.html#55, June 5, 1996.

Haizen's Astrology FAQ. [Online] Available http://www.sedona.net/nen/haizen/faq.html, April 12, 1996.

Hamilton, Calvin J. Chronology of Space Exploration. [Online] Available http://bang.lanl.gov/solarsys/craft2.html, April 22, 1996.

Hamilton, Calvin J. Magellan Mission to Venus. [Online] Available http://bang.lanl.gov/solarsys/magellan.html, April 22, 1996.

Hamilton, Calvin J. Neptune. [Online] Available http://bang.lanl.gov/solarsys/neptune.html, July 11, 1996.

Hamilton, Calvin J. Saturn. [Online] Available http://bang.lanl.gov/solarsys/saturn.htm#stats, March 26, 1996.

Hamilton, Calvin J. Sun. [Online] Available http://bang.lanl.gov/solarsys/sun.html, April 22, 1996.

Hamilton, Calvin J. Uranus. [Online] Available http://bang.lanl.gov/solarsys/uranus.html, April 22, 1996.

Hamilton, Calvin J. Venus Introduction. [Online] Available http://bang.lanl.gov/solarsys/venus.html, April 22, 1996.

Hamilton, Calvin J. Venusian Impact Craters.[Online] Available http://bang.lanl.gov/solarsys/vencrate.html, April 22, 1996.

Hamilton, Calvin J. Venusian Volcanic Features. [Online] Available http://bang.lanl.gov/solarsys/venvolc.html, April 22, 1996.

Hamilton, Calvin J. Voyager Uranus Science Summary: December 21, 1988. [Online] Available http://bang.lanl.gov/solarsys/vgrur.html, April 22, 1996.

Harris, Pete. Star Facts: The Andromeda Galaxy—The Most Distant Thing Human Eyes Can See. [Online] Available http://ccnet4.ccnet.com/odyssey/sfa995.html, April 30, 1996.

Harvard-Smithsonian Center for Astrophysics (CfA). [Online] Available http://sao~www.harvard.edu/hco~home.html, July 17, 1996.

Hathaway, David H. Skylab. [Online] Available http://ally.ios.com/~skylab19/skylab19.html, March 22, 1996.

Hill, Frank. The National Solar Observatory at Kitt Peak. [Online] Available http://www.nso.noao.edu/nsokp/nsokp.html, July 17, 1996.

Hoffman, Kay. Shuttle/Mir. [Online] Available http://shuttle-mir.nass.gov/, May 8, 1996.

The Infrared Space Observatory (ISO). [Online] Available http://isowww.estec.esa.nl/ISO/ISO.html, March 27, 1996.

Intelsat. [Online] Available http://www.intelsat.int:8080/info/html/intelsat.html, May 21, 1996.

International Space Station: Frequently Asked Questions. [Online] Available http://issa-www.jsc.nasa.gov/ss/sshpt.html, March 28, 1996.

International Ultraviolet Explorer Satellite. [Online] Available http://inewwww.gsfc.nasa.gov/iue/iue_homepage.html, March 27, 1996.

Introduction to SOHO. [Online] Available http://vulcan.sp.ph.ic.ac.uk/SOHO/soho/html, July 22, 1996.

Irving, Don. Mt. Hamilton and Lick Observatory. *XPLORE Tours*. [Online] Available http://www.ucolick.org/, June 5, 1996.

James Clerk Maxwell. [Online] Available http://www~groups.dcs.st~and.ac.uk/~history/Mathematicians/, June 5, 1996.

Jenkins, Dawn. Maya Astronomy Page. [Online] Available http://www.astro.uv.nl/michielb/maya/astro.html, July 25, 1996.

Johannesson, Anders. Big Bear Solar Observatory www page. [Online] Available http://sundog.caltech.edu/, July 26, 1996.

JPL Space Very Long Baseline Interferometry Project. [Online] Available http://sgra.jpl.nasa.gov/mosaic_v0.0/svlbi.html, June 3, 1996.

Judith Resnik. *STS 51-L (Challenger) Crew Biography.* [Online] Available http://flight.osc.on.ca/documenta-tion/judy.html, May 9, 1996.

Judith A. Resnik: Biography. *The Challenger Accident: January 28, 1986.* [Online] Available http://www.dartmouth.edu/~wsk/challenger/resnik.html, May 9, 1996.

King, J. H. Pioneer 10. *NSSDC Master Catalog Display Spacecraft.* [Online] Available http:nssdc.gsfc.nasa.gov/cgi-bin/database/www-nmc?72-012A, June 18, 1996.

King, J. H. Pioneer 11. *NSSDC Master Catalog Display Spacecraft.* [Online] Available http:nssdc.gsfc.nasa.gov/cgi-bin/database/www-nmc?73-019A, June 18, 1996.

King, J. H. Voyager Project Information. [Online] Available http:nssdc.gsfc.nasa.gov/planetary/voyager.html, June 18, 1996.

Kitt Peak. [Online] Available http://www.noao.edu/kpno/pubpamph/pub.html, April 7, 1996.

Launius, Roger D. Chronology of Selected Highlights in the First 100 American Spaceflights, 1961-1995. [Online] Available http://www.hq.nasa.gov/office/pao/History/Time-line/100flt.html, April 4, 1996.

Levine, Deborah A. Brief Introduction to IRAS. [Online] Available http://www.gsfc.nasa.gov/astro/iras/iras_home.html, March 27, 1996.

Liebacher, John. Global Oscillation Network Group. [Online] Available http://www.gong.noao.edu/, July 17, 1996.

Lyndon B. Johnson Space Center. Biographical Data: Shannon W. Lucid. [Online] Available http://www.jsc.nasa.gov/Bios/htmlbios/lucid.html, May 9, 1996.

Maarten Schmidt. *The Bruce Medalists-Brief Biogra-phies.* [Online] Available http://yorty.sonoma.edu/people/faculty/tenn/BM2S.html#85, June 5, 1996.

MacRobert, Alan. When, Where, and How to See Comet Hyakutake. [Online] Available http://www.skypub.com, March 23, 1996.

Malin, David. General Information About the AAO. [Online] Available http://www.aao.gov.au/general.html, April 4, 1996.

Mariner Space Probes. [Online] Available http://www.hq.nasa.gov/office/pao/History/mariner.html, May 30, 1996.

Mars 96. [Online] Available http://www.iki.rssi.ru/mars96/mars96hp.html, July 2, 1996.

Mauna Kea Observatories. [Online] Available http://www.ifa.hawaii.edu/mko/mko.html, April 7, 1996.

McClaughlin, Siobhan. Anglo-Australian Observatory. [Online] Available http://www.aao.gov.au/aaohome-page.html, April 4, 1996.

McCurdy, Andrea and Mark Stokes. Jim Lovell: An As-tronaut's Story. [Online] Available http://www.mcn.org/Apollo 13/Home.html, May 9, 1996.

McDonald Observatory Visitors Center Home Page. [On-line] Available http://vulcan.as.utexas.edu//vc/vc_home.html, June 5, 1996.

McDonnell Douglas Spacelab Homepage. [Online] Avail-able http://hvsun21.mdc.com:8000/~mosaic/main.html, July 15, 1996.

Napier, Beth. Activity: Precession of the Equinoxes. [On-line] Available http://cea-ftp.cea.berkeley.edu/Edu-cation/beth/precess.html, April 12, 1996.

NASA Headquarters. International Space Station. [On-line] Available http://www.dfrc.nasa.gov/PAIS/HQ/HTML/FS-004-HQ.html, May 8, 1996.

NASA Headquarters. An Overview of NASA. [Online] Available http://www.dfrc.nasa.gov/PAIS/HQ/HTML/FS-001-HQ.html, May 8, 1996.

National Solar Observatory. [Online] Available http://argo.tuc.noao.edu/, March 22, 1996.

Naumann, Michael. ESO Telescopes, Instrumentation & Detectors. [Online] Available http://www.hq.eso.org/telescopes-instruments.html, April 7, 1996.

Nemiroff, Robert and Jerry Bonnell. Astronomy Picture of the Day. M31: The Andromeda Galaxy. [Online] Available http://antwrp.gsfc.nasa.gov/apod/ap950724.html, May 1, 1996.

Neufeld, Christopher. The Physics of Solar Sailing. [On-line] Available http://caliban.physics.utoronto.ca/neufeld/sailing.txt, March 21, 1996.

Pluto Express Home Page. [Online] Available http://www.jpl.nasa.gov/pluto/, July 22, 1996.

Project Mercury. [Online] Available http://www.osf.hq.nasa.gov/mercury/, May 8, 1996.

Rapp, Michael. Dr. Carl Sagan Honorary Page. [Online] Available http://wwwvms.utexas.edu/~mrapp/sagan/sagan.html, March 18, 1996.

Reflection. [Online] Available http://covis.atmos.uiuc.edu/guide/optics/html/reflection.html, June 14, 1996.

Refraction. [Online] Available http://covis.atmos.uiuc.edu/guide/optics/html/refraction.html, June 14, 1996.

Rudd, Richard. Voyager Project Home Page. [Online] Available http://vraptor.jpl.nasa.gov/voyager/voyager.html, July 2, 1996.

Sally Kristen Ride. Juanita Kreps Award. [Online] Available http:www.jcpenney.com/nrelease/jkreps/content/sride.html, May 9, 1996.

Sargent, Wallace W. Caltech Astronomy: Keck Observatory. [Online] Available http://astro.caltech.edu/observatories/keck/bluebook.html, April 7, 1996.

Satellite Tracking of Threatened Species. [Online] Available http://sdcd.gsfc.nasa.gov/ISTO/satellite_tracking/satelliteDRO.html, June 25, 1996.

Search for Extraterrestrial Radio Emissions from Nearby Developed Intelligent Populations (SERENDIP). [Online] Available http://albert.ssl.berkeley.edu/serendip/, April 12, 1996.

Simmons, Michael. The History of Mount Wilson Observatory. [Online] Available http:www.mtwilson.edu/history/history.html, June 5, 1996.

Simon Newcomb. *The Bruce Medalists-Brief Biographies*. [Online] Available http://yorty.sonoma.edu/people/faculty/tenn/BM2MN.html#1, June 5, 1996.

Smith, Woody. The Flights of Project Gemini. [Online] Available http://www.osf.hq.nasa.gov/gemini/, May 8, 1996.

Smith, Woody. STS-71 Press Kit: The Space Station Mir. [Online] Available http://www.osf.hq.nasa.gov/shuttle/sts71/mir.html, May 8, 1996.

Smithsonian Astrophysical Observatory. [Online] Available http://cfa~www.harvard.edu/sao~home.html, May 27, 1996.

SOHO Ultraviolet Coronograph Spectrometer-UVCS. [Online] Available http://sao~www.harvard.edu/uvcs/, July 17, 1996.

SOHO-CDS at Imperial College. [Online] Available http://www.sp.ph.ic.ac.uk/SOHO/, July 22, 1996.

Solar and Heliospheric Observatory (SOHO). [Online] Available http://www.hq.nasa.gov/office/oss/enterprise/II/ii-soh82.html, July 22, 1996.

Space Shuttle Launches. [Online] Available http://www.ksc.nasa.gov/shuttle/missions/missions.html, July 15, 1996).

Space Telescopes. [Online] Available http://meteor.anu.edu.au/anton/astro_space.html, March 27, 1996.

Spacecraft: SOHO Brief Description. [Online] Available http://www~istp.gsfc.nasa.gov/ISTP/soho.html, July 22, 1996.

Spacelab. [Online] Available http://www.ksc.nasa.gov/shuttle/technology/sts-newsref/spacelab.html, July 15, 1996.

Spend an Out-of-this-World Evening at McDonald Observatory. [Online] Available http://numedia.tddc.net/hot/bigbend/mdo, June 5, 1996.

Stanton, Ed. Six Reasons Why America Needs the Space Station. [Online] Available http://issa-www.jsc.nasa.gov/ss/prgview/prgview.html, March 28, 1996.

STS-75 Payloads: TSS-1R, USMP-3 & MGBX. [Online] Available http://liftoff.msfc.nasa.gov/sts-75/welcome.html, May 8, 1996.

Tethered Satellite System (TSS-1R). [Online] Available http://liftoff.msfc.nasa.gov/sts-75/tss-1r/tss-1r.html, May 8, 1996.

Tribute to Carl Sagan. [Online] Available http://wea.mankato.mn.us:80/tps/sagan.html, March 18, 1996.

Urbain Jean Joseph Le Verrier. [Online] Available http://www~groups.dcs.st~and.ac.uk/~history/Mathematicians/, June 5, 1996.

Weisstein, Eric. Janksy, Karl (1905-1950). *Eric's Home Page*. [Online] Available http://www.gps.caltech.edu/~eww/bios/jnode2.html#SECTIONO, June 5, 1996.

Welcome to CTIO! [Online] Available http://www.ctio.noao.edu/ctio.html#visitors, April 7, 1996.

Welcome to Lowell Observatory.[Online] Available http://www.lowell.edu/, May 27, 1996.

Welcome to the Yerkes Observatory Virtual Tour! [Online] Available http://astro.uchicago.edu/vtour/, June 5, 1996.

What is the VLA? [Online] Available
http://www.nrao.edu/doc/vla/html/VLAintro.html,
June 5, 1996.

Wirth, Fred. Pioneer Project Home Page. [Online] Available
http://pyroeis.arc.nasa.gov/pioneer/PNhome.html,
July 2, 1996.

Wyoming Infrared Observatory. [Online] Available
http://faraday.uwyo.edu/physics.astronomy/
brochures/wiro.html, July 17, 1996.

Yerkes Observatory, University of Chicago. [Online]
Available http://astro.uchicago.edu/Yerkes.html,
June 5, 1996.

Index

Italic type indicates volume numbers;
boldface type indicates entries and their page numbers;
(ill.) indicates illustrations.

Astrometric binary star *1:* 53, 63; *3:* 623

Astrometry *3:* 658

Astronomer Royal *1:* 69, 207, 216

Astronomical Almanac 3: 659

Astronomical Society of the Pacific *3:* 536

Astronomical unit (AU) *1:* 85; *2:* 305

Astronomy 3: 557

Astronomy websites *1:* 15

Astrophysical Journal 3: 501

Astrophysics *1:* 94, 200

AT&T *1:* 104

Attila the Hun *1:* 98

Atlantis 1: **42-44,** 43 (ill.), 90, 96, 106, 127, 149, 172, 176; *2:* 336-37, 349, 385, 395; *3:* 580, 586, 591, 607, 636

Atlas rocket *2:* 316, 369

Atmospheric Compensation Experiment *2:* 394

Atomic bomb *1:* 55, 145

Aurora australis *1:* 44, 117

Aurora borealis *1:* 44, 45 (ill.), 117

Aurorae *1:* 9, **44-45;** *3:* 573, 630, 638, 662

Autumnal equinox *1:* 152

B

Baade, Walter *1:* 19, **47-50,** 48 (ill.); *2:* 256, 421, 436; *3:* 704

Ballistic missile. *See* Intercontinental ballistic missile (ICBM)

Barnard, Edward E. *3:* 701

Barnard Observatory *3:* 539

Barred spiral galaxy *1:* 168; *3:* 615

Barringer meteor crater *2:* 375 (ill.)

Bassett, Charles A. *1:* 180

Baum, L. Frank *1:* 129

Bean, Alan *1:* 108

Bell Burnell, Jocelyn *1:* 47, **50-52,** 192; *2:* 244-45, 412, 461; *3:* 494, 520

Bell Telephone Laboratories *1:* 104

Belyayev, Pavel *2:* 323; *3:* 680

Bennett, David *1:* 124

Benzenberg, Johann *2:* 376

Beregovoy, Georgi *3:* 576

Berlin Observatory *1:* 2; *2:* 325

Bessel, Friedrich *1:* **52-53,** 52 (ill.), 62, 70; *2:* 428

Bethe, Hans *1:* **53-56,** 54 (ill.), 140

Big bang theory *1:* 31, **56-59,** 57 (ill.), 61, 113, 117, 120, 176-77, 191-92; *2:* 250, 256, 262, 267, 320, 410, 438-39, 449, 451-52; *3:* 489, 494, 498, 515, 546, 619

Big Bear Solar Observatory *1:* **59-60;** *2:* 402

Big bore theory *1:* 60

Big crunch theory *1:* **60-61,** 125

Big dipper *1:* 159; *2:* 445; *3:* 570

Billion-channel Extra-Terrestrial Assay *1:* 159

Binary star *1:* **62-63,** 66; *2:* 328, 387, 419; *3:* 541, 621-22, 651, 676, 694, 696

Binary star system *1:* 62 (ill.)

Biot, Jean-Baptiste *2:* 376

Black dwarf star *1:* 61, 123; *2:* 394, 398-400; *3:* 506, 513, 532, 580, 586, 593, 596-97, 599, 605, 636-38, 653, 691, 705

Black hole *1:* 3, 18, 22, 61, **63-66,** 64 (ill.), 93, 106, 123, 140, 167, 169, 175-76, 195, 214, 220; *2:* 274, 311, 314, 328, 380, 411, 417, 420-21; *3:* 488, 503, 589, 614, 622, 631, 651, 676, 691, 695, 697, 701, 705

Bloch, Felix *2:* 463

Blue-shift *3:* 504, 552

Bluford, Guion *1:* **66-68,** 90

Bode, Johann Elert *1:* 37, **68-69,** 68 (ill.), 111

Bode's Law *1:* 37, 68-69

Bohr, Neils *1:* 176

Bolometer *1:* 147; *2:* 309

Bolshevik Revolution *3:* 648

Bonaparte, Napoleon *2:* 308

Bondi, Hermann *1:* 121; *2:* 250

Bondone, Giotto Ambrogio di *1:* 183

Borman, Frank *3:* 545

The Boston Herald 1: 188

Bradley, James *1:* **69-70,** 69 (ill.); *3:* 514, 612

Brahe, Tycho *1:* **70-73,** 71 (ill.), 85, 119; *2:* 294, 390, 420, 446; *3:* 553

Brand, Vance *1:* 27

Brandes, Heinrich *2:* 376

Braun, Wernher von *1:* **73-76,** 74 (ill.), 156; *2:* 425; *3:* 513, 532, 665

Brezhnev, Leonid *1:* 27; *2:* 323

A Brief History of Time 1: 215

Brown dwarfs *1:* 61, **76-77,** 77 (ill.), 123; *2:* 300, 406-07; *3:* 624, 659, 705

Brownian movement *1:* 143

Brunhes, Bernard *1:* 138

Bunsen, Robert *2:* 297

Bureau of Longitudes *1:* 28

Burke, Bernard *3:* 494

Burney, Venetia *3:* 646

Burrell-Schmidt telescope *2:* 299

Butler, Paul *1:* 159; *2:* 445; *3:* 569

Bykovsky, Valery *3:* 635

C

C. Donald Shane Telescope *2:* 328

C-141 Starlifter *2:* 302

Caesar, Julius *1:* 79, 98

Calendar *1:* 8, 10-11, 14, **79-81,** 80 (ill.); *2:* 453, 459; *3:* 514, 625

Calendar of Works and Days, 1281 1: 9

Callipus *1:* 13

Caloris Basin *2:* 368

CalTech Submillimeter Observatory *2:* 362

Cambridge Observatory *1:* 2, 140; *2:* 325; *3:* 517

Cannon, Annie Jump *1:* **81-83,** 82 (ill.)

Cape Canaveral *1:* 24; *2:* 293, 337, 398; *3:* 505

Capture trajectory *3:* 604

Carnegie, Andrew *1:* 200; *3:* 516

Carnegie Institution *1:* 152; *2:* 391, 437; *3:* 515-16, 661

Carpenter, Scott *2:* 369, 371

Carter, Jimmy *3:* 658, 686

Cassini, Gian Domenico *1:* **83-85,** 84 (ill.); *3:* 513, 530

Cassini 3: 531, 581

Cassini Division *1:* 85; *3:* 530

Catherine Wolfe Bruce Medal *3:* 536

Cavendish, Henry *1:* 193

Cavendish Laboratory *1:* 54

Celestial mechanics *2:* 319

Celestial Mechanics 2: 311, 413

Celestial Police *1:* 69

Celestial sphere *1:* 42, 108

Centaur rocket *1:* 174; *2:* 317, 400; *3:* 510 (ill.)

Centaurus A *2:* 449

Cepheid variables *1:* 19, 49, **85-87,** 220; *2:* 248, 254, 318, 404, 436; *3:* 541-42, 618, 632, 666

Ceres *1:* 36-37, 119, 178; *2:* 427; *3:* 566

Cernan, Eugene *1:* 182

Cerro Tololo Interamerican Observatory *1:* **87-89,** 88 (ill.), 130, 152; *2:* 298, 313, 400, 402

Cesarsky, Catherine *2:* 274

CGRO. *See* Compton Gamma Ray Observatory

Chaffee, Roger *1:* 23; *3:* 596, 689

Challenger 1: 36, 44, 66, **90-92,** 91 (ill.), 94, 96, 114, 125, 127, 134, 149, 161-63, 173; *2:* 257, 316, 395; *3:* 505-07, 513, 585 (ill.), 586, 592, 653, 685

Chandrasekhar, Subrahmanyan *1:* **92-94,** 93 (ill.), 140; *2:* 417, 421; *3:* 701

Chandrasekhar's limit *1:* 93; *2:* 421

Chang-Diaz, Franklin *1:* 96

Charged coupling device (CCD) *1:* 20; *2:* 440

Charon *2:* 305, 388, 456-57; *3:* 659

Chiron *1:* 38

Chladni, E. F. F. *2:* 375

Christian constellations *1:* 111

Christian IV *1:* 73

Christy, James *3:* 659

Chromatic aberration *2:* 432

Chromosphere *2:* 394; *3:* 555-56

Chronometer *2:* 402

Civil War *2:* 414

Clairaut, Alexis *1:* 209

Clark, Alvan G. *1:* 53; *2:* 335

Clark Telescope *2:* 336

Clarke, Arthur C. *1:* 102

Clementine 2: 345

Clocks *1:* 9; *2:* 263; *3:* 514, 642

Coal Sack nebula *2:* 406

COBE. See Cosmic Background Explorer

Cochran, Anita L. *2:* 306

Cold war *1:* 26; *2:* 321; *3:* 513, 582

Collins, Eileen M. *1:* 127

Collins, Michael *1:* 6, 23, 35; *3:* 582, 592, 596

Columbia 1: 44, 90, **94-96,** 95 (ill.), 125, 127, 149, 162; *2:* 338, 394-95; *3:* 507, 584, 586, 606-07

Comet Grigg-Skellerup *1:* 184

Comet Hale-Bopp *3:* 694

Comet Hyakutake *1:* **96-98,** 97 (ill.); *3:* 694

Comet Kohoutek *3:* 550, 588

Comet Shoemaker-Levy *2:* 280; *3:* 676

Comet Tempel-2 *2:* 271

Comets *1:* 7, 12, 71, 96-97, **98-100,** 136, 182, 184, 204, 206-07, 209, 211-12, 216-17; *2:* 253, 260, 271, 280, 291, 296, 298, 300, 306, 335, 373, 377, 386, 389, 401, 406-07, 426-31, 437, 443, 445, 454, 458; *3:* 531, 535, 565-66, 573, 590, 602, 646-47, 652-54, 659, 692, 694

Command module *1:* 22, 25, **100-02,** 101 (ill.); *2:* 345; *3:* 565, 596, 689

Communications satellite *1:* 44, 66, **102-05,** 103 (ill.); *2:* 438

Communications Satellite Corporation (Comsat) *1:* 104; *2:* 274

Compass *2:* 402

A Compendium of Spherical Astronomy 2: 415

Compton, Arthur Holly *1:* 105

Compton Gamma Ray Observatory *1:* 44, **105-06,** 176; *3:* 591

Comsat. *See* Communications Satellite Corporation (Comsat)

Concerning a New Star 1: 71

Congreve, William *3:* 511

Connaissance des Temps 2: 372

Connelly, Mary Lois *3:* 528

Conrad, Charles *1:* **107-08,** 180

Constellations *1:* 13, 42, 66, **108-11,** 109 (ill.), 206, 217; *2:* 282, 285, 295, 306, 373, 377, 404, 406, 444, 452, 459; *3:* 488, 493, 500, 519, 569, 631, 652, 694-95, 697

Convection *3:* 555

Convection zone *3:* 627

Cook, James *1:* 125, 149

Cooper, Gordon *1:* 107, 180; *2:* 369, 371

Copernican model. *See* Heliocentric model

Copernicus, Nicholas *1:* 14, 40, 53, **111-113,** 111 (ill.), 119, 131, 138, 171-72; *2:* 253, 390, 416-17, 445-46, 460; *3:* 660

Corona *1:* 4; *3:* 554-56, 558, 572-73, 627, 652, 654

Coronagraph *3:* 571

Corrective Optics Space Telescope Axial Replacement (COSTAR) *2:* 258

Cosmic Background Explorer 1: 58, **113-15,** 192; *2:* 252-53; *3:* 620

Cosmic dust *3:* 281-82, 387

Cosmic radiation *2:* 279

Cosmic rays *1:* **115-17,** 212; *2:* 243, 253, 442; *3:* 590, 629-30, 654, 661, 663, 688

Cosmic rays research *1:* 116 (ill.)

Cosmic string *1:* **117-18**

Cosmological constant *3:* 546

Cosmological principle *3:* 619

Cosmology *1:* **118-21,** 191; *2:* 256

Cosmos 3: 592

COSPAS-SARSAT 2: 403

COSTAR. *See* Corrective Optics Space Telescope Axial Replacement (COSTAR)

Coudé telescope *2:* 328

Countdown 3: 596

Cowan, Clyde L. Jr. *2:* 410

Crab nebula *2:* 373, 405, 412, 461; *3:* 494, 688, 696-97

Crafoord Prize *3:* 526, 528

Crookes, William *2:* 450

Curtis, Heber *3:* 542

Cygnus *1:* 111; *2:* 406; *3:* 493, 519, 694, 696-97

Cygnus 1992 *3:* 694

Cygnus X-1 *1:* 66

Cyril *2:* 266

D

Daguerreotype camera *1:* 163

Dark matter *1:* 18, 61, **123-25,** 124 (ill.), 148, 168; *2:* 365, 381, 436; *3:* 515-16, 614, 703, 705

Dark rift *2:* 281, 387

Daylight savings time *3:* 644

De caelo 1: 13, 32

De nova stella 1: 71

De Revolutionibus Orbium Coelestium 1: 112-13, 119, 171

Decan stars *1:* 10

Deep Space Network *3:* 554

Deimos *2:* 355; *3:* 657

Delaunay, Charles-Eugene *2:* 326

Delisle, Joseph Nicolas *2:* 372

Delta rocket *2:* 316

Deoxyribonucleic acid (DNA) *3:* 522

Depot of Charts and Instruments *3:* 657

Descartes, René *2:* 262, 264, 416; *3:* 553

Deslandres, Henri-Alexandre *3:* 571

Détente *1:* 27

Dialogo di Galilei linceo . . . sopra I due massimi sistemi del mondo 1: 172

Dialogue Concerning the Two Chief World Systems 1: 172

Differential forces *3:* 639

Differential rotation *3:* 562

Diffraction of light *1:* 197

Dinosaurs *1:* 38

Dirac, Paul A. M. *1:* 21

Discovery 1: 44, 67, 90, 96, **125-27,** 126 (ill.), 149; *2:* 257, 337, 395; *3:* 505-06, 590, 653

Dobrovolsky, Georgi *3:* 578

Doppler, Christian Johann *1:* 119; *3:* 503

Doppler effect *3:* 503

Dörffel, Georg Samuel *1:* 98, 208

Douglass, Andrew *2:* 333

Draco *3:* 488

Drake, Frank *1:* **128-30,** 129 (ill.), 159

Draper, Henry *1:* 82

Dresden Codex *1:* 17

Druids *3:* 624

Druyan, Anna *3:* 523

Dryden Flight Research Center (DFRC) *2:* 400

Dwarf galaxy *1:* 123, 149; *2:* 272; *3:* 616, 693

Dynamical system *1:* **130-31**

Dynamics *1:* 130

E

E=mc² *1:* 144

Early Bird 2: 276-77

Earth Radiation Budget Satellite (ERBS) 1: 134; *3:* 507

Earth Resources Technology Satellite (ERTS) 1: 133

Earth survey satellite *1:* **133-34**

Earth's atmosphere *1:* 3, 8, 26, 43-44, 59, 87, 92, 94, 98, 100, **134-37,** 135 (ill.), 153, 167, 175, 185, 188; *2:* 243, 246-47, 272, 279, 302, 309, 316, 341, 360, 365, 369, 374, 376-77; *3:* 511, 521, 524-25, 550, 564, 572-73, 576, 584, 587, 589, 591, 593-94, 597-600, 604, 636-38, 651-52, 661, 682, 688, 695, 697, 700

Earth's magnetic field *1:* 44, **137-38,** 178, 207, 402; *3:* 573, 661

Earth's rotation *1:* 9, 108, **138-39,** 152; *2:* 380, 414; *3:* 498, 602, 639, 659

Earth's rotation experiment *1:* 139 (ill.)

Echo 1: 104; *2:* 317, 438

Eclipse. *See* Lunar eclipse *and* Solar eclipse

Goddard, Robert *1:* 6, **188-91,** 189 (ill.); *2:* 423; *3:* 511
Goddard Space Flight Center (GSFC) *2:* 280, 399; *3:* 554
Gold, Thomas *1:* 51, 121, **191-93,** 191 (ill.); *2:* 245, 250, 412, 461; *3:* 619
Goldin, Daniel *1:* 160; *2:* 357
Gordon, Richard *1:* 107
Goryacheva, Valentina Ivanovna *1:* 167
Göttingen Observatory *1:* 178
Grand Unified Theory *1:* 215
Grant, Ulysses S. *2:* 377
Granules *3:* 561, *3:* 627
Gravity *1:* 56, 61-62, 107, 120, 131, 139-40, 142, 145, 172, 182, **193-95,** 206, 208, 214-15; *2:* 320, 340, 412, 418; *3:* 546, 598, 600, 602, 609, 622, 631, 639, 666, 690
Gravity assist *1:* 172; *3:* 604
Grazing incidence telescope *2:* 246
Great Debate *3:* 542
Great Galaxy *1:* 19
Great Mathematical Compilation 1: 12; *2:* 459
Great Pyramid *1:* 10-11
The Greatest 2: 459
Green Bank Telescope *3:* 675
Greenhouse effect *1:* **195-97,** 196 (ill.); *3:* 673
Greenstein, Jesse *3:* 536
Greenwich Observatory *1:* 207
Gregorian calendar *1:* 81; *3:* 514
Gregory X *3: 1:* 80
Grimaldi, Francesco *1:* 83, **197-98**
Grissom, Virgil "Gus" *1:* 23, 76, 179; *2:* 369; *3:* 594, 596, 689
Group for the Study of Jet Propulsion (GIRD) *2:* 300
Gurman, Joseph *3:* 555
Guth, Alan *1:* 58; *2:* 267-68
Gyroscope *1:* 164; *2:* 259

H

H-K Project *2:* 394
Haise, Fred *1:* 24
Hale, George *1:* **199-203;** *2:* 249-50, 253, 261, 391, 435; *3:* 571, 700
Hale Observatories *3:* 527, 534, 536
Hale Telescope *1:* 202 (ill.), **203-04;** *2:* 250, 256, 314, 435, 436 (ill.); *3:* 488, 535
Hall, Asaph *3:* 657
Halley, Edmond *1:* 98, **204-07,** 205 (ill.), 208; *2:* 296, 307, 375, 417-18
Halley's comet *1:* 52, 96-97, 99, 155, 182, 184, **207-09,** 208 (ill.), 210; *2:* 304, 306, 372, 428; *3:* 564, 667-68, 694
Halo *1:* 18, 168; *2:* 381; *3:* 614
Halo orbit *3:* 554
Hard X-rays *1:* 3; *3:* 695, 697

Hariot, Thomas. *See* Harriot, Thomas
Harlan Smith Telescope *2:* 366
Harper, William Rainey *1:* 200; *3:* 701
Harriot, Thomas *1:* **209-10**
Harvard College Observatory *1:* 81, 199; *2:* 318, 414; *3:* 542-43, 687
Harvard-Smithsonian Center for Astrophysics *1:* **210-13;** *3:* 687
Hawking, Stephen *1:* 65, **213-15,** 213 (ill.)
Hawking radiation *1:* 65, 214
HEAO-1 *2:* 246
HEAO-3 *2:* 246
Heavenly Spheres 1: 112
Helen B. Warner Prize *3:* 536
Heliacal rising *1:* 17
Heliocentric model *1:* 72, 112, 118, 131, 138, 172; *2:* 445; *3:* 567
Helios 1 3: 629
Helios 2 3: 629
Helioseismograph *1:* 60
Heliosphere *3:* 553
Heliostat *2:* 401; *3:* 571-72
Heliotrope *1:* 178
Hellas *2:* 355
Henry, Joseph *2:* 413
Henry Draper Catalogue of Stars *1:* 82
Heraclitus *1:* 12
Hercules *1:* 111
Hermes *1:* 38
Hero of Alexandria *3:* 509
Herschel, Caroline *1:* **215-16,** 215 (ill.)
Herschel, John *1:* 2, 62, 216
Herschel, William *1:* 1, 37, 62, 119, 215, **216-18,** 217 (ill.); *2:* 444; *3:* 654, 656
Hertz, Rudolf Heinrich *1:* 147
Hertzsprung, Ejnar *1:* **218-20;** *3:* 518
Hertzsprung-Russell diagram *1:* 219 (ill.), 220; *3:* 518, 631
Hess, Victor *1:* 115; *2:* **243,** 243 (ill.)
Hevelius, Johannes *1:* 98, 208; *2:* 390
Hewish, Antony *1:* 47, 50, 192; *2:* **244-45,** 244 (ill.), 412, 461; *3:* 494, 520
High Energy Astrophysical Observatories *1:* 4, 106; *2:* **246;** *3:* 590, 696
High Precision Parallax Collecting Satellite *2:* 247
Hipparchus *1:* 13, 14; *2:* 247, 459
Hipparcos 2: 247
Hitler, Adolf *1:* 54, 73, 145; *3:* 543
Hobby-Eberly Telescope (HET) *2:* 364
Hogg, Frank *2:* 248
Hogg, Helen Sawyer *2:* **247;** *3:* 667
Homogeneity *1:* 58; *2:* 268
Hooker, John D. *1:* 201; *2:* 249, 393
Hooker Telescope *1:* 201; *2:* **248-50,** 254, 256, 380, 404, 435
Horoscope *1:* 42
Horowitz, Paul *1:* 160

Hourglass *3:* 642
House Un-American Activities Committee *3:* 543
Hoyle, Fred *2:* **250-53,** 251 (ill.); *3:* 619
Hubble, Edwin *1:* 19, 49, 58, 86, 114, 120, 169, 192; *2:* 249, 252, **253-57,** 255 (ill.), 261, 267, 320, 382, 391, 404, 430; *3:* 504, 526-27, 542, 548, 552, 619
Hubble constant *2:* 259
Hubble Space Telescope *1:* 2, 19, 87, 97, 118, 121, 127, 151, 155, 160, 169; *2:* 256, **257-59,** 258 (ill.), 280, 305, 314, 318, 395, 434, 455; *3:* 531, 589-90, 592
Hubble's Law *2:* 256, 261; *3:* 527
Huggins, William *2:* **259-60,** 260 (ill.)
Humason, Milton *1:* 58; *2:* 254, 256, **261-62;** *3:* 504, 527
Hummel, Mathilde *2:* 424
Huxley, Aldous *2:* 417
Huygens, Christiaan *1:* 83; *2:* **262-64,** 262 (ill.), 364; *3:* 530-31, 553
Huygens 3: 531, 581
Hyakutake, Yuji *1:* 96
Hyakutake. *See* Comet Hyakutake
Hydrometer *2:* 265
Hydroscope *2:* 265
Hypatia of Alexandria *2:* **264-66,** 265 (ill.)

I

Icarus 3: 523
Ida *1:* 174
Inertia *1:* 131
Inflationary period *2:* 267
Inflationary theory *1:* 58; *2:* **267-68**
Infrared Astronomical Satellite *2:* **268-71,** 269 (ill.), 273, 305, 449; *3:* 590
Infrared astronomy *1:* 52, 77; *2:* **271-73,** 302, 335; *3:* 494, 518, 605, 692
Infrared galaxy *2:* 268, 363
Infrared radiation *1:* 20; *2:* 270-73, 302, 363, 393, 406, 449; *3:* 487, 491, 518, 539, 652
Infrared Space Observatory *2:* 271, **273-74;** *3:* 590
Infrared Spatial Interferometer *2:* 393
Infrared telescope *2:* 271, 273, 382, 406, 431; *3:* 701
Intelligent Life in Space 1: 130
Intelsat *1:* 104, 151; *2:* **274-77,** 275 (ill.)
Intensity curve *2:* 440
Intercontinental ballistic missile (ICBM) *2:* 301, 317; *3:* 512
Intercontinental VLBI *3:* 496
Interferential refractometer *2:* 379
Interferometer *1:* 160; *2:* 379, 393

532, 534, 544-45, 555, 566, 575, 579, 582, 587, 592-93, 596, 602, 639-40, 658

The Moon Car 2: 426

Moon rover 3: 601 (ill.)

Moonlets 2: 409

Moonscape 2: 390

Morelos 1: 337

Morley, Edward 2: 277, 379

Mount Hopkins Observatory 3: 687

Mount Wilson Institute 2: 393

Mount Wilson Observatory 1: 47, 86, 169, 199, 201, 203; 2: 248-49, 254, 261, 380, 382, **391-94**, 392 (ill.), 404, 435; 3: 526, 539, 541, 700, 703

Multi-Element Radio-Linked Interferometer Network (MERLIN) 3: 495

Multiple Mirror Telescope (MMT) 1: 212; 3: 687

Murmurs of Earth 3: 685

Muses-A 2: 345

Museum of Alexandria 2: 265

Musgrave, Storey 2: **394-95**, 394 (ill.)

My Grandmother Is an Astronomer 3: 517

Mysterium Cosmographicum 2: 295

Mystery of the Universe 2: 295

Mysticism 2: 294

Mythology 3: 655

N

NAFTA 1: 188

Napoleon. *See* Bonaparte, Napoleon

NASA. *See* National Aeronautics and Space Administration

NASA Infrared Telescope Facility 2: 362

Natal astrology 1: 42

National Academy of Sciences 3: 516

National Advisory Committee for Aeronautics (NACA) 1: 35, 156, 161; 2: 397, 399-400

National Aeronautics and Space Administration 1: 2, 22, 24, 35-36, 42, 58, 67, 76, 90, 104-07, 114, 130, 133, 149, 155, 159-61, 173, 180, 185, 192, 204; 2: 246, 252, 256, 278, 287, 293, 302, 304, 316-17, 329, 331, 337-38, 349, 351, 356, 366, 369-70, 372, 394, **397**, 400, 437, 442, 456-57; 3: 496, 506-07, 509, 512, 523, 531, 543, 550, 553-54, 563, 579-80, 582-84, 589-90, 594, 596, 605, 620, 636, 638, 651, 653, 663, 681, 683, 685, 696

National Geographic Society 2: 437

National Medal of Science 1: 76

National Optical Astronomy Observatories (NOAO) 1: 89; 2: 298, 313, 400

National Radio Astronomy Observatory (NRAO) 1: 129-130, 159; 3: 493, 498, 675

National Science Foundation 1: 29; 2: 299, 313

National Solar Observatory 1: 89; 2: 298, **400-02**; 3: 572

Navigational satellite 2: **402-04**

Navstar 2: 403

Nazis 1: 55, 75, 145, 156, 166; 2: 429; 3: 512, 543

Neap tides 3: 640

Nebula 1: 19, 86, 109, 148, 167, 216, 218; 2: 254, 257, 260, 281, 311, 334-35, 372, 387, **404-06**, 405 (ill.), 461, 494; 3: 503-04, 526, 542, 551, 568, 614, 622, 691

Nebular hypothesis 2: 311; 3: 568

Nelson, Bill 1: 96

Nemesis 2: **406-07**

Neptune 1: 1, 29, 69, 120, 134, 196; 2: 261, 305, 325, 334-35, 366, **407-09**, 408 (ill.), 444, 454-56; 3: 530, 565, 580, 604, 655, 685, 701

Nereid 2: 409

Neutrino 2: **409-11**, 412, 421

Neutrino research 2: 410 (ill.)

Neutron star 1: 22, 47, 51, 65, 93, 140, 192; 2: 243, 245, **411-12**, 420-21, 436, 449, 460; 3: 503, 520, 622, 691, 703-04

"New Mathematical Theory of Jupiter's Satellites" 3: 546

New Methods for the Determination of Orbits of Comets 2: 319

New moon 2: 348

Newcomb, Simon 2: **413-15**; 3: 657

Newton, Isaac 1: 99, 119, 131, 171, 178, 193-94, 208, 213, 215; 2: 297, 308, 311, 413, **415-18**, 416 (ill.), 419, 445-47; 3: 660

Newton's laws of motion 1: 215; 2: 296, **418-19**, 447

Nikolayev, Andrian 3: 635

Nixon, Richard 1: 27, 36

Nobel Prize 1: 22, 51, 94, 143; 2: 243, 245; 3: 526

North magnetic pole 1: 137

North pole 3: 574

North star 1: 8, 210; 3: 575

Northern lights 1: 117; 3: 573, 630, 638

Nouvelles méthodes pour la détermination des orbits des comets 2: 319

Nova 1: 8, 71, 106, 211; 2: 260, 280, 419-20; 3: 590, 647, 652-53, 692, 704

Nova and supernova 2: **419-21**

Nuclear bombs 3: 703

Nuclear fusion 1: 53, 55, 65, 76, 106, 140, 175-76; 3: 560, 569, 624, 628, 631, 690

Nuclear magnetic resonance (NMR) 2: 464; 3: 493

Nuclear resonance absorption 2: 461

Nutation 1: 70

O

Oak Ridge Observatory 1: 211-12

OAO Copernicus 3: 652

Oberon 3: 656

Oberth, Hermann 2: **423-26**, 424 (ill.); 3: 511

Observatorio del Teide 2: 402

Ocean Topography Experiment (TOPEX) 1: 134

Oersted, Hans Christian 1: 146

Olbers, Heinrich 1: 38, 52; **426-28**

Olbers' paradox 2: 428

Olympus Mons 2: 354

On the Heavens 1: 13, 32

Onizuka, Ellison 1: 127

Oort, Jan 1: 99, 120, 169; 2: 305, **429-30**, 429 (ill.), 494, 535

Oort cloud 1: 99; 2: 305-06, 407, 430, 445, 456; 3: 566

Open cluster 2: 453; 3: 617

Ophelia 3: 657

Oppenheimer, Robert 1: 55

Oppolzer, Theodor 2: **430-31**

Optical telescope 2: **431-34**,

Orbiting Solar Observatories 3: 652

Orestes 2: 265

Origins Project 1: 160

Oschin Telescope 2: 437

Osiander, Andreas 1: 113

Osiris 1: 11

Otto Struve Telescope 2: 365

Outside the Earth 3: 698

Owen, Toby 2: 291

Ozma of Oz 1: 129

Ozone layer 1: 106, 134, 136

P

Pacini, Franco 1: 51, 192; 2: 245, 461

Pale Blue Dot 3: 523

Palisa, Johann 1: 38

Pallas 1: 38; 2: 428

Palomar Observatory 1: 47, 49, 204; 2: 250, 256, 314, 433, **435-37**; 3: 488, 515-16, 526, 535

Palomar Observatories 3: 703

Palomar Sky Survey 2: 433, 437

Parallax 1: 52, 62, 69-70, 85; 3: 517

Paris Observatory 1: 28, 83, 85; 2: 326, 374

Parmenides 1: 12

Particle accretion theory 2: 311

Patsayev, Viktor 3: 578

Pauli, Wolfgang 2: 410

Pauling, Linus 1: 53

Payne-Gaposchkin, Cecilia 1: 83; 3: 705

Peebles, Jim 2: 439

Pegasus 1: 159; 2: 445; 3: 569

Penrose, Roger 1: 214

Penumbra 3: 558, 629

Penzias, Arno *1:* 58, 114, 177, 192; *2:* **438-39,** 438 (ill.); *3:* 494, 620

Perihelion *2:* 457

Period-luminosity curve *3:* 541

Perkins Observatory *2:* 335

Perseid meteor shower *2:* 377

Perseus *2:* 377

Perth Observatory *2:* 335

Peter the Great *1:* 207

Peterson, Donald *2:* 395

Philip II *1:* 32

Philolaus *1:* 14

Philosophiae Naturalis Principia Mathematica 1: 131, 193; *2:* 417-18, 447

Phobos *2:* 355; *3:* 657

Pholus *1:* 36

Photoelectric effect *1:* 143

Photometry *2:* **439-40**

Photopolarimeter *1:* 183

Photosphere *3:* 555-56, 561, 627, 630

Physics *1:* 55; *2:* 439, 450, 463-64; *3:* 520

Piazzi, Father Giuseppe *1:* 37, 119, 218; *2:* 427

Pierce, John *1:* 104

Pioneer program *2:* 344, 399, **440-44;** *3:* 523, 629

Pioneer-Venus Multiprobe 2: 443

Pioneer-Venus Orbiter 2: 443

Pioneer 1 2: 442

Pioneer 3 3: 664

Pioneer 4 2: 344, 442

Pioneer 5 2: 442; *3:* 629

Pioneer 6 3: 629

Pioneer 7 3: 629

Pioneer 8 3: 629

Pioneer 10 2: 441 (ill.), 443; *3:* 580, 604, 683, 685

Pioneer 11 2: 443; *3:* 580, 604, 683, 685

Plages *3:* 556, 627

Planet X *2:* 334, **444-45,** 454; *3:* 566, 644

The Planetary Hypothesis 3: 460

Planetary motion *1:* 9, 73, 131; *2:* 294, **445-48**

Planetary Society *1:* 159; *3:* 523, 685

Planetesimals *1:* 37; *2:* 305; *3:* 568

Planetesimals and protoplanets *2:* **448-49**

Plasma *1:* 44, 61; *2:* 359, **449-51,** 452; *3:* 561, 572-73, 606, 630, 638, 683

Plasma theory *1:* 61; *2:* **451-52**

Plateau theory *1:* 60

Plato *1:* 12, 32; *2:* 390

Pleiades star cluster *1:* 4, 129; *2:* **452-53**

Plinth *1:* 14; *2:* 460

Pluto *1:* 69; *2:* 261, 304-05, 331, 366, 388, 407, 409, 443-45, **453-56,** 454 (ill.), 457-58; *3:* 565, 579-81, 644, 646, 659

Pluto Express 2: 456, **457-58,** 457 (ill.); *3:* 581

Population I stars *1:* 49

Population II stars *1:* 49

Poseidon 1: 134

Positional astronomy *3:* 658

The Primeval Atom 2: 321

Probes *1:* 108, 155, 172, 174, 182; *2:* 288, 316, 333, 338, 342, 345, 349, 351, 353, 357-59, 368, 390, 399, 440, 443, 457; *3:* 553, 582, 592, 602, 628, 647, 654-55, 667-68, 676, 683

Proceedings of the Institute of Radio Engineers 3: 499

Progress 3: 525

Project Matterhorn *3:* 661

Project Orbiter *3:* 665

Project Ozma *1:* 129

Project Paperclip *1:* 75

Project Pathfinder *1:* 160

Prominence *1:* 45; *3:* 556, 571, 573, 627

Proper motion *1:* 207

Proton rocket *3:* 575

Protoplanetary systems *2:* 449

Protoplanets *3:* 568

Proxima Centauri *2:* 305; *3:* 607-08, 627

Ptolemaic model. *See* Geocentric model

Ptolemy *1:* 14, 42, 110, 112, 118, 131, 207; *2:* 445, **458-460,** 457 (ill.); *3:* 567

Pulitzer Prize *3:* 521

Pulsar *1:* 3-4, 31, 47, 50, 106, 176; *2:* 246, 405, 412, **460-61;** *3:* 494, 496, 498-99, 520, 590, 651, 688, 695, 697, 705

Purcell, Edward *2:* **461-64,** 462 (ill.); *3:* 493

Pythagoras *1:* 12

Q

Quadrant *1:* 72

Quantum mechanics *1:* 215

Quantum physics *1:* 92

Quasars *1:* 3-4, 21, 50, 65, 106, 121, 176, 204; *2:* 244, 252, 271-72, 280, 300, 328, 412, 437, 461; *3:* **487-89,** 488 (ill.), 495, 526-27, 534, 536, 539, 591, 620, 651-53, 695

Quasi-stellar radio source *3:* 527, 534

Queloz, Didier *1:* 159; *2:* 445; *3:* 569

R

Rabi, Isidor Isaac *2:* 463

Radiation *1:* 3, 20, 30, 105, 114, 174, 214; *2:* 243, 247, 267, 270, 273, 279, 337, 406, 439, 452, 460; *3:* 491, 494, 589, 620, 652, 695-96

Radiative zone *3:* 561, 627

Radio astronomy *1:* 30-31; *2:* 244, 283, 285, 429, 438, 463; *3:* **491-94,** 492 (ill.), 495-96, 518, 520

Radio galaxies *1:* 20; *3:* 493, 519

Radio interferometer *2:* 278, 361; *3:* 493, **494-96,** 499, 519, 674

Radio interferometry *1:* 212; *2:* 433; *3:* 520

Radio telescope *1:* 30, 89, 129, 153, 158-59; *2:* 244, 382, 431, 449, 461, 464, 487, 491; *3:* 493-95, **496-99,** 497 (ill.), 498-501, 518, 668, 674

Radio wave *1:* 105, 146-47, 174; *2:* 298, 363, 402, 412, 429, 439; *3:* 491, 493-94, 539, 652, 695

Radioisotope thermal generator (RTG) *2:* 458; *3:* 581 (ill.)

Raleigh, Walter *1:* 210

Ranger probes *2:* 344, 399; *3:* 579

Reagan, Ronald *2:* 278

Reber, Grote *2:* 285; *3:* 492, 498, **499-501,** 500 (ill.), 518

Red dwarf *2:* 406; *3:* 517

Red giant star *1:* 220; *2:* 282, 404, 419; *3:* **502-03,** 502 (ill.), 517, 622, 624, 628, 666, 691

Red-shift *2:* 256, 261, 272, 428; *3:* 487, **503-04,** 527, 535, 552, 688

Redstone rocket *1:* 75; *2:* 369, 399; *3:* 512, 532

Reflection of light *2:* 460

Reflector telescope *1:* 59, 128, 204, 212; *2:* 249, 314, 392, 431, 435; *3:* 659, 687, 699

Refraction of light *2:* 311, 460

Refractive indexes *1:* 210

Refractor telescope *1:* 59, 199-201, 211; *2:* 249; *3:* 644, 659, 699

Reines, Frederick *2:* 410

Relay 1: 104

Resnik, Judith *1:* 127; *2:* 337; *3:* **504-06,** 505 (ill.)

Retrograde motion *1:* 9, 13; *3:* 568

Return to Earth 1: 7

Revolution of the Heavenly Spheres 1: 112-13, 119, 171

Riccioli, Giovanni *1:* 83, 197

Richer, Jean *1:* 85

Ride, Sally *1:* 90; *2:* 337; *3:* **506-09,** 508 (ill.), 633

The Right Stuff 3: 545

Ring galaxy *1:* 169

Ring nebula *2:* 404

Rocket fuel *1:* 188

Rocketry *1:* 73, 75, 188, 190; *2:* 300, 329, 398-99, 423, 425; *3:* 509, 511, 648

Rockets *1:* 23, 35, 73, 114, 155, 174, 180, 188, 190, 212; *2:* 247, 294, 300, 316-17, 329, 346, 369, 398, 400, 423, 425-26; *3:* 506, **509-13,** 532, 534, 564, 575, 591, 597, 602-03, 648, 651, 661, 665, 695, 697

Rockoon technique *3:* 662

Roemer, Olaus *1:* 83; *3:* **513-14,** 514 (ill.), 612

Roosevelt, Franklin D. *1:* 55

ROSAT satellite *1:* 4

Royal Astronomical Society *1:* 2, 216

Royal Irish Academy *1:* 216

Royal Observatory *1:* 21, 51

Royal Radar Establishment *3:* 519

Royal Society of Edinburgh *2:* 364

Royal Society of London *2:* 364

RR Lyrae stars *3:* 666-67

Rubin, Vera *1:* 125; *3:* **515-17**

Rudolph II *1:* 73

The Rudolphine Tables *2:* 296

Russell, Henry *1:* 219; *3:* **517-18,** 517 (ill.), 541

Russian Space Agency *2:* 458

Rutherford, Ernest *1:* 176

Ryle, Martin *1:* 51; *2:* 244-45; *3:* 493, **518-20,** 519 (ill.)

S

Sacramento Peak Observatory *2:* 400-01

Sagan, Carl *1:* 130, 159; *2:* 357; *3:* **521-23,** 522 (ill.), 685

Sagittarius *2:* 282, 285; *3:* 500

Salyut program *2:* 324, 340; *3:* **523-26,** 578, 583

Salyut 1 *2:* 383; *3:* 523, 525, 576, 587

Salyut 2 *3:* 524

Salyut 3 *3:* 524

Salyut 4 *3:* 525

Salyut 5 *3:* 524

Salyut 6 *3:* 525, 587

Salyut 7 *3:* 525, 587

Sandage, Allan *3:* 487, **526-28,** 534

Saturn *1:* 2, 9, 13, 38, 45, 68, 112, 119, 134, 171, 218; *2:* 262, 310, 333, 335, 364, 366, 386, 409, 440, 443, 445; *3:* **528-31,** 529 (ill.), 565, 567-68, 580, 604, 655, 683-85

Saturn I rocket *3:* 532

Saturn IB rocket *3:* 532

Saturn V rocket *1:* 23, 76, 190; *3:* 513, **532-34,** 533 (ill.)

Schiaparelli, Giovanni *2:* 333, 357, 377

Schiller, Julius *1:* 111

Schirra, Walter *2:* 371

Schmidt, Maarten *3:* 488, **534-36**

Schmidt telescope *2:* 433

Scientific American *2:* 306

Search for Extraterrestrial Intelligence (SETI) *1:* 158 (ill.), 159-60

Seasat 1: 134

Seasons *3:* **536-38,** 537 (ill.)

See, Elliot M. *1:* 180

Service module *1:* 22

SETI. *See* Search for Extraterrestrial Intelligence (SETI)

Seven Sisters *2:* 453

Sextant *1:* 40

Seyfert, Carl *3:* **539-40**

Seyfert galaxies *3:* 539-40

Shapley, Harlow *1:* 86, 220; *2:* 254; *3:* **540-43,** 540 (ill.)

Sharpe, Mitchell *3:* 636

Shepard, Alan *2:* 331, 370; *3:* **543-46,** 544 (ill.)

Shooting stars *2:* 376

Shuttle Autonomous Research Tool for Astronomy (SPARTAN) *2:* 337

Sidereus Nuncius *1:* 171

Sigma *2:* 371

Sitter, Willem de *1:* 56, 120; *3:* **546-48,** 547 (ill.)

61 Cygni *1:* 52

Sky & Telescope *3:* 705

Skylab **space station** *1:* 108; *2:* 394, 399; *3:* 534, **548-51,** 549 (ill.), 583-84, 587, 589, 601, 629

Slayton, Donald "Deke" *1:* 27

Slipher, Vesto Melvin *3:* 548, **551-53,** 551 (ill.)

Small Astronomical Satellite 1 *3:* 651

Small Magellanic Cloud (SMC) *1:* 4, 86, 89, 168, 220; *2:* 312, 318; *3:* 542

Smithsonian Astrophysical Observatory (SAO) *3:* 687

Smithsonian Submillimeter Array *2:* 362

Snell, Willebrord *3:* **552-53**

Snell's law *3:* 553

Snow, Helen *1:* 201

Snow Solar Telescope *1:* 201; *2:* 391, 393-94

Society for Space Travel *1:* 73

Society of Jesuits *1:* 197

Soft X-rays *1:* 3; *3:* 695, 697

Sokolov, Andrei *2:* 324

Solar and Heliospheric Observatory *3:* **553-55,** 629

Solar atmosphere *3:* **555-57**

Solar chromosphere *1:* 29

Solar eclipse *1:* 12, 13, 45; *2:* 243, 246, 340, 374; *3:* 556, **557-60,** 559 (ill.), 570

Solar energy transport *3:* **560-62**

Solar flare *1:* 45, 59, 106, 137; *2:* 246; *3:* 550, 556, 571, 573, 588, 627, 629-30

Solar Maximum Mission *3:* 592, 629

Solar rotation *3:* **562-63**

Solar sail *3:* **563-65,** 564 (ill.)

Solar system *1:* 9, 13-14, 24, 37, 56, 99, 111, 118-19, 131, 134, 138, 140, 167, 171, 174, 193, 207, 217; *2:* 253, 273, 290, 295, 305-06, 308, 310-11, 334, 342, 354, 366, 368, 376, 381, 397, 399, 406-09, 411, 417, 429-30, 438, 440, 443-45, 448, 454, 456-57, 459; *3:* 488, 494, 513, 527, 535, 551,

553, 557, 562, 564, **565-70,** 567 (ill.), 572, 579, 583, 591, 596, 598, 602, 604, 626, 652, 655, 683, 685

Solar telescope *1:* 199; *2:* 298, 391-92, 394, 400; *3:* 525, **570-72**

Solar wind *1:* 44, 98, 116, 137, 158, 183; *2:* 347, 352, 442, 449, 553; *3:* 557, 566, **572-73,** 627, 629, 654

Solstice *1:* 9, 14, 151; *3:* **573-75,** 625

Sommerfeld, Arnold *1:* 53

Sosigenes *1:* 79

South magnetic pole *1:* 137

South pole *3:* 574

Southern lights *1:* 117; *3:* 573, 630, 638

Soyuz program *1:* 167; *2:* 278; *3:* **575-79,** 605, 679-80

Soyuz T series *3:* 578

Soyuz TM series *3:* 578

Soyuz TM-11 3: 577 (ill.)

Soyuz 1 2: 323; *3:* 575-76

Soyuz 2–9 3: 576

Soyuz 10 3: 524, 576

Soyuz 11 3: 524, 576

Soyuz 12 3: 578

Soyuz 17 3: 578

Soyuz 19 1: 6, 27; *2:* 324; *3:* 578, 583

Space age *2:* 442

Space Infrared Telescope Facility *3:* 591

Space probe *1:* 24, 172; *2:* 301, 354, 368, 390; *3:* **579-81,** 586, 653-54, 673-74

Space race *1:* 26, 179; *2:* 302, 321, 343, 351, 369; *3:* 513, 523, 543, **582-84,** 586, 593, 616, 665, 679, 681

Space shuttle *1:* 6, 24, 42, 66-67, 90, 94, 96, 114, 125, 127, 134, 149, 161, 172-73, 176; *2:* 257-58, 276, 278, 287, 291, 294, 316, 331, 336-37, 349, 384; *3:* 505, 507, 564, 583, **584-86,** 592, 601, 604, 606, 685

Space Shuttle Orbiter *1:* 162

Space sickness *2:* 288; *3:* 682

Space station *1:* 127, 156; *2:* 247, 278, 317, 324, 336, 338, 340, 359, 382, 394, 425; *3:* 511, 523-24, 534, 548, 551, 575-76, 578, 583-84, **586-89,** 591-92, 596, 602, 605, 629

Space telescope *3:* **589-91**

Space-time continuum *1:* 144

Space trash *3:* **591-93**

Spacecraft, piloted *3:* **593-96**

Spacecraft design *3:* **596-99**

Spacecraft equipment *3:* **601-02**

Spacecraft voyage *3:* **602-05**

Spacelab *1:* 67, 90, 96, 155; *2:* 288, 399; *3:* 586, **605-07**

Spacelab 1 *3:* 606

Spacelab 2 *2:* 395; *3:* 606

Spacelab 3 *3:* 606

Spacesuits *1:* 101; *2:* 394; *3:* 598, 601, 605, 680

V

V-2 rockets *1:* 190; *2:* 425; *3:* 512, 662
Vacuum Solar Telescope *2:* 401
Vacuum tower *3:* 572
Valle Marineris *2:* 355
Van Allen, James *1:* 116, 156; *3:* **661-63,** 662 (ill.)
Van Allen belts *1:* 44, 116, 129, 137, 156; *3:* 661, **663-64,** 664 (ill.)
Van de Hulst, Hendrik *2:* 429
Vanguard program *1:* 156; *3:* **665-66**
Variable stars *1:* 85-86; *2:* 248, 318; *3:* **666-67**
Vega program *3:* 580, **667-68**
Vega 1 *1:* 183; *3:* 667
Vega 2 *1:* 183; *3:* 668
Velas *1:* 106, 175
Venera program *3:* 580, **668-71**
Venera 1 *3:* 670
Venera 2 *3:* 670
Venera 3 *2:* 301; *3:* 669 (ill.)
Venera 4 *3:* 670
Venera 5–14 *3:* 671
Venera 15 *3:* 670-71
Venera 16 *3:* 670-71
Vengeance Weapon 2 *1:* 75
Venus *1:* 13, 31, 68, 135, 172, 174, 196, 218; *2:* 290, 296, 301, 333, 340, 349, 351, 368, 440, 443, 445, 458; *3:* 498, 506, 521, 564-65, 567-68, 579-80, 592, 667-68, **672-74,** 672 (ill.)
Venus Orbiting Imaging Radar *2:* 349
Venus Radar Mapper (VRM) *2:* 349
Vernal equinox *1:* 80, 152
Verne, Jules *2:* 423
Very Large Array *1:* 130; *2:* 278; *3:* 493, 495, **674-76,** 675 (ill.)
Very Long Baseline Array (VLB) *2:* 361; *3:* 496
Very Long Baseline Interferometry (VLBI) *1:* 212; *3:* 495
Vesta *1:* 38; *2:* 356, 428
Viking program *2:* 317; *3:* 523, **676-79**
Viking 1 *2:* 356; *3:* 579, 677-79, 677 (ill.)
Viking 2 *2:* 356; *3:* 579, 677-78
Virtual particles *1:* 65
Visible light *1:* 147; *2:* 412

Visual binary star *1:* 53, 62; *3:* 623
VLBI Space Observatory Program (VSOP) *3:* 496
Volkov, Vladislav *3:* 578
Voskhod program *3:* **679-80**
Voskhod 1 *3:* 680
Voskhod 2 *2:* 321; *3:* 680
Vostok program *1:* 165, 167; *2:* 317; *3:* 633, 679, **680-83**
Vostok 1 *1:* 165; *2:* 301; *3:* 543, 594, 633, 680, 682
Vostok 2 *3:* 682
Vostok 3 *3:* 635, 682
Vostok 4 *3:* 682
Vostok 5 *3:* 635, 682
Vostok 6 *3:* 633, 635, 681 (ill.), 682
Voyager program *1:* 85; *2:* 317, 366, 399; *3:* 523, **683-86**
Voyager 1 *1:* 45, 173; *2:* 291, 349, 458; *3:* 528, 530-31, 580, 598, 604, 683-85, 684 (ill.)
Voyager 2 *1:* 173; *2:* 291, 349, 407, 458, 528; *3:* 530, 573, 580, 598, 604, 655-56, 683-85
Vulcan *2:* 326; *3:* 566

W

Wakata, Koichi *1:* 151
Waldheim, Kurt *3:* 686
Waning crescent phase *2:* 348
Waning gibbous phase *2:* 348
Washington Monument *2:* 415
The Washington Post *3:* 555
Waxing crescent phase *2:* 348
Waxing gibbous phase *2:* 348
Ways to Spaceflight *2:* 425
Weber, Wilhelm *1:* 178
Weightlessness *1:* 194 (ill.)
Weiler, Edward *2:* 259
Westar *1:* 105
Wheeler, John A. *1:* 65
Whipple, Fred L. *3:* 687
Whipple Observatory *1:* 210, 213; *3:* **687-89**
Whirlpool galaxy *2:* 273
White, Edward *1:* 23, 180; *3:* 596, **689-90,** 689 (ill.)
White dwarf star *1:* 47, 51, 53, 61, 65, 93-94, 123, 140, 192, 220; *2:* 245,

335, 411, 419, 461; *3:* 503, 518, 622, 628, 631, **690-91,** 691 (ill.), 694, 701, 705
William III *1:* 52
Wilson, Robert *1:* 58, 114, 177, 192; *2:* 438-39; *3:* 494, 620
WIMPs *1:* 123
Winter solstice *3:* 573, 575
Woodward, Charles *3:* 694
World Ocean Circulation Experiment *1:* 134
World War I *1:* 201; *2:* 249, 254, 320, 379, 393, 423
World War II *1:* 26, 166, 185, 190, 203-04; *2:* 293, 301, 335, 337, 399, 424-25, 429, 463; *3:* 493, 495, 498, 501, 512, 519, 532, 535, 543, 545, 633, 661-62, 703
World Wide Web. *See* Astronomy web-sites
Wyoming Infrared Observatory *3:* **692-94,** 693 (ill.)

X

X-ray astronomy *2:* 246, 337; *3:* 494, 605, 651, **695-96**
X-ray stars *2:* 363; *3:* **696-98,** 697 (ill.)
X-ray telescope *1:* 4; *3:* 695, 697

Y

Yeager, Chuck *2:* 371
Yegorov, Boris *3:* 680
Yeliseyev, Aleksei *3:* 576
Yerkes, Charles *1:* 200; *3:* 701
Yerkes Observatory *1:* 94, 200; *2:* 249, 432; *3:* **699-701,** 700 (ill.)
Yohkoh *3:* 629
Young, John *1:* 179
Young, Judy *3:* 516
Young, Thomas *2:* 264

Z

Zodiac *1:* 42 (ill.)
Zwicky, Fritz *1:* 47, 124; *2:* 421, 436; *3:* 516, **703-05,** 704 (ill.)